CONCEPTUAL FRAMEWORKS IN GEOGRAPHY

General Editor: W. E. Marsden

The Location of Manufacturing Industry

An Introductory Approach

John Bale

Lecturer in Geography, Avery Hill College of Education, London

Maps and diagrams drawn by Tim Smith

AUT:

T:

A

Oliver & Boyd

Oliver & Boyd

Croythorn House
23 Ravelston Terrace
Edinburgh EH4 3TJ

A Division of Longman Group Ltd

ISBN 0 05 002901 0

Printed in Great Britain by Willmer Brothers Limited, Birkenhead

Contents

Editor's Note

An encouraging feature in geographical education in recent years has been the convergence taking place of curriculum thinking and thinking at the academic frontiers of the subject. In both, stress has been laid on the necessity for conceptual approaches and the use of information as a means to an end rather than as an end in itself.

The central purpose of this series is to bear witness to this convergence. In each text the *key ideas* are identified, chapter by chapter. These ideas are in the form of propositions which, with their component concepts and the inter-relations between them, make up the conceptual frameworks of the subject. The key ideas provide criteria for selecting content for the teacher, and in cognitive terms help the student to retain what is important in each unit. Most of the key ideas are linked with assignments, designed to elicit evidence of achievement of basic understanding and ability to apply this understanding in new circumstances through engaging in problem-solving exercises.

While the series is not specifically geared to any particular 'A' level examination syllabus, indeed it is intended for use in geography courses in polytechnics and in colleges of education as well as in the sixth form, it is intended to go some way towards meeting the needs of those students preparing for the more radical advanced geography syllabuses, such as those of the JMB, the Oxford and Cambridge Board and the Scottish Higher Grade.

It is hoped that the texts contain the academic rigour to stretch the most able of such candidates, but at the same time provide a clear enough exposition of the basic ideas to provide intellectual stimulus and social and/or cultural relevance for those who will not be going on to study geography in higher education. To this end, a larger selection of assignments and readings is provided than perhaps could be used profitably by all students. The teacher is the best person to choose those which most nearly meet his students' needs.

W. E. Marsden
University of Liverpool.

February 1975

Preface

There are too many exciting and important concepts in the contemporary geographical viewpoint to eliminate them from the school curriculum.

Peter Gould and Rodney White, *Mental Maps*, Penguin, 1974, page 186.

Three threads have run through my thinking in writing this book.

First, the views of educational psychologists who stress that cognitive development does not consist solely of the acquisition of facts. I have, therefore, tried to aid the development of comprehension, the acquisition of skills and an ability to analyse in presenting necessary factual content. At times the reader may also detect an incursion into the affective domain.

The second thread has been woven by the persuasive writing of J. S. Bruner whose view that the fundamental concepts of any discipline can be taught in a meaningful way to students of any age has been a rallying cry of many educationists in recent years. Thus, I have tried to deal with contemporary knowledge in a way which I hope will be digestible to students beginning an advanced course in geography.

Finally, my thoughts have been profoundly influenced by the changing paradigm within geography itself. From the start, therefore, I nail my flag to the spatial and conceptual masthead. At the same time I have tried to achieve a greater balance between geography and pedagogy than is found in most texts at this level.

Throughout the writing of this book I have recognized the need for a *structure* which binds the chapters together. Essentially, the unifying theme is embodied in the question 'why are manufacturing industries located where they are?' Thus traditional inductively derived explanations, interpretations based on classical models and aids to explanation based on the infusion of concepts from economic theory have all been included.

Textbook activity in the concept-based human geography field has been dominated by works from the field of urban geography. This appears to have been at the expense of similar work from economic geography. Thus this book tries to fill a lacuna in the literature of economic geography arising from the absence of an introductory text in modern industrial geography.

Many people have played a part in the preparation of this book, and my thanks go to numerous people – mainly professional geographers – who have stimulated me through their writings. My debt to them will be obvious from the captions to many maps and from the references at the end of the book. My own geographic education has been greatly influenced over the past six or seven years by irregular meetings with Rex Walford and John Everson, both of whom have helped me in more ways than they realize. I am also most grateful to my friends Dave Smallbone, Roger Cracknell and David Mills who all read crude early drafts of the manuscript and made most useful and discerning comments. Bill Marsden has been a far from nominal editor and it is due to his persistent yet friendly badgering that much of the pedagogic merit that this book may possess owes its inclusion.

In addition, of course, no book can be completed without the co-operation of the author's family and I am thus indebted to my wife and son for their patience and consideration. The comments of family and friends have improved this book considerably. Any shortcomings are, of course, the fault of the author.

John Bale
Avery Hill College

February 1975

Acknowledgments

The author and publishers wish to thank the following for permission to make use of copyright material in this book:

Areofilms Ltd. Plates 3.3, 8.2; George Allen & Unwin Ltd. and University of Toronto Press Fig. 4.10; The editor, Area (Institute of British Geographers) the verse 'Industry grows where the grass is greener'; Edward Arnold (Publishers) Fig. 2.4; Association of American Geographers Figs. 3.8, 9.6, 9.7; K. L. Bale Plate 4.6; The editor, Barclays Bank Review, Table 8.2; B. T. Batsford Ltd. Figs. 8.2, 8.3; Bell & Sons Ltd. Table 3.5, Fig. 9.3; Bolton Metropolitan Borough Table 3.2; British Steel Corporation Plates 4.3, 8.4; The editor, Cahiers de Geographie de Québec, Fig. 7.2; Cambridge University Press Fig. 3.6; Cumbria County Council Fig. 8.11; T. Dalton Plates 4.1, 4.2; Doncaster Metropolitan Borough Council Fig. 6.16; Duxbury Press Fig. 5.11; The editor, The Economist, Table 8.6; Esso Petroleum Company Limited Plate 3.2; Ford Motor Company Table 3.1; The editor, Geografiska Annaler, Fig. 5.9; The Controller, Her Majesty's Stationery Office Tables 2.1, 2.2, 7.1, 8.1, 8.7; Dr D. E. Keeble and the editor, Town Planning Review, Fig. 9.2; Dr D. E. Keeble, M. Chisholm and G. Manners (and Miss M. Thomas, cartographer) Figs. 3.2, 9.9; The editor, Lloyds Bank Review, Table 3.3, Fig. 6.18; Jamieson Mackay & Partners and the editor, Urban Studies, Fig. 4.16; Mackenzie Hill Holdings Ltd. Fig. 4.15; R. L. Mackett, University of Leeds Fig. 9.10; Methuen & Co. Ltd. Table 5.3; MIT Press Fig. 4.6; National Museum of Wales (Welsh Folk Museum) Plate 8.1; North West Industrial Development Association Fig. 6.15; Pergamon Press Ltd. Table 9.1; The editor, Private Eye, Fig. 8.18; The director, Second Land Utilisation Survey Fig. 4.8; M. Taylor, University of Auckland Fig. 7.1; The editor, Tijdschrift voor Economische en Sociale Geografie, quotations on page 34, Fig. 4.11, Table 9.2; University of London Institute of Education and George Philip & Son Ltd Fig. 4.7; University of Wales Press Fig. 4.1; H. D. Watts and the editor, Geography, Fig. 6.1.

Although every effort has been made to trace copyright owners, in some cases this has not proved possible, and we apologise for any omission in the above list.

Introduction: the spatial view

The American geographer, E. J. Taaffe, has written:

> If we were to concentrate less on factual coverage and more on the development of higher level generalizations and theories, we would leave the student with a larger and more useful set of residual ideas.[1]

The aim of this book is not to catalogue the world's manufacturing industries or to provide long lists of products and places. Instead it seeks to introduce the ways in which modern geographers view manufacturing industry, and concentrates on 'ideas'; it uses facts which are relatively fleeting to illustrate generalizations which are relatively durable.

A. Concepts in Geography

By the time you have finished reading this book you should be able to see how the basic concepts which hold together all branches of geography are applied to the study of the location of manufacturing industry. Concepts are 'abstract ideas generalized from innumerable experiences'[2] and certain key abstract concepts can be identified in geography. There are various ways of structuring the study of geography. For instance, in the 'man and environment approach' many key concepts are involved (such as the ecological) which stress man's adaptation to his environment. Key concepts related to the spatial view of geography, however, include:

1. *Location*—where things are located and the reasons for their location;
2. *Spatial organization* – the way in which the space making up the earth's surface is organized;
3. *Surfaces* – the arrangement of various forms of surface which can be identified by the use of contours of various kinds;
4. *Points* – the patterns and locations of the many forms of points which are distributed over the surfaces;

5. *Movement* – between points and over surfaces, either along different kinds of lines or in the form of 'mass' movement;
6. *Scale* – geographers reduce the scale of reality so that it may be represented on a map; many different scales are adopted in geographic enquiry;
7. *Distance* – geography has been called a discipline in distance,[3] and this concept is, perhaps, the most basic of all. If everything occurred at the same point in space there would be no subject called geography;
8. *Direction* – which permits us to relate one object to another by means of reference to points of the compass.

These concepts can be illustrated in diagrammatic form, as in Fig. 1.1 where examples of physical and economic points and surfaces are illustrated, and in Fig. 1.2 where the contents of this book are summarized within a structure of industrial geography.

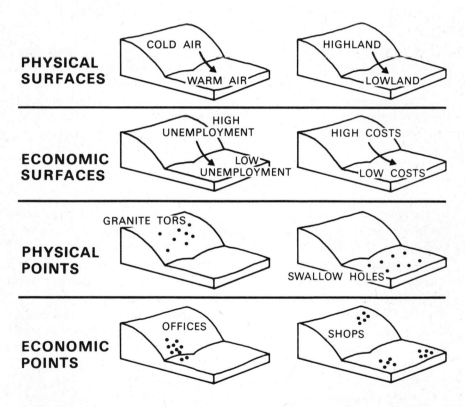

Fig. 1.1. Surfaces and points illustrated by examples from physical and human geography. (After an idea in K. W. Rumage & L. D. Cummings, 'Introduction to Geography; A Spatial Approach', in *New Approaches in Introductory College Geography*, Association of American Geographers Commission on College Geography, Publication **4**, 1967, p. 141)

Fig. 1.2 centres on three basic concepts – surfaces, points and movement. It shows you how the contents of this book involve the study of different kinds of points, surfaces or movements. Many would argue that all branches of geography study these concepts in some form.

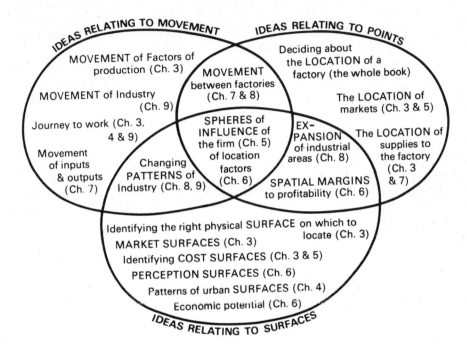

Fig. 1.2. The basic themes of industrial geography in relation to the contents of this book.

The concepts discussed in this section and in Figs. 1.1 and 1.2 are not the only key concepts in geography, but they are those most in accord with the spatial approach to it which is stressed in this book.

'Spatial' derives from the noun 'space'. Geographers are not interested in the extremes of space. They leave the study of outer space to the astronomer, of the inside of a house to an architect and of a crystal to a crystallographer. Hence geographers are not unique in studying space, but they can be distinguished by the fact that they study it at a scale which comes between that of the astronomer and the architect. They are interested in phenomena at local, regional, national and global scales.

In this book we are looking at the spatial organization of manufacturing industry – why factories are located where they are, what movement or interaction occurs between factories, and how this interaction affects location.

To return to our key concepts, in industrial geography we might conceive of a region as a *surface*, over which *move* goods and workers between *points* (towns for example). By changing the *scale* at which we look at a given phenomenon, what was formerly a point may be interpreted as a surface. For instance, a town may be looked on at different scales; it may change on enlargement of scale from a point to a surface, and so may contain points such as factories, between which movement similarly takes place. Equally, the scale of factories can be enlarged to make them into surfaces.

Perhaps more than anything else, however, we are concerned in this book with recurring and predictable patterns of location, particularly those which are reflected in the spatial organization of manufacturing industry in western societies.

B. Models in Geography

During the course of reading this book you will also be introduced to what are called *models* of industrial location. The use of models is especially prominent from Chapter 4 onwards. We need, therefore, to introduce briefly what is meant by a geographical model so as to set the scene for later work.

We can perhaps best understand the use of models if we think of an aircraft designer faced with the problems of building an ultra-sonic jet. He would become very muddled indeed if he set about his project by building a full-scale plane, trying to fly it and then scratching his head because it did not perform too well. Instead, he has to construct a geometrical and then a hardware model, on the drawing board and in the wind tunnel respectively, progressively testing and improving the model until it reflects reality, and he has a full understanding of the processes which make it work. To take another example, we may understand how the earth rotates on its axis much better by using a model globe, than by trying to gatecrash the next lunar launching to observe it from space.

Thus, if we want to understand the complexities of industrial location, we would be wiser to work from theoretical models which are logically consistent than to build up an enormous gazetteer of industries from all over the world which would probably prove more confusing than enlightening. Models strip away the confusing and irrelevant detail from the real world (the background 'noise') and concentrate on the essential components. Models may also have a useful teaching function; although a general model may not describe accurately every single situation, that does not mean to say that it is not an economical form of communicating the general properties of a phenomenon.

To many readers the term 'model' might still evoke anything from 36–23–36 to *papier maché*. Indeed, geographers do sometimes use the term to mean 'ideal' or 'scaled down version'. But geographers also define models as:

4

verbal or mathematical abstractions from reality, emphasizing certain character-istics of that reality and discarding others. The development of models usually involves a discarding of the unique or irrelevant characteristics of phenomena and a focus on the characteristics which phenomena share.[4]

Thus geographical models can range from 'youth, maturity and old age' to the geometry of central place theory, and from a wave tank to the algebra of the gravity model (see page 212).

C. Quantification in Geography

Models are often expressed quantitatively as the last quotation suggests. In addition, quantitative techniques provide geographers with sharper tools of analysis and more precise results than vague verbal statements. Such increased precision should be welcomed but it is interesting to note that some people have talked of a quantitative and model-based 'revolution' sweeping through the subject so that it has lost sight of the world of reality and become ensnared in a jungle of formulae and theory. An amusing view of this alleged revolution is shown in Fig. 1.3. Here we see the nasty, brutish Quantifactus carrying Fair Geographia away from the verdant pastures of the 'real world' inhabited by Qualifactus, into the arid and sterile world of models and quantitative techniques. It has been suggested that Geographia is older and more able to take care of herself than the cartoonist suggests![5]

D. Systems thinking in Geography

A system may be defined as a collection of components with a set of links between them. The most obvious example to most readers will be the hot water system of their houses. While a system is essentially a form of model, it is also a way of thinking about things, emphasizing not only the wholeness of the environment but also the interdependence of the system's various components.

The beauty of the systems approach is that it applies to all levels of scale. In this book, for example, systems may be illustrated by examples at the level of the individual firm (page 25) and the individual industry (page 141) to the town (page 67) and the region (page 179). Fig. 1.4 illustrates a hypotheti-cal spatial system consisting of workplaces, links between them, and regional boundaries. It will be observed that some regions in Fig. 1.4 are relatively self-contained with regard to the links connecting their workplaces (for example, regions A and F). Such regions might be described as relatively *closed systems* and in these the workplaces depend very little on units in other regions. In regions E, B and C, however, almost all the workplaces are linked with units in other regions and are, therefore, much more *open systems*.

Fig. 1.3. The Rape of Geographia? (After L. Curry, 'Quantitative Geography', *The Canadian Geographer*, **2**, 1967)

Of course, each workplace in Fig. 1.4 may itself be thought of as a system, while if all the regions were combined to form a nation that, too, could be interpreted as a complex spatial system.

Systems are useful conceptual devices since they enable us to envisage the impact of change of (perhaps) one component or link on the total system. If, for example, workplace X in Region E (in Fig. 1.4) was forced to go out of business, the effect would be felt on many other workplaces within the system. The systems concept, therefore, stresses *wholeness*, the *interdependence* of

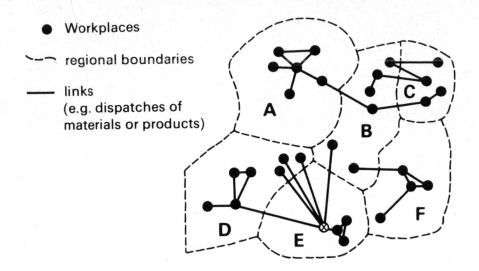

Workplaces

regional boundaries

links
(e.g. dispatches of
materials or products)

A B C D E F

Fig. 1.4. A hypothetical spatial system.

elements within the economic (and physical) environment and *dynamic* relationships within a system.

E. The Plan of this Book

Chapter 2 introduces the main sub groups of 'industry' and then considers the nature of manufacturing geography. Chapter 3 is a guide to the confusing variety of factors which apparently affect the location of industry in the real world. Chapter 4 introduces you to some generalizations about the location of industry in towns. We thus start at a local level of scale – the scale at which readers of this book will be most familiar with industry.

Chapters 5 to 7 offer possible solutions to the apparent complexity of the real world by trying to explain industrial location through the use of models. Some of these models (see Chapter 5) try to explain industrial location by making very rigid assumptions about how human beings behave, while others recognize the importance of the vagaries of human nature and are thus 'behavioural' models (see Chapter 6).

Chapter 8 is concerned with the way in which the central government influences the location of industry and the way in which regional policy has (or has not) worked. This chapter also provides the reader with some simple quantitative techniques for use in industrial geography. These can be supplemented by reference to the rapidly growing number of books on quantitative methods.

Chapter 9 deals with industrial movement, a subject closely allied to that of government policy. But movement can be interpreted at different levels of scale and so this chapter considers also the movement of industry within towns as well as between regions.

Each of these chapters may appear self-contained. The reader is warned, however, that later sections do build on ideas introduced earlier and, while chapters can be read in isolation, careful use of the index will be required if this is done.

F. Using this Book

So far we have stressed that this book is concerned essentially with key geographical ideas as applied to industrial geography. In order to help the reader grasp the concepts reflected by these key ideas each chapter is followed by three components which are essential elements of the book. These are:

(a) A summary of the key ideas contained in the chapter; these are propositions built up from basic concepts, mostly of an economic or spatial nature.

(b) Readings, which supplement the relevant chapter in the book; the books and articles referred to are fairly accessible and an attempt has been made to avoid esoteric references which might look impressive but which are difficult to obtain. If your own library does not possess those suggested, you can place an order with your librarian for them to be obtained on an inter-library loans system. References which the student may find too difficult but which may be of interest to his teacher, have been indicated by an asterisk (*).

(c) Assignments, which occur both in the body of the text in many chapters as well as at the end of each chapter; those listed at the ends of chapters are more concerned with integrating key ideas in rather lengthier exercises than those found within chapters. The nature of the assignments varies considerably: some are simply suggestions for discussion; others are essay-type questions; others are simulations or games; elsewhere the student is asked to respond to various forms of information and data presented; other assignments may be incorporated into fieldwork projects.

It is important to emphasize that the summaries of the key ideas, the suggested additional readings and the assignments are not intended as 'additional extras' or time-consuming luxuries. Instead they are intended to be integral parts of this introductory course in modern industrial geography.

8

Key Ideas

A. *Concepts in Geography* (pages 1–4)
1. The identification of basic concepts provides a set of unifying themes for a given discipline.
2. Concepts are abstract generalizations based on innumerable practical experiences.
3. Major abstract concepts in geography include location, spatial organization, surfaces, points, movement, distance, scale and direction. They can be built up into propositions or key ideas which provide a means of selecting important content and act as aids to understanding.
4. The spatial approach to geography emphasizes how the space occupying the earth's surface is organized.

B. *Models in Geography* (pages 4–5)
1. Models are simplifications of reality which focus on the essential characteristics of a given phenomenon.
2. Models are, therefore, aids to understanding complex situations.
3. Models may be quantitative expressions, verbal statements or hardware models.
4. Models are useful teaching devices because they concentrate on basic ideas and ignore irrelevant detail.

C. *Systems thinking in Geography* (pages 5–7)
1. A system is a collection of components with a set of links between them.
2. Systems thinking emphasizes the wholeness and inter-relatedness of various environments.
3. The scale of systems in industrial geography can vary from that of an individual firm to the world as a whole.
4. Self-contained systems are called closed systems and those which are linked to other systems are called open systems.

Additional Activities

1. (a) Identify some of the basic concepts which recur throughout urban, physical, industrial and all other geographies.
(b) Fig. 1.1 (page 2) shows examples of surfaces and points taken from physical and human geography. Identify the nature of the movements in each diagram and draw similar diagrams illustrating the concept of movement in different branches of geography.
(c) Take examples from physical or urban geography to show how the concepts of 'surfaces', 'points' and 'movement' form three basic components of geographical study. Draw a diagram like Fig. 1.2 (page 3) to illustrate the contents of your physical or human geography course.

9

2. Review the models which you have encountered so far in your school geography course. Of the types described in this chapter, which do those models you have already studied best fit?
3. (a) In what way is a river basin an open system?
(b) What do you understand by the view that a city is a system within a system of cities?

Reading

A. AMBROSE, P., *Analytical Human Geography*, Longman, 1970, pp. 283–93.
B. HAGGETT, P., 'Changing concepts in economic geography', in CHORLEY, R. & HAGGETT, P., (eds.), *Frontiers in Geographical Teaching*, Methuen, 1970, pp. 106–09.
C. ELIOT HURST, M., A *Geography of Economic Behavior*. Duxbury Press, 1972, pp. 32–8.

Manufacturing industry: some introductory ideas

A. Classification of Industries

The government recognizes 27 main groups of industries in its *Standard Industrial Classification* and each of these 27 *Main Order Headings* (MOHs) is broken down into varying numbers of *Minimum List Headings*. Thus, under MOH 'Instrument Engineering', for example, are given the Minimum List Headings of 'photographic and document copying equipment', 'surgical instruments and appliances' and 'scientific and industrial instruments and systems'. Each month the *Department of Employment Gazette* prints the numbers employed in each industry for each of the economic planning regions of Britain. A summary of the way in which these data are presented is shown in Table 2.1 (pages 12–13). In this table the Minimum List Headings have been omitted to save space.

Table 2.1 lists the regions along the top and the MOHs down the left hand side. Clearly, such a readily available source of information is useful for anyone wishing to make a comparative study of the economic structure of British regions.

Locationally, the industries included in Table 2.1 can be broken down into three or four basic groups. These groups are:

1. Primary industries

These are MOHs 1 and 2 and are concerned with extracting material direct from the earth (or sea) and do not involve the processing or fabrication of a finished product. By definition, economic activity in the primary industries is located at the source of the raw materials – it cannot be located anywhere else (i.e. coal can only be extracted from a coalfield and trees can only be felled in a forest).

2. Tertiary industries

These are concerned with providing a service and tend to be located where services are required, at the market. We therefore call industries such as

Table 2.1. Estimated numbers of employees at June 1971. Regional analysis by Main Order Heading of the Standard Industrial Classification. (Source: *Department of Employment Gazette*, 1971)

Industry (Standard Industrial Classification 1968)	ECONOMIC PLANNING			
	South East	East Anglia	South West	West Midlands
1 Agriculture, forestry, fishing	86.5	46.7	37.8	25.3
2 Mining and quarrying	15.6	2.5	14.7	31.2
3 Food, drink and tobacco	219.6	43.1	70.2	75.5
4 Coal and petroleum products	21.9			1.3
5 Chemicals and allied industries	154.7	12.6	12.7	22.0
6 Metal manufacture	49.3	3.7	8.2	143.3
7 Mechanical engineering	337.9	30.4	68.4	154.1
8 Instrument engineering	84.7	5.5	14.0	8.5
9 Electrical engineering	380.3	26.3	35.0	118.8
10 Shipbuilding and marine engineering	49.2	4.3	18.0	1.4
11 Vehicles	230.7	18.6	62.5	218.0
12 Metal goods not elsewhere specified	158.9	5.4	16.1	211.9
13 Textiles	30.9	3.8	14.6	31.7
14 Leather, leather goods, leather fur	16.9	1.2	3.5	5.0
15 Clothing and footwear	120.3	13.1	25.5	22.4
16 Bricks, pottery, glass, cement, etc.	78.6	7.9	10.4	76.7
17 Timber, furniture, etc.	116.0	10.6	18.9	22.5
18 Paper, printing and publishing	297.6	17.9	39.1	33.5
19 Other manufacturing industries	129.2	10.2	18.9	55.4
20 Construction	408.9	44.2	89.6	115.8
21 Gas, electricity and water	127.5	11.4	26.7	35.4
22 Transport and communication	677.2	42.9	85.4	106.6
23 Distributive trades	1 001.6	70.9	169.7	207.0
24 Insurance, banking, finance and business service	574.3	17.6	39.1	56.7
25 Professional and scientific services	1 042.7	89.8	195.3	257.6
26 Miscellaneous services	723.4	57.4	143.1	137.0
27 Public administration and defence	605.9	38.9	103.8	98.6

Primary

Secondary

Tertiary

12

REGIONS				Wales	Scotland	Great Britain
East Midlands	Yorks. and Humberside	North West	North			
28.4	29.0	14.0	19.8	12.1	58.7	358.4
80.4	92.9	22.0	70.0	51.0	42.5	422.9
50.3	88.3	135.1	43.8	22.8	113.9	862.6
3.2	7.3	9.7	3.7	8.1	3.5	59.1
19.5	36.9	114.6	56.4	17.7	29.6	476.6
45.1	104.4	34.4	51.4	88.2	48.7	576.1
103.6	113.3	153.6	74.8	32.8	107.2	1 176.0
5.0	5.7	10.5	3.6	3.6	19.5	160.0
36.1	30.4	131.3	57.8	31.2	52.4	898.0
1.5	8.0	31.0	38.5	1.7	46.7	200.3
54.3	45.5	123.1	14.0	26.1	39.0	832.8
27.9	83.5	60.8	15.0	24.9	31.3	635.7
116.2	141.2	170.6	23.7	20.5	80.8	633.9
4.9	5.7	8.6	2.5	1.6	3.7	53.6
70.3	68.9	81.9	36.5	17.5	35.1	481.2
23.2	36.0	46.9	19.9	11.5	24.3	335.5
19.8	29.3	35.0	13.7	9.5	27.1	302.2
27.8	37.4	87.3	20.2	14.0	55.8	630.7
19.6	17.4	52.0	14.0	20.3	17.3	354.4
77.3	116.9	150.4	101.4	77.6	184.0	1 366.1
23.4	34.0	45.7	20.9	21.5	31.0	377.6
69.0	121.3	215.9	74.1	65.2	146.7	1 604.3
150.2	221.7	330.1	148.1	95.4	253.3	2 648.1
33.8	52.5	96.3	28.4	20.1	67.9	986.6
153.1	241.0	357.4	160.8	130.6	294.2	2 972.7
86.8	319.0	202.2	108.5	76.7	174.7	1 848.8
66.9	90.1	151.9	82.7	63.9	133.4	1 445.6

retailing market-oriented. In the Standard Industrial Classification the Tertiary industries include MOHs 20 to 27.

3. Quaternary industries

Some geographers identify a group of activities, which are undifferentiated in Table 2.1, as Quaternary industries. These are concerned with the provision of information and expertise. Included in this group would be universities, 'think tanks' and research establishments. Such activities also tend to be market-oriented but could theoretically be located almost anywhere since information, which is what they deal in, can be transmitted easily from place to place by electronic media.

4. Secondary industries

This group has been left until the end of this summary because it is with the industries in MOHs 3 to 19 that this book is chiefly concerned. Industries in this group are characterized by the variety of their locations. Some are clearly located with reference to the final purchaser, others are strongly tied to their raw materials, while some are in between these two extremes. Because of the great variety of manufacturing industry it will be helpful, therefore, if we can discern valid general patterns of locational behaviour which help in understanding the principles of industrial location.

The information provided in Table 2.1 is in a rather indigestible form and it is only by working through it very carefully that any patterns can be discerned. It might be useful, therefore, to use a visual aid which depicts the information more clearly. Two simple ways of showing such data are, therefore, introduced here, while in Chapter 8 certain simple numerical methods of analysis are suggested.

1. The triangular graph

Let us assume, first, that we wish to show the difference between the proportions of employees in primary, secondary and tertiary industry in each of the economic planning regions of Britain. We can do this by drawing a triangular graph consisting of an equilateral triangle with each side divided into percentage scales. Fig. 2.2 shows how the 100% end of one scale is the 0% end of another. (In this case our three sides represent primary, secondary and tertiary industry. We will include quaternary industry with tertiary because of the lack of delimitation between these two in Table 2.1.) From our data we can calculate, for example, that in the South East 1.3% are employed in primary, 31.9% in secondary and 66.8% in tertiary industry. Each of the points is located on the appropriate axis and a tri-linear co-ordinate (this is self-explanatory if you look at the diagram) drawn parallel with the next scale.

Fig. 2.1. Primary, secondary, tertiary and quaternary industry – some examples.

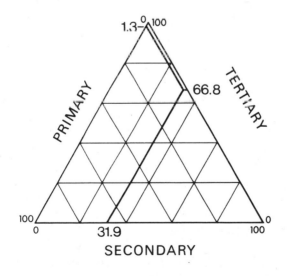

Fig. 2.2. Triangular graph to illustrate employment data.

Where the three lines meet we mark a dot illustrating the position of the South East on the graph. By plotting other areas a quick visual comparison of industrial specialization in each region is obtained.

2. The star diagram

The triangular graph deals with only three classes of data and, as we have seen, the Standard Industrial Classification involves far more. A larger number of classes can effectively be presented by means of a star diagram. Using a type of graph paper called 'polar-co-ordinate' any number of classes can be plotted on individual lines radiating a central point, each radius representing one industry group. Employment in each industry group is marked on each radius and if the marks on the radii are joined up a star-like effect is produced. Thus the longer the radius, the greater the proportion of total employment in that industry group (see Fig. 2.3).

ASSIGNMENTS

1. *Using the information provided in Table 2.1 and the triangular graph method described above, draw a graph to show the different percentages of employment in primary, secondary and tertiary industries in Scotland and Wales.*
2. *On a star diagram illustrate the nature of employment in three standard regions of Britain for the MOHs 3 to 19 inclusive, and compare the result with Fig. 2.3.*

B. The Nature of Manufacturing Industry

Manufacturing industry involves the conversion of raw materials or the assembly of parts to form a finished or semi-finished product. Such production is undertaken in *establishments* which may be parts of *enterprises* or *firms*. Manufacturing industry encompasses a vast range of products and because of this is found in a wide variety of types of location, as will be seen in subsequent chapters.

Some manufacturing industry has to be close to its raw material; in other cases it is located nearer its markets; and in others seems able to be almost anywhere and is thus called 'footloose'. Thus the industrialist is faced with the problem of weighing up the individual factors he believes to be important and selecting the location which best suits his particular case. Because manufacturing involves taking in raw materials or semi-finished products, and subsequently distributing completed or further-assembled products, the origins of the inputs and the destinations of the outputs may be important considerations.

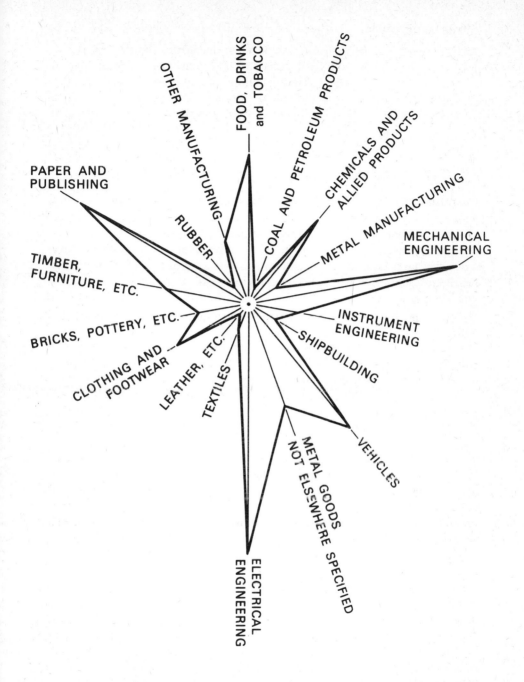

FOOD, DRINKS and TOBACCO

OTHER MANUFACTURING

COAL AND PETROLEUM PRODUCTS

CHEMICALS AND ALLIED PRODUCTS

PAPER AND PUBLISHING

RUBBER

METAL MANUFACTURING

MECHANICAL ENGINEERING

TIMBER, FURNITURE, ETC.

BRICKS, POTTERY, ETC.

INSTRUMENT ENGINEERING

CLOTHING AND FOOTWEAR

LEATHER, ETC.

SHIPBUILDING

TEXTILES

METAL GOODS NOT ELSEWHERE SPECIFIED

VEHICLES

ELECTRICAL ENGINEERING

Fig. 2.3. Star diagram showing relative percentages in different manufacturing industries for South East England.

17

Firms and plants

At this stage it is useful to distinguish between the factory and the firm.

1. *Firms* are economic and legal units and may consist of a large number of factories or plants as well as individual offices and research establishments.
2. *Plants* or factories have individual locations, and because of this geographers have tended to devote more energy to the study of factories than to that of firms.

Size and distribution of plants

Manufacturing establishments range in size from the small family works employing a man and a boy to the giant multi-national corporation with many thousands of employees. Most firms are small and few are big; over 25 000 in Britain employ 25 or fewer workers while only about 220 firms employ over 5 000. The large firms, however, account for over 45% of total employment and nearly 50% of output while those employing under 25 people account for 4% and 6% respectively. Although size is usually thought of in terms of number of workers, it can also be measured by value of output, extent of floorspace and site area.

Interestingly, the size distribution of a population of manufacturing establishments in a given town, region, or nation seems to form a pattern similar to that of settlement size distribution. The regular pattern produced when size is plotted against rank for a given object is found in a population of factories just as it is for many other phenomena. From common observation, we realize that there are few large objects and lots of small objects, but we may be less aware that when we draw a graph to show their rank-size distribution there is a striking amount of regularity and predictability. This regularity is illustrated in Fig. 2.4, which illustrates the number of industrial establishments plotted against their sizes for the province of Ontario in Canada. In this diagram the scales on each of the axes are plotted logarithmically. Such logarithmic scales are very useful when a wide range of values needs to be plotted. For instance, the graph is able to accommodate values from 1 to over 6 000. One would need a very large sheet of paper to draw such a graph using normal scales.

The graph shows that there are nearly 5 000 firms in the smallest category for all industries but only 20 in the largest. Almost parallel curves have been drawn for two individual industries. To a large extent geographers and other social scientists remain rather baffled by the regularity of such size distribution curves. Some have suggested that they represent some kind of underlying logic in the minds of men, others that they represent some kind of optimal or equilibrium position. They do illustrate the truth of the oft-quoted words of Sigwart, 'That there is more order in the world than appears at first sight is not discovered until the order is looked for.'[1] The search for *spatial order* forms a central theme of this book.

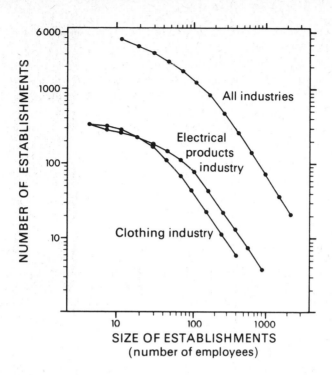

Fig. 2.4. Cumulative size distributions for permanent establishments and selected industries in Ontario 1965. (Source: L. Collins, 'Industrial size distributions and stochastic processes', *Progress in Geography*, **5**, 1973, p. 137)

C. Sources of Information for Industrial Geographers

We have already referred to the data provided each month in the *Department of Employment Gazette*, but these are provided at a rather aggregated level of scale; in other words, the size of the regions chosen as areal units is large and information about smaller areas (such as individual towns) is subsumed within them. In this section we shall consider some other sources of information: first, for industry *within* the urban area, and secondly, for industry aggregated at the urban, as opposed to the regional scale.

1. Intra-urban industry

The best way to establish the present-day distribution of industry and employment in your own (or any other) urban area is to go and look for yourself. This method does present some disadvantages, however. First, it is time and energy consuming; secondly, you may not be sure where to look for industry; thirdly, you may not be able to find the name of the firm, the reasons for its location, the nature of the product it manufactures or the number employed unless you obtain an interview with a member of the firm. This final point needs elaboration. Members of management – those members of the firm most likely to be able to give you accurate information about the firm and the factors influencing its location – are busy people; they are not employed to provide fieldworkers with information. The works superintendent of one factory recently wrote to the author, following a request to visit his factory, as follows:

> We thank you for your letter of … but regret to advise you that we shall be unable to grant your request to visit our works on the…. We get so many requests of a similar nature and being at the moment a small establishment employing less than 100 people, we simply cannot afford the time.

Such a response is not uncommon. Some firms may employ personnel officers, part of whose job is in the field of public relations. Even if a personnel manager is available, however, he is often not acquainted with the geographical aspects of the enterprise and is more aware of the techniques of production than the location factors considered by the firm or the locational attitudes of the top decision makers. Indeed, a problem with all interview/questionnaire surveys in industrial geography is that the respondent is very probably unaware of the factors influencing the location decision since he may not have been with the firm (or he may not even have been born) when the decision was made.

It may be best to avoid interviewing members of factory management for another reason: the composition of a questionnaire is, in itself, something of a science, needing great care in its construction and presentation. If in the final analysis, however, you do decide to make a personal survey of the factory, be sure to write first and arrange a mutually convenient time.

There are, in fact, other sources of information available for the urban industrial geographer, such as maps and directories.

(a) *Maps* The Second Land Utilization Survey maps provide an easily available source of information about the location of industry in towns. Unlike the monumental First Land Use Survey, undertaken in the 1930s by Britain's most famous geographer, Sir Dudley Stamp, the second survey divides urban land use into residential and industrial components. What is more, the type of industry is also specified. Now the maps have their limitations; the most basic objection for the industrial geographer being that they only show the *area* occupied by industry and not numbers employed or value of output. A strong positive relationship does exist, however, between area of factory and workforce so this objection may not be too important. Although land use survey maps represent a static picture of land use in the early sixties, they are useful in providing raw material for formulating and testing models, as the exercises in Chapter 4 will show. (The maps are available from The Director of the Second Land Utilization Survey of Britain, Department of Geography, University of London, Kings College, Strand, London, WCR2 2LS.)

Unfortunately, maps for all areas have not yet been published so you should investigate whether your local planning department has produced a map of urban land use in its Master Plan. Such documents are usually available in your local reference library.

(b) *Directories and newspapers* Directories are useful in locating industries in towns, not only at the present time, but also for the past. They are, therefore, useful for those interested in reconstructing past urban industrial geographies.

Perhaps the best known, *Kelly's Directory* lists every occupant of every building in every street of most British towns. All that is needed, therefore, is a street map to locate the industrial establishments in the appropriate place. As *Kelly's Directory* stretches back over many years and has run to over 160 editions, it is especially useful for the reconstruction of past urban industrial geographies. The Yellow Pages of the *Telephone Directory* provide another possible source. Some areas are catered for by specialist industrial and trade directories – *An Industrial Directory of Wales and Monmouthshire* has been published on several occasions since the war. In some cases individual industries produce their own directories. Your local reference library is the best place to enquire about the availability of such material.

Local newspapers provide a further source for the industrial geographer. The close examination of the local press often reveals the opening of new factories, the addition of extra floorspace or the closure of a plant. A typical press report on an individual industrial development is reproduced in Chapter 3 (page 29). Such press coverage often also includes one of the most difficult items to obtain – the numbers employed in the factories. At the urban or micro level these data are very difficult to obtain unless personal visits are made to the factories. Advanced research workers have used data from the Factory Inspectorate but it is not suggested that readers of this book should try this source.

A final source of data worthy of mention at this micro-scale is *Trade and Industry*, the journal of the Department of Trade and Industry. This is especially useful for checking on newly opened and expanded government-built factories in many of the towns in our older industrial regions.

2. The industrial structure of towns

Instead of wishing to know where industry is located *within* towns we may be more interested in contrasting industrial structures of *different* towns, in the way we compared different regions in the exercises on page 16.

One possible source, though of limited value because of its datedness, is the 1966 Sample Census *Economic Activity County Leaflets*. These provide the number of persons in employment for each county, county borough, urban area with a population of over 50 000, new town and conurbation centre for each MOH and Minimum List Heading of the S.I.C. Leaflets based on the 1971 census should be available by 1976.

Information of other use to industrial geographers may be obtained from the Department of Employment's Employment Record II (ERII) forms for each employment exchange area in the country. Employment exchange areas do not correspond exactly with urban areas, but the differences between the two need not concern us at this stage. For the years up to 1971 it is not unduly difficult to obtain data on the employment for each of the MOHs in any town from the Statistics Division of the Department of Employment. It is not current practice, however, to provide this information in a fully disaggregated form. Instead, figures are provided for employment in exchange areas under nine headings, as shown for the example of Oxford in Table 2.2. (Figures for a single industry might reveal confidential information about the numbers employed by individual firms.) The main value of such data is to show the proportion of total employment in the town engaged in primary, secondary and tertiary industries, although it is to be regretted that employment in manufacturing is presented in such a highly aggregated manner.

Table 2.2. Nature of data contained in Employment Record II forms. Employees in employment in Oxford/Wallingford, June, 1971. (Source: Department of Employment)

	Males	Females	(Thousands) Total
Primary industries (orders 1 & 2)	1.5	0.4	1.9
Manufacturing industries (orders 3–19)	27.2	5.1	32.2
Construction (order 20)	4.5	0.4	4.8
Gas, electricity and water (order 21)	0.8	0.2	1.1
Distributive trades (order 23)	5.6	6.7	12.3
Miscellaneous services† (order 26)	3.5	3.9	7.4
Public administration (order 27)	6.9	5.4	12.3
Other service industries* (orders 22, 24 & 25)	17.1	21.6	38.7
Not classified by industry	0.0	0.0	0.0
Total all industries and services†	67.0	43.6	110.6

* Transport and communication; insurance, banking, finance and business services, and professional and scientific services.

† Excluding private domestic service.

Key Ideas

A. *Classification of industries* (pages 11–16)
1. There is a basic distinction between primary, secondary, tertiary and quaternary industries which are respectively concerned with extracting raw materials, processing or manufacturing, providing services and providing expertise.
2. Locationally, primary industry is raw material-oriented; tertiary industry is market-oriented, quaternary industry is also market-oriented but is potentially footloose, while secondary industry possesses a wide range of locational attributes.

B. *The nature of manufacturing industry* (pages 16–19)
1. Manufacturing industry is undertaken in plants (factories or establishments) which may be only part of the system of a firm.
2. Most firms are small in scale and only relatively few are large.
3. For most regions firms seem to exhibit a regular rank-size distribution.

Additional Activities

1. From members of your group ascertain the percentage of parents engaged in the three main sections of employment. How does this compare with the national figures? (See Table 2.1.)
2. Attempt a short definition of industrial geography.

Reading

A. ODELL, P., 'Britain and the Golden Triangle', *New Society*, 14 May 1970, pp. 821–3.
B. Central Statistical Office, *Standard Industrial Classification*, HMSO, 1968.
C. OLIVER, J. L., 'Directories and their use in geographical enquiry', *Geography*, **49**, 1964, pp. 400–9.

Factors of production as factors in location

Before reading on in this chapter imagine yourself to be an industrialist faced with the problem of setting up for the first time a factory concerned with the production of, say, cardboard packing cases. One of the things about which you have to decide is a location for your factory. Make a list of 10–15 factors which you might consider before choosing the location and rank them in order of importance. (As you read through the chapters which follow, you might like to look back at this list from time to time and see if your hunches are borne out by the work of others.)

This chapter is designed to introduce you to the basic requirements of all manufacturing industries and the fact that these requirements vary in quality and quantity from place to place. If all location factors did not differ in such a way, any place would be as good as another as a factory location.

A. A Systems Approach to Manufacturing

The fundamental factors influencing practically every manufacturing establishment may be regarded as part of a simple system. On the one hand there are many inputs, the factory itself processes these inputs (they become 'throughputs') and the finished or semi-finished products emerge as outputs. This concept is illustrated in Fig. 3.1. Input factors are shown on the left hand side of the diagram and the finished products as outputs on the right. These inputs and outputs are moved along transport networks.

The inputs and transportation of materials may be regarded as *cost* factors while the sale of goods to the market produces *revenue* for the firm, the difference between cost and revenue being *profit*.

In this chapter we will look at some of the more important components of Fig. 3.1.

At a different level of scale, as we have already noted (on page 5), the individual firm can also be regarded as a system. While some small firms are,

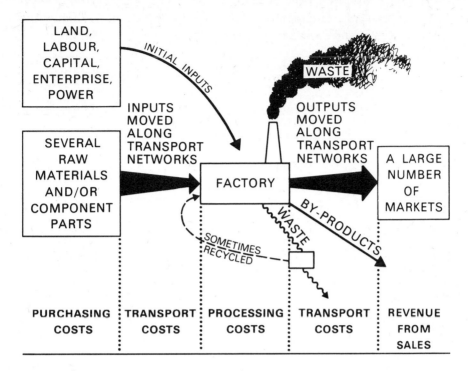

LAND,
LABOUR,
CAPITAL,
ENTERPRISE,
POWER

INITIAL INPUTS

WASTE

INPUTS
MOVED
ALONG
TRANSPORT
NETWORKS

OUTPUTS
MOVED
ALONG
TRANSPORT
NETWORKS

SEVERAL
RAW
MATERIALS
AND/OR
COMPONENT
PARTS

FACTORY

A LARGE
NUMBER
OF
MARKETS

BY-PRODUCTS

WASTE

SOMETIMES
RECYCLED

PURCHASING COSTS	TRANSPORT COSTS	PROCESSING COSTS	TRANSPORT COSTS	REVENUE FROM SALES

Fig. 3.1. Location factors for manufacturing. Notice how several initial costs are incurred before the purchase of raw material or component parts takes place. Some firms may be pulled to the raw materials, others to the markets and the final locational choice may be influenced by a variety of factors not even on the diagram.

indeed, single entities operating from one plant, many firms – especially large corporations like Ford (Table 3.1), the British Steel Corporation or Esso – may be aggregates of many different activities. Each of these activities could theoretically (and often does in practice) possess an independent location, thus necessitating links between them. Fig. 3.2 shows how a firm may consist of a 'packet' of manufacturing functions, made up of several activities, four of which are likely to be locationally independent in the case of a large firm. These are end-product manufacture, component manufacture, research and development, and sales, marketing and distribution. On the other hand, storage and administration are likely to be at the same location as the plant manufacturing the end-product. Thus, when we talk about a manufacturing location, we ought to be quite clear that we know which part of the packet we are talking about. Fig. 3.2 also suggests that different location factors may influence different parts of the firm's manufacturing system.

Table 3.1 shows how it is impossible to talk of 'location of the Ford company' without considering at least 18 different locations. The registered office is in London – the centre of the spatial organization of the country – the

25

production of Ford's carburettors and rear axles, on the other hand, is in places like Belfast and Swansea.

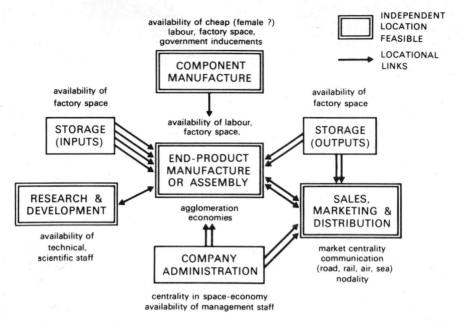

Fig. 3.2. The 'packet' of manufacturing functions and some suggested location factors. (Source: D. Keeble, 'Employment mobility in Britain', in M. Chisholm & G. Manners (eds.), *Spatial Policy Problems of the British Economy*, Cambridge University Press, 1971, p. 36)

ASSIGNMENTS

1. *Suggest why, in the 'packet of manufacturing functions' (Fig. 3.2) the storage and administrative components of the firm's system are likely to be at the same location as the plant manufacturing the end-product, whereas marketing and distribution might be expected to be located elsewhere.*

2. *Consider Table 3.1 and discuss to what extent the Ford company fits into the idea of the manufacturing 'packet'. Can you draw maps based on this sort of information for any other companies?*

B. Factors affecting the Location of Manufacturing Industry

1. Capital

By capital is meant not only financial capital but fixed capital equipment such as plant, machinery and buildings. Fixed capital is vitally important as a factor

26

Table 3.1. Ford locations in the United Kingdom in 1974

	Location	Employment (including staff)	Floor space ('000 square feet)	Main function
1	Belfast	1100	281	Carburettor and distributor production
2	Halewood	14000	4991	Production of Capris, Escort car and van range/Transmission for vehicle range
3	Leamington	1300	229	Production of truck and tractor transmission castings
4	Daventry	1550	1772	Parts headquarters and depot, and service training college
5	Langley	2400	1130	Medium and heavy truck assembly
6	Enfield	1350	301	Electrical components manufacture
7	Harold Hill	600	68	Apprentice training school
8	Warley	2000	440	Administrative headquarters
9	Dunton	3300	912	Research and Engineering Centre
10	Basildon Tractor	3300	1360	Production of tractors and engines
11	Basildon Radiator	900	330	Radiator production
12	Aveley	950	682	Ford Advanced Vehicle Operations (specialist car production)
13	Dagenham	27500	9571	Cortina and Consul-Granada production/Engine manufacture
14	Woolwich	700	203	Parts machining
15	Croydon	300	114	Manufacture of small stampings
16	Southampton	3750	1164	Production of Transits and truck cabs
17	Swansea	2550	1103	Production of rear axles and heavy CV
18	Treforest	360	60	Production of spark plug ceramic insulators

Other facilities include:
Six District Sales Offices, 16 Ford Motor Credit Offices, a Marketing School and a Service Training College, 11 Service and Administration Offices and 7 Storage and Workshop areas.

influencing the present-day location of industry, since buildings and 'social capital' (i.e. houses, schools) are not easily written off and thus tend to perpetuate industrial areas, even though the original occupants of the factories may have long since disappeared.

Such *Industrial Inertia* means that industrial areas may survive for many years even though the regional location factors which led to their initial development may have been outdated by technological progress. Industrial inertia is classically illustrated by the British iron and steel industry. In a large-scale industry such as this, it has been frequently felt advisable to update existing plant and equipment rather than to establish brand new factories at different locations. Thus Kenneth Warren has written colourfully about the location of the present-day British sheet steel industry being explained largely by 'the locational commitment of history'. The factories are 'relics, the flotsam of locational history' operating 'in locations moulded in the past'.[1] A notable example is the Ebbw Vale steel plant in South Wales which, on the basis of site and locational characteristics, is unsuitable as a modern steelworks.

Just as the forces of the past are invariably felt in the present-day industrial landscape, 'undoubtedly the greatest influence on the future location of people and activities is their present location.'[2] We will see later in this chapter that, over time, the pull of location factors has changed in emphasis – the pull of the market, for example, gradually becoming more important than the pull of raw materials. The value of capital in the form of industrial inertia remains, however, as the continued importance of many old industrial regions testifies.

In many parts of Britain, factories erected originally for one purpose have been converted for a different use at the present day. This is exemplified by the conversion of a large number of former cotton mills in Lancashire to smaller manufacturing units. Table 3.2, for instance, shows the changing use of cotton mills in Bolton. Many wartime ordnance factories have been similarly converted, while Plate 3.1 and the newspaper extract (Fig. 3.3) show that the fact that a building was not originally built for manufacturing purposes may not prevent it being converted. Although capital equipment is rarely mobile between different *places*, therefore, it can certainly be very mobile between *uses*.

Obviously, the firm setting up in business for the first time, or one which is looking for room to expand, may find the availability of fixed capital such as the old post office (Fig. 3.3), an important location factor. A readily available, and easily convertible, building saves the industrialist time and, therefore, money.

The cost of fixed capital varies spatially. This partly reflects the spatial variations in industrial land costs (see Fig. 3.5) and partly the variations in demand for industrial premises. In addition, costs of factory construction and costs of raw materials may vary spatially in large political units such as the USA. The variations in the costs of buildings certainly contribute an important part to the construction of total cost surfaces.

Plate 3.1. The conversion of existing fixed capital. The former British Railways repair works at Caerphilly, South Wales, is now the Harold Wilson Industrial Estate. *(Author's photograph)*

Mini-factory opens in old post office

A former post office has taken on a new lease of life with the sale of postage stamps being replaced by the production of women's underwear, and if the venture by a Midland firm is successful another four "mini-factories" may be set up in the area.

Walker Reid Ltd., of Nottingham, a subsidiary of the giant Courtaulds combine, have opened a small works in the former post office at Llanidloes as the nucleus of a chain of units to be created within 25 miles of Newtown.

By concentrating on small works instead of one large factory, the company are confident that they will get the labour they need to cope with production.

The man behind the idea is Mr. Joseph Foster, a con-sultant with Courtaulds, who lives at Cwm Rheidol, near Aberystwyth.

"We are confident that there are pockets of labour available, but we realise the transport difficulties in Mid-Wales and that workers would have great difficulty in travelling to one central spot." he said.

"By using small works in several towns we are optimistic we will get staff and the venture will be a success."

The Llanidloes unit went into production this week with a labour force of 12, mostly women. Within a month 33 will be employed.

Later this year the works will switch to manufacturing disposable paper underwear.

Suitable sites for the four other small works are being considered by the firm.

Fig. 3.3. (*Western Mail*, 16 May 1969)

Table 3.2. The changing use of selected former cotton mills in Bolton. (Source: Bolton Public Relations Department)

Name of mill	Taken over by	New use(s)	Approx total floor area	Approx area re-occupied	Estimated labour force
Flash Street Mills (3) Great Moor Street	Leslie Fink Ltd (for letting-off in portions)	Occupied by almost 30 tenant firms for variety of purposes including: manufacture of rainwear, shopfittings, confectionery, photo-electric and electronic control equipment, cane baskets, engineering patterns, signs and light engineering products; also for printing, wholesale and retail distribution, storage and offices	198 000	180 000	250–300
Columbia Mill, Bedford Street	ditto	Poultry processing and packing	120 000	10 000	20
Albion No. 4 Mill, Coe Street	ditto	Engineering, assembly and distribution of office furniture	118 000	30 000	40
Grecian Mill, Lever Street	ditto	Engineering, textile printing; manufacture of dyes and chemicals; wholesale distribution and offices	237 000	100 000	150
Haslam Nos. 2 & 3 Mills, Chorley Old Road	ditto	Being let in portions, as yet only three tenant firms in occupation (pharmaceutical chemicals, engineering and printing)	218 000	25 000	50
Bradford Mill, Weston Street	Kaylis Chemical Co Ltd	Manufacture of thermoplastic moulding compounds	140 000	140 000	40

Mill / Address	Company	Description		
Milton Mill, Mule Street	Vantona Textiles Ltd	Engineering; storage	25 000	25 000	15
Orient Mill, Brandwood Street	Jas Lever & Sons Ltd	Rope and twine manufacture	61 000	61 000	120
Gibraltar Mill, Gibraltar Street	Turner & Brown Ltd	(1) Plastic fabricating; (2) Painting and decorating	45 000	45 000	100
Haslam Street Mill	Hawker Siddeley Dynamics Co Ltd	Engineering and storage	50 000	50 000	40
Woodside Nos. 1, 2 & 3 Mills, Rishton Lane	Farnworth Engineering Co Ltd	Engineering	169 000	169 000	180
Gilnow Mill, Spa Road	Southern Bros Ltd	Manufacture of tubular steel furniture and car seats	159 000	159 000	450
Brownlow Fold Mill, Tennyson Street	De Luxe-Topper Ltd	Toy manufacture	63 000	63 000	120
Egyptian Mill, Slater Street	Vernon & Co Ltd	Manufacture of moulded paper products	135 000	135 000	30
Mossfield Mill, Vernon Street	Whewells (Soft Drinks) Limited	Manufacture and bottling of aerated waters; bottling and distribution of wines and spirits	227 000	227 000	150
Haslam No. 1 Mill, Chorley Old Road	Jos Maude & Co Ltd	Yarn processing	164 000	164 000	100
Garfield Mill, Cannon Street	F. Tyrell & Co Ltd	Manufacture of animal feeding stuff additives (part let off to manufacturers of mineral waters)	39 000	35 000	35

Financial capital is also essential before any enterprise can commence. Its availability is far from ubiquitous, and for small firms the availability of local pools of financial capital may be critical. Capital for forming a new plant may be more forthcoming from an area in which the industrialist is well known to the local bank, since his personal credentials and repute will count for something in the eyes of the bankers. The large corporation, on the other hand, does not have such worries. It can finance its new developments internally by ploughing back its profits and through the issue of shares on the national stock market. It is thus independent of local capital supplies.

Some authorities have assumed that financial capital is perfectly mobile spatially. This seems far from being the case, however, especially in the early stages of economic growth. Estall illustrates this with a case study from New England:

> The early 19th century distribution of cotton textile manufacture within New England was significantly affected by the geographical immobility of capital. Investment funds came chiefly from shipping and commercial interests located in coastal settlements, especially at Boston and in communities around Narragansett Bay, and the prospective investors showed a marked reluctance to put money into projects that were very far from home. This was one consideration among several that contributed to the great concentration of cotton textile capacity in and around Boston and the Providence – Pawtucket areas at that time. Gradually, the parochial outlook was overcome and by the 1830s Boston capital was supporting textile mills at Manchester and Nashua in southern New Hampshire, and at Lewiston and other points in Maine. Subsequently investment funds from Boston reached further and further from the city. The key elements in this progression were, naturally, advances in communications, in security and in the organization of financial affairs. With such advances, Boston capital was made available for investment up to, and then beyond, the boundaries of the New England region.[3]

Certain types of capital are far from mobile even in developed countries, however, especially if that capital is provided by the government (see Chapter 8), which is highly selective in its choice of sites and locations to be helped in this way.

While the cost of financial capital (i.e. the rate of interest) does not vary spatially, we should remember that we should think of it in conjunction with the cost of fixed capital which, as we have seen, can vary considerably from place to place.

ASSIGNMENTS

1. Can any common features be distinguished in the firms taking over the old cotton mills listed in Table 3.2?
2. From the example of the New England cotton industry described on page

32, show how the location of the nineteenth-century cotton textile industry was influenced by the immobility of financial capital.
3. From examples in your own town or region, illustrate the concept of industrial inertia.
4. Locate buildings in your local area which are today occupied by manufacturing industry but which were formerly erected for another purpose (or another industry). What kinds of buildings are most common? What kind of pattern does a map of such buildings produce?

2. Land

In its broadest sense, land consists of soil, minerals and climate – in other words, the 'natural environment' or 'natural endowment' of the earth's surface. While formerly in the Western World, and in some parts of the so-called 'underdeveloped' world today, environment greatly influenced human response, it is often now a case of man influencing his environment rather than vice versa. Today it is technically possible for a factory making matchsticks to be located in the Sahara Desert – if someone is prepared to overcome the environmental cost involved. What tends to happen, however, is that businessmen do not set up at such a costly location unless absolutely necessary; it is the cost involved, and not the environment of the Sahara, which inhibits them. The way geographers today look at the natural environment has been summarized by Morrill:

> the natural environment of an area is significant only insofar as it is easier or more difficult to carry on a particular activity in a particular place. The environment should be evaluated in terms of its cost to development desired by man.[4]

Similarly, the space-economist Walter Isard, notes the relationship between changing technology and the landscape:

> physical factors have critical value as barriers only with respect to a given or assumed state of technology.[5]

In other words, as technology improves former physical constraints become less significant.

(a) Sites for industry

Land requirements vary tremendously among the large number of different industries. A small plot for a workshop employing a man and a boy may be only a few square metres. On the other hand, factories are taking up more space since the development of conveyor belt technology favours single storey buildings. In addition, the increased use of cars for the journey to work necessitates large spaces for car parks. The shape of the land, therefore, must partially control the location and the cost of the individual enterprise and consequently decisions about location. The land requirements for an integrated steel plant have been usefully summarized by Trevor M. Thomas:

A steelworks with a continuous strip mill having a capacity of three million ingot tons a year requires a flat site about 5 km long by 1.5 km wide with the subsoil and underlying formations having good load bearing properties sufficient to carry heavy plant without resorting to excessive expense for extensive foundation piling. For reasons of land economy good farmland should be avoided. Large quantities of suitable soft water, up to 90 000 m³ per day, are essential, particularly for the production of sheet tinplate. Unlike power stations with a coastal or estuarine location no use can be made of sea water and hard water requires special treatment which would add to production costs.[6]

In the 1950s Richard Thomas and Baldwin faced a difficult problem over the siting of a major steelworks. A short list of ten possible sites was drawn up by a firm of consulting engineers before Llanwern, just to the east of Newport in Monmouthshire, was chosen. Even this site, however, needed some modification by man before the building of the steelworks could commence. Trevor Thomas continues:

After a careful analysis of all the relevant factors the promoting Company reached their decision that from nearly every conceivable aspect the best available site in the country was Llanwern, the western edge of which lies less than a km east of the eastern built up limits of Newport. This comprised 1 040 ha of flat, ill drained, agricultural land, all lying below the 8 m contour line and located within a few km of the Bristol Channel coastline. Apart from a few isolated farms the site area was uninhabited. This was drained by a complicated system of 22 km of reens and in addition there were 9 km of reens, maintained by the local drainage authority, which would be severed from their outfall by the construction works on the site.

The site area forms about a tenth of the so called Monmouthshire Moors which stretch eastward for nearly 16 km and at their maximum north-south width extend inland for 5 km from the Bristol Channel coastline. Government approval had previously been given for a £1 million scheme of drainage improvement, irrigation and sea defence works embracing the whole of this low lying area. With regard to the actual steelworks site the Ministry of Agriculture, Fisheries and Food classified more than half of its acreage as low producing with the change of user not giving rise to a serious loss of agricultural production. The area lying immediately to the east was also of very low productive value and could at some future date provide space for tipping slag and refuse. Only minor modifications of the original drainage scheme would be required to allow for the additional run off caused by the steelworks development.

To provide a better foundation for some of the buildings and also to raise the greater part of the site above possible flood level it was later found necessary to import nearly 10 million tons of ballast in the form of quarry waste or burnt colliery shale from locations as far away as the Rhondda and Merthyr Tydfil.[7]

In some areas man has gone so far as to win land back from the sea, in order to find suitable sites for giant processing plants such as oil refineries. This sort of constructive work is illustrated by the Dutch Europort complex, west of Rotterdam.

Land reclamation for industry can also occur on a much smaller scale. In many areas land for industry is scarce: in valleys it is often too steep for industry; marshy areas may not be able to support heavy weights; what land is available may be derelict. Fig. 3.4 illustrates how man can transform a derelict site such as that of a former colliery, and convert it into a thriving industrial area. Such land conversions are possible through the willingness, resourcefulness and ability of local engineers, plus a considerable amount of money; in such cases industry exists in spite of, not because of, the local environment.

Thus it is clear that the number of sites with precisely prescribed conditions is decreasing and, from necessity, man is having increasingly to modify sites to suit himself. Nevertheless, site constraints do exist. Landform conditions do have a critical effect on an enterprise if, for example, the cost of clearing land to extend a factory is prohibitive. Apart from its inland location, the Ebbw Vale steel plant in South Wales has been hampered by being located in a narrow valley with steep sides. Thus the shape of the land, being a spatial variable, has the same effect upon the location of industry as it does upon the cultivation of certain crops.

Just as physical gradients tend to repel factories so, too, may cost gradients; just as the stability and flatness of land may vary from place to place so, too, does its cost. Fig. 3.5 shows a 'rent-surface' map of South Wales and Severnside. The lines are not height but rent contours (drawn by plotting the rent per sq ft on industrial estates in 1969). It is clear that there is considerable spatial variation in rents, with high cost 'peaks' around Cardiff and Bristol and a lower cost 'trough' in the heart of the South Wales coalfield.

We have seen several examples of land as a spatial variable. It is obviously not spatially mobile, but it is economically mobile – that is, it can move from one use to another. The inter-industry mobility of a piece of land is, however, influenced by the range of uses for which the land is suitable (for instance, a site housing a light industrial plant could only accommodate an oil refinery or integrated steel plant at prohibitive cost).

(b) *Amenity factors*

Land can affect industry in other ways. Industrialists are increasingly having to blend their plants into the landscape for environmental purposes, and the preservation of amenities for the public may be reflected in increased costs to the firm. In the case of oil refineries which have been forced to locate at deepwater sites because of the increasing size of tankers, the environments selected for location are often ones of outstanding natural beauty, such as Milford Haven in south-west Wales where much of the area around one of Britain's best deepwater tanker terminals is in a National Park. 'A refinery covering about a square mile, with chimneys 300 feet high, is bound to be

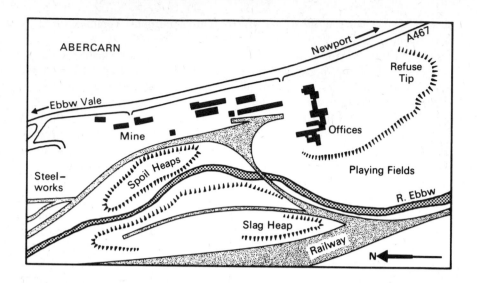

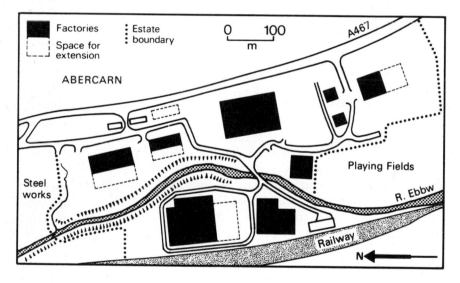

Fig. 3.4. The formerly derelict site of the Prince of Wales Colliery (top) has been transformed into the Prince of Wales Industrial Estate (bottom) at Abercarn, Monmouthshire.

rather noticeable in a rural landscape only 200 feet above sea level. By overwhelming its surroundings it could cause considerable scenic damage and result in unpleasantness and inconvenience to local people.'[8] As far as possible refineries are blended into the landscape (see Plate 3.2).

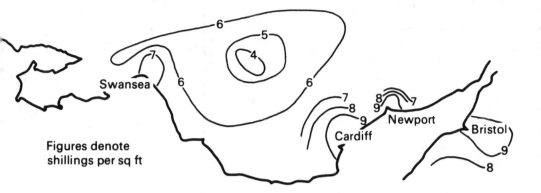

Fig. 3.5. Generalized industrial estate rent-surface map for South Wales and Severnside, 1969.

(c) Land as wealth

One of the main reasons why land is important to manufacturing as a factor of production is that, in its broadest sense, it provides wealth in the form of minerals. Minerals which need processing before they become worth purchasing may attract processing plants to them if they are bulky or lose a large proportion of their weight in the production process. The iron industry is a classic example of an industry said to be raw material-oriented – a subject which we discuss in greater detail in Chapter 5. On the other hand, some minerals, such as oil, lose hardly any weight in the production process and so exert a less strong influence on the location of refineries. Other industries, it must be emphasized, are not directly concerned with taking in raw materials as such, but use semi-finished components as inputs. The sources of these inputs may again influence the location of the plant, as we will see in Chapters 5 and 7.

Minerals are rarely exhausted; as they become increasingly inaccessible the cost of mining them becomes too expensive to be worthwhile. In the case of South Wales, for instance, the local iron ore on the northern outcrop of the South Wales Coalfield became increasingly costly to mine in competition with cheaper, imported ores. This resulted in many iron works in the north being closed down, and new developments taking place on the coast to deal with imported supplies.

Similarly, increasing costs of mining iron ore in the Lake Superior region of North America have meant that new fields have had to be opened up in, for example, Labrador and Venezuela.

Plate 3.2. Esso Terminal and Refinery, Milford Haven, 1973. As the installation lies across the boundary of a National Park, the main processing areas and tankage have been landscaped into a valley on the refinery site to minimise visual impact. The tankage outside the valley has been installed so as to minimise the visual impact when viewed from a distance by the creation of an unbroken skyline. In order to assist in obtaining the result, tanks are now being painted to merge in with the surrounding countryside – (see tankage on left of photograph where the tanks have been painted). (Esso photograph)

(d) Land as a provider of power

Since land also provides varying forms of energy for industrial use this, too, can be a localizing factor for industrial establishments.

(i) *Water* provided a ready source of power for many centuries and man responded by selecting industrial sites near swiftly flowing streams which provided the energy to drive his mills and machines. Fig. 3.6 illustrates the location of cloth-making in late fourteenth-century Somerset. The narrow valleys of the Mendips could be easily dammed to provide the water power to drive the overshot water wheel. Similar locations were developed for the textile industry of Yorkshire and for the milling of various products by water power in many parts of the country. Eventually, of course, water was replaced as a source of energy by coal and oil.

Water still remains an important location factor. Indeed, it is still used to provide power, not direct to the factory but by means of hydro-electric power stations generating electricity which is fed via a grid to houses and factories some distance away. Nevertheless, for many industries, access to water still

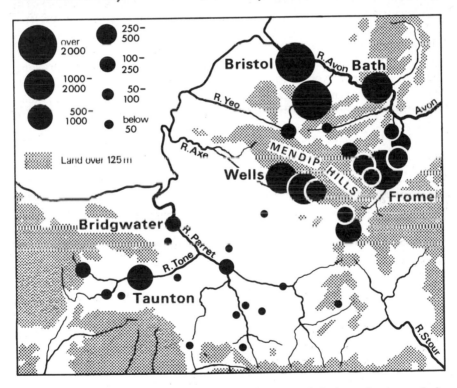

Fig. 3.6. Notice the relationship between the location of cloth production and the location of rivers in the fourteenth-century Somerset textile industry. (Source: R. A. Pelham, 'Fourteenth-century England', in H. C. Darby (ed.) *An Historical Geography of England before 1800*, Cambridge University Press, 1963, p. 252)

39

remains important. The iron and steel industry, for example, uses water in three main ways:

(a) in transporting raw materials to the blast furnace and moving finished products to markets;

(b) in satisfying the large and varied needs of the iron and steel mills (e.g. cooling, quenching coke);

(c) in facilitating waste disposal.

In the mid-1950s it was estimated that 57 tonnes of water were used in the production of one tonne of pig iron in the American steel industry.[9] The equivalent amount of solid material used was 3.2 tonnes. In fact, much water is re-cycled in the iron and steel industry and in the case of North America less than 2% of the circulated supply is not re-used.

In addition to the uses noted above, water is required by many factories for other purposes, for example washing plant and materials, staff hygiene and the testing of equipment such as pumps.

(ii) *Coal's* impact in the shape of what has been called 'carboniferous capitalism' was first felt in Britain near the end of the nineteenth century. The development of the steam engine and the use of coking coal in the iron industry have led Estall and Buchanan to aver that by the nineteenth century 'the optimum location for many industries was where large quantities of coal could be procured economically – on the coalfield. This was the principal reason for the growth of the great industrial concentrations on the coalfields of the United Kingdom.'[10] Towards the end of the nineteenth century technical advances in the iron industry began to reduce the importance of coal on industrial locations. Whereas Newcomen's steam engine in 1708 required 9 kg of coal per horse power hour generated, James Watt's engine (1770s) consumed about 3–4 kg. By the early 1920s only 500 g were required in electricity generation using large turbines. Today, coal used in power stations provides the basis of power for much industry by means of the electricity grid, and so electricity as a source of power has become virtually ubiquitous – it is found almost everywhere. This has led geographers to coin the term 'footloose' to describe those industries which are relatively untied to localized sources of energy.

(iii) *Oil* refining on a national scale is a raw material-oriented industry, the refineries being located mainly at tidewater sites. (Note that on a world scale the industry is market-oriented, being located mainly at the markets and not in the oil producing countries – with notable exceptions.) To some extent – though not as much as with coal in the nineteenth century – other industries using products made in oil refineries are being attracted to the source of oil imports near the refinery. The growth of chemical factories linked to the Fawley refinery near Southampton illustrates how such industrial agglomerations have developed at 'modified raw material' sites (in this case points of entry of oil to the country).

(e) Climate

This is included here as part of the 'natural environment' though it is not so easy to assess the importance of climate as an industrial location factor.

North American advertisements show how the industrial climate for profits may coincide spatially with a favourable physical climate.

> Denver (Colorado) is the only major city in the US to combine the maximum amount of sunshine with the optimum comfort index.... It's why Denverites are able to play shirt-sleeve golf in January while skiers are on the powder snow only 50 miles away.

> The climate of the Okanagan Valley (British Columbia) is second to none, passing even Bermuda and the Bahamas in total hours of summer sunshine. The atmosphere is generally mild and dry, with an average rainfall of only 10 inches.... You don't have to retire to the country if your plant is in the Okanagan.[11]

It seems that science-based industries have, in fact, gone to the sunnier parts of USA (California, for example) but to what extent climate alone is responsible is debateable. This topic will be discussed more fully in Chapter 6 where consideration is given to how factory managers perceive their environment.

ASSIGNMENTS

1. *Draw a cross section (a section similar to a relief section) across the South Wales area from the northern edge of the region to Cardiff, using the information provided in Fig. 3.5. What does it show?*
2. *On the basis of information from local estate agents, see if it is possible to construct a cost surface map of your local region. The information required to produce such a map would be the rents for factory floor space.*
3. *Suggest why major industrial regions are less likely to grow up around oil ports than they did around coalfields in the nineteenth century.*

3. Labour

Like land, labour varies spatially in quality and quantity. It also varies in cost, in its ability and in its reputation for militancy. For some industries labour costs form a very high proportion of total costs and, if costs vary from place to place, may exert a strong locational influence. Other industries, employing few workers, may be capital intensive and thus less tied to sources of labour.

(a) *The nature of local labour* A large urban area possessing a labour force with a variety of skills might seem a more appropriate location for a firm needing a large labour force than would a small town. On the other hand, if a particular place had a bad reputation in the field of labour relations, firms might be repelled for this reason. For example, the Pilkington Company planned a new glass-producing factory at Skelmersdale New Town but are said to have moved it because the area had such a reputation. In the period before World War Two many industrialists thought that places like South Wales possessed such militant labour that industry would never function satisfactorily there. The fact that the region did attract industry shows how the actual nature of a place may differ considerably from how potential industrialists may think of it. People can be prejudiced against places, as well as against other people. (See Chapter 6.)

In some areas, over a period of time, local pools of skilled labour may develop, thus making such regions more likely to attract any new industries requiring the skills concerned. In other cases, a predominantly female labour force may be required thus favouring mining areas and other regions with few possibilities for female employment. For this reason, many female intensive industries are found in industrial South Wales and in Yorkshire.

The absence of a pool of unemployed labour need not be a deterrent to industry; the arrival of a new firm may simply mean that workers leave existing jobs and transfer to the new arrival. This may even occur where unemployment rates are high (see page 184 for an example). Despite this, however, labour reserves are often quoted by industrialists when asked to name important location factors, as Table 3.5 indicates.

(b) *The cost of labour* is another spatial variable though it is fair to say that national unionization of labour has significantly reduced regional disparities. However, as Table 3.3 shows, regional disparities in average hourly earnings, albeit small in degree, do exist. In Table 3.3, an index of 100 is adopted for the national average, so that regional divergences from this national figure can be easily appreciated. Note how, for example, the average hourly earnings in paper and printing in Wales are over ten points below the national average. In addition, the actual average figures in pence per hour are provided. It should be added that productivity (to which earnings may be related) may also vary regionally.

In countries where unionization is less developed, variations are likely to be much higher. If a manufacturer wishes to minimize his costs, a low labour cost area could be an important influence on the final location of his plant.

(c) *Labour mobility* can be divided into spatial mobility and economic mobility – workers being less mobile between places than between jobs. In many older industrial areas where traditional employment is in decline workers *have* to be economically mobile if they wish to remain in work. Often government retraining centres help to increase the job mobility of, for example, former coal miners. The relative lack of spatial mobility of labour is reflected in the fact that government regional policy (Chapter 8) has overwhelmingly concentrated on taking work to the workers, rather than vice versa. It is not difficult to understand why most workers are reluctant to move from their home areas.

Table 3.3. Average hourly earnings of adult male manual workers, October, 1972. (Source: E. V. Morgan 'Regional problems and common currencies', *Lloyds Bank Review*, **110**, 1973, p. 24)

	National average	North West	North	Scotland	Wales
	p	p	p	p	p
Food, drink	77.05	75.80	71.89	76.79	69.22
and tobacco	*100.0*	*98.4*	*93.3*	*99.7*	*89.8*
Chemicals	83.19	86.50	89.23	81.70	81.71
	100.0	*104.0*	*107.3*	*98.2*	*98.2*
Metal	85.13	80.71	83.55	85.36	92.92
manufacture	*100.0*	*94.8*	*98.1*	*100.3*	*109.2*
Mechanical	79.84	77.19	83.49	85.07	78.38
engineering	*100.0*	*96.7*	*104.6*	*106.6*	*98.2*
Electrical	79.45	81.05	81.64	78.31	82.32
engineering	*100.0*	*102.0*	*102.9*	*98.6*	*103.6*
Vehicles	98.42	94.60	84.98	94.95	91.85
	100.0	*96.1*	*86.3*	*96.5*	*93.3*
Clothing and	71.13	68.50	73.41	69.42	69.64
footwear	*100.0*	*90.3*	*103.2*	*97.0*	*97.9*
Paper and printing	92.19	91.31	91.72	82.28	80.42
	100.0	*99.0*	*99.5*	*89.3*	*87.2*

Their families may be unable to move; housing may be expensive where job vacancies exist; friends and local ties are not easily severed.

This is not to say that no movement of labour takes place. In the inter-war years workers from many of Britain's peripheral areas migrated to the South East to find work and, similarly, new industrial towns like Corby inevitably have a high proportion of 'immigrant' workers.

Movement of labour, like everything else, can be studied at different levels of scale. All workers undertake some movement each day – unless they actually live in the factory. As a general rule low-income workers live closer to a given factory than high-income workers who are able to overcome the friction of distance and commute from some distance away. (See page 208 for some variations on this theme.) Daily movements are over relatively short distances but other work-movement types may involve anything up to continental-scale migration, as Table 3.4 shows. We return to the question of journey to work in the later sections of Chapter 9 (pages 206–09).

Table 3.4. Movements of labour

Time period	Size of group	Example
1 Daily	Single person	Journey to work
2 Seasonal	Group	Students in summer jobs
3 Long term but not intended to		
be permanent	Mass migration	Turks to West Germany
4 Intended to be permanent	Mass migration	Britons to Australia

ASSIGNMENTS

1. *Consider the locational implications for industries in which a large proportion of total costs are made up of labour costs (e.g. the production of lace goods or dresses), rather than capital costs (e.g. oil refining, production of industrial gases).*

2. *Analyse the movement pattern of one 'worker' in your family and compare the results with others in your group. For one day, ask each worker to keep a 'time-space' diary – records of the times and places they move to and from. Does any pattern emerge from the results when they are recorded on a diagram such as that in Fig. 3.7? How much time is taken on average in simply travelling between places?*

4. Entrepreneurial ability

Setting up a factory is a risky business. There is a chance that the business will never get off the ground and financial investment may be lost for ever. The ability of an entrepreneur (a person co-ordinating and controlling other factors of production, who often makes major industrial innovations and changes) to take risks or resist taking risks at a given point in time and space can often make a great deal of difference to the operation (or even survival) of a firm. Like land, labour and capital, business skill varies from place to place. You would not expect a large number of entrepreneurs to emerge from a rural area. Thus, the Industrial Revolution in South Wales, for example, was achieved more through the efforts of Bristolians, Londoners, Midlanders and Germans – areas which have for generations bred families of businessmen – than of native Welshmen. At the same time 'only with difficulty does the son of the founder retain the same drive as his father, or the changing board of directors of a

44

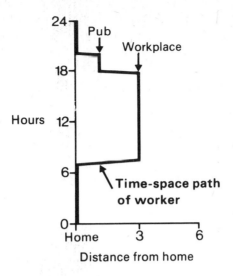

Fig. 3.7. Time-space activity of one worker over 24 hours. The diagram shows that the worker leaves his home at about 7 am arriving at his workplace, 3 km away at about 7 30. He stays at work all day leaving just before 18 00 (6 pm). On the way home he stops off at the pub (just over a mile from home and stays there till 20 00 (8 pm). He gets home just after 20 00 in the evening. The time-space path of workers will differ according to their ocupation, their location of residence, the location of their workplace and their leisure activities. The vertical scale could be modified to embrace a longer time period.

successful company continue to exhibit the willingness to innovate which its predecessors showed when making the first initial thrusts.'[12]

In Britain, London and the South East are believed to contain a larger number of good quality executives than other regions. An area's traditional economic specialisms may affect the supply of businessmen on the market. Indeed, for most manufacturing firms, transport costs represent less than 10% of total costs. Thus a region with a highly competitive industrial structure may provide a 'breeding ground' for businessmen whereas the region with an industry organized as a monopoly may not. Nevertheless, it is often pure chance that a brilliant businessman was born or happened to live in the place where he decided to set up an industry. Classic examples are Ford at Detroit, Morris at Oxford, Player and Boot at Nottingham and Wedgewood in the Potteries.

It is important to emphasize, however, that many businessmen may not aspire to the heights of a Henry Ford or a William Morris. For some, motives may be psychological as well as economic, their aims may be satisfied by relatively low profit margins rather than huge ones. This point has important spatial implications and is examined further in Chapter 6.

It must be remembered that if a large number of industrialists were asked to say which factors were important to them in their choice of location, it is highly unlikely that they would all answer in the same way – even if they were all in the same industry. An example of the variety of factors influencing industrialists in their location decisions is illustrated in Table 3.5. It illustrates the responses of 25 industrialists in new factories in the Bristol region to a survey undertaken in the mid-sixties. They were asked to state the four location factors of greatest significance to them. Twenty-two respondents included 'available labour', thus bearing out the importance of the labour factor; the land and capital factors were also well represented. What is interesting, however, is the great variety of factors cited. It is tempting to ask, therefore, whether we can usefully generalize about industrial location factors, or is human behaviour too inconsistent to make valid generalizations possible? This, of course, is an invitation to discuss theories and models of industrial location, which we shall begin to do in subsequent chapters.

Table 3.5. Ranked location factors for 25 industrialists locating in the Bristol region since 1945. (Source: J. Britton, *Regional Analysis and Economic Geography*, Bell, 1967, p. 134)

Location factor	Frequency
Availability of labour in the area	22
Scope for expansion on site	14
Attractive price of land or building	13
Presence of suitable building	11
Adequate supply and satisfactory type of water	6
Access to markets	5
Regional location of firm's headquarters	5
Good labour relations in the area	4
Availability of raw materials and components	4
Personal—with economic advantages	3
Anticipation of market growth	3
Low freight cost on raw materials and components	2
Flat land	2
Personal—without economic advantages	2
Low freight cost to markets	1
Low cost of fuel and power	1
Availability of local capital	1
War dispersal	1

ASSIGNMENT

Carry out a survey of local industrialists (note the cautionary comments on page 20 and compare their reasons for setting up nearby factories as closely as possible to the location factors given in Table 3.5. Which factors were regarded as very important, important and irrelevant?

5. The market

As the pulls of raw material and of localized energy sources have declined as location factors, the market has gradually become more important as a factor in the location of modern industry. So far we have concentrated on the location and varying qualities of the manufacturer's inputs as influences on plant location. We must now introduce the location of his potential customer, the market. Because the customers for manufactured goods are not evenly spread all over the surface of the regions in question, differences in market strength seem most likely to influence industrial location. This is even more obviously the case when one is reminded that electric power is found almost everywhere and that many inputs are easily and cheaply transported.

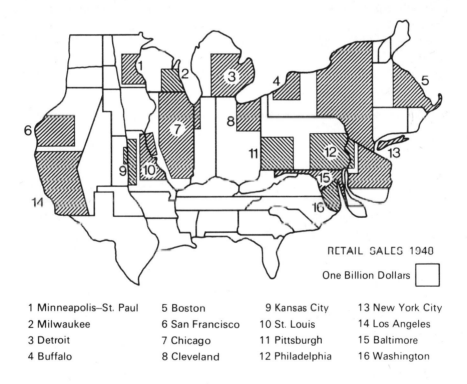

RETAIL SALES 1948

One Billion Dollars

1 Minneapolis–St. Paul	5 Boston	9 Kansas City	13 New York City
2 Milwaukee	6 San Francisco	10 St. Louis	14 Los Angeles
3 Detroit	7 Chicago	11 Pittsburgh	15 Baltimore
4 Buffalo	8 Cleveland	12 Philadelphia	16 Washington

Fig. 3.8. A market view of the United States. Cartogram in which the areas of the cities and states are shown in proportion to their retail sales. (Source: C. Harris, 'The market as a factor in the localization of industry in the United States', *Annals of the Association of American Geographers*, **44**, 1954, p. 320)

While the term market might be conveniently thought of as 'population', geographers often employ other measures of market strength, for example, the volume of retail sales. An interesting way of depicting the location of major markets based on this criterion is illustrated in Fig. 3.8 which was originally produced in 1953 by the American geographer, Professor Chauncy Harris, in a pioneering work on the importance of the market as a factor in the location of American industry.

Fig. 3.8 shows the states (and major towns) of the USA with their size drawn in proportion to the amount of retail sales in 1948. Notice how the southern states represent a very small part of the 'national retail sales space' and how the great markets of the eastern and midwest cities have 'pushed' the Mississippi westwards and 'compressed' the states of the Great Plains. Such stretching of conventional geographic space produces an example of what is called a cartogram or map transformation.

Thus, if a large percentage of firms' sales were in, say, New York, it might appear logical to locate as near New York as possible, assuming of course, that the 'pull' of raw materials was not stronger than that of the market.

Industries which locate at their markets tend to make products which gain in weight during the production process.

The whole question of market- versus raw material-oriented industries will be considered further, with examples, in Chapter 5, while the concept of 'market potential' is illustrated on page 135.

6. Transport

Linking the inputs, the processing plant and the market is the all-important factor of transport. Indeed transport appears so important to some enterprises that it is almost worth thinking of it as another factor of production. After all, we have seen in Fig. 3.1 that all firms need to transport their finished products to market. We will discuss this question in the following chapter but at this stage we may note that for many firms costs of other factors of production are more important than those of transport.

Few forces have been more important in modifying the landscape than transportation. Transport routes, be they on land, over the sea or, today, in the air have a strong impact on industry.

Transport technology may be producing a 'global village' whereby the 'friction of distance' or the 'tyranny of space' is being overcome. Transportation produces interaction between places which, in its absence, would be part of a spatially restricted society. Throughout this book we shall refer to the question of transport in a variety of contexts and on a variety of scales. Chapter 4, for example, notes the importance of transport routes on industrial location within the urban area; Chapter 5 deals at some length with the importance of transport costs. Ports, canals, roads, railways and airports have all, at different times and to different degrees, been important influences on industrial location. Thus industrial location and technological change in transport are inextricably linked together.

ASSIGNMENT

Refer to the industrial property page of one of the 'quality' newspapers. List the transport factors which are stressed in the advertisements. Reconstruct an imaginary advertisement for the equivalent property page for the years 1750 and 1880.

C. Conclusion

The various factors of production which we have discussed in this chapter together form part of the complex, interacting manufacturing system. Two main points can be emphasized. First, what we see in the industrial landscape today is the outcome of a complex inter-relationship between past and present. In attempting to explain industrial locations, therefore, we may have to consider (a) the original location factors at the time of the establishment of the firm, and (b) the factors which have operated to permit the firm to continue in its location. Early in this chapter it was stressed that inertia is a strong force influencing location and it is one of the less obvious factors which are not evident from maps or from fieldwork. Secondly, the relative importance of the location factors discussed above has changed over time. Whereas in the seventeenth and eighteenth centuries water and then coal power were import-ant, present-day industry is released from the grip of such factors by elec-tricity. The market has assumed much more importance than hitherto.

Finally, because entrepreneurs are individual human beings, each with different aspirations and abilities, we should not underrate the human factor in location, a subject taken up in greater detail in Chapter 6.

ASSIGNMENTS

1. *In this chapter we have suggested that many factors influence the location and siting of an industrial establishment. Discuss how the relevant significance of industrial location factors has changed over time.*
2. *What evidence is there in the photograph (Plate 3.3) of the Port Talbot steelworks that any of these factors were influential in the siting of the factory? What other information would you need to give you a better understanding of the location of the plant?*

Plate 3.3. Port Talbot Steelworks. (*Aerofilms*)

A cautionary word about photo interpretation and map reading

Maps and air photographs on their own cannot tell us *why* any given location is chosen over another. Knowledge derived solely from these sources is almost useless as an aid to explanation. It is often dangerous to try to *explain* the location of a factory by physical site and communications factors. Present-day environmental circumstances cannot tell us much about the founding of a factory. Also, from a map it is almost impossible to distinguish between those factors which may have been responsible for the original choice of location and those which have contributed to its subsequent survival. Maps and photographs simply set the scene, and students hoping to find *reasons* for a factory's location will have to look elsewhere. Searching the map or photograph for explanation is indulging in what K. L. Wallwork has called 'little better than an elaborate parlour game.'[13]

Key Ideas

A. *A Systems Approach* (pages 24–26)
1. The individual factory is part of the manufacturing system in that it processes or assembles inputs and dispatches outputs.
2. The individual firm is also part of a smaller-scale system – the 'manufacturing packet'.
3. Different components of a firm's system may possess separate locations.

B. *Capital as a Location Factor* (pages 26–33)
1. Capital (referring to man-made phenomena for use in the production process) may be fixed capital or financial capital.
2. Fixed capital is spatially immobile but mobile between uses.
3. The spatial immobility of fixed capital has contributed largely to the phenomenon of industrial inertia.
4. Financial capital is more spatially mobile than fixed capital.
5. But in the early stages of economic growth especially, financial capital may be relatively fixed spatially.

C. *Land as a Location Factor* (pages 33–41)
1. The natural environment is a less potent influence on industrial location today than in the nineteenth century and before.
2. The natural environment may be evaluated in terms of its cost of development by man.
3. Sites for manufacturing industry vary in physical quality and so have implications for cost.
4. While not physically mobile, land is mobile between users.
5. Large enterprises are increasingly having to take into account environmental standards in their siting.

51

6. Land provides raw material inputs, though in many cases such inputs may be in the form of semi-finished products.
7. Land has provided, and continues to provide, power to drive machines, water and coal both exerting a strong locational pull particularly during the Industrial Revolution.

D. *Labour as a Location Factor* (pages 41–44)
1. The quality, quantity, and reputation for militancy of labour vary spatially.
2. Areas of high unemployment can be attractive to labour-intensive industries.
3. Regional variations exist in the earnings of labour.
4. Labour is mobile between jobs and places, though less so between places.

E. *Entrepreneurial Ability as a Location Factor* (pages 44–47)
1. The availability of skilled controllers of factors of production varies spatially.
2. Many important industrial areas developed their specialisms because the inventor or innovator was born or lived there.
3. Individual entrepreneurs may perceive the same location factor in different ways.

F. *The Market* (pages 47–48)
1. The market is tending to become more important as a location factor than the location of raw material inputs.
2. Spatial variations in market strength exist, the strength of the market often being interpreted as a measure of populations or purchasing power.

G. *Transport* (pages 48–49)
1. Transportation is vitally important to industry since it links inputs, plant and markets.
2. Improved transport technology reduces the friction of distance (i.e. the effect which distance exerts on the ease of movement).

Additional Activities

1. Map the location of the different components of the manufacturing packet for a firm for which you have been able to obtain the relevant information. To what extent are the suggested locations in Fig. 3.2 (page 26) borne out by your case study?
2. Lancashire and South Wales both possess similar environments yet one developed a great specialization in cotton manufacturing whereas the other did not. Having read the relevant pages in Chisholm's book (see Reading section C below), can you suggest why?
3. If you were a businessman setting up operations for the first time, in what

ways would you be constrained from locating in areas other than your local region?

4. Outline the reasons why the market is considered more important than the source of raw materials as a location factor for many modern industries. Relate the reasons to examples.

5. From a local land use map attempt to relate industrial location to transport. Is it possible to categorize industry on the basis of the type of transport (e.g. road, rail, water) to which it is related. (N.B. You cannot say with certainty that because a factory is next to a railway it necessarily uses that railway.)

Reading

A. *LANGTON, J., 'Potentialities and problems of adopting a systems approach to the study of change in human geography', *Progress in Geography*, **4**, 1972, pp. 125–79.
B. ESTALL, R. & BUCHANAN, R. O., *Industrial Activity and Economic Geography*, Hutchinson, 1964, pages 95–8.
   *ESTALL, R., 'Some observations on internal mobility of investment capital', *Area*, **4**, 1972, pages 193–8.
C. CHISHOLM, M., *Geography and Economics*, Bell, 1965, pages 13–25.
D. ESTALL, R. & BUCHANAN, R. O., *op. cit.*, pages 82–95.
   *CHISHOLM, M., *op cit.*, Chapter 5.
E. ELIOT HURST, M., *A Geography of Economic Behavior*, Duxbury Press, 1972, pages 142–50.
F. HOUSE, J. W., (ed.), *The UK Space*, Weidenfeld & Nicolson, 1973, pages 259–63.
G. HOUSE, J. W., *op cit.*, Chapter 5.
   *HARRIS, C. D., 'The market as a factor in the localization of industry in the United States,' in BLUNDEN, J. *et al.* (eds.) *Regional Analysis and Development*, Harper & Row, 1973, pp. 141–54.

4 Industry in the urban area

Because the factories and industry with which most readers of this book will be familiar are likely to be in their nearest town, this chapter is focused on the location of industry in the urban area. The geographer's scale concept reminds him that factors which might influence industrial location at the national level of scale may differ from those which influence industrial location within the town or city. In addition to seeking explanatory generalizations about intra-urban industrial location, this chapter also provides some initial simple quantitative techniques for use on some of the data sources mentioned in Chapter 2 (pages 20–21).

A. Models of Urban Growth and Manufacturing Location

Manufacturing industry, like service trades and extractive industries, provided the *raison d'être* for many of our present-day urban areas. A number of factories utilizing locally available raw materials or power supplies produced urban nuclei which in time coalesced to form continuously built up urban areas. Our nineteenth-century areas of heavy industry grew up in this way since, because of the limited transport technology of the times, the workers had to live near their place of work. An example of such a development is seen in Fig. 4.1 which illustrates the location of former iron works in Merthyr Tydfil. Workers' homes were in built up areas which developed around each works until a continuous urban area gradually emerged.

It is important to notice, however, that even if localized raw materials or energy sources did not exist, we would still find industrial locations scattered around our urban areas. What, then, are the factors which have led present-day industry to be located in some parts of our towns and cities and not in others? Do towns illustrate recurring patterns of industrial location? In order to answer these questions, geographers have utilized several models which, in a general sense, go part of the way towards explaining intra-urban industrial location. We may consider four quite well-known models in turn:

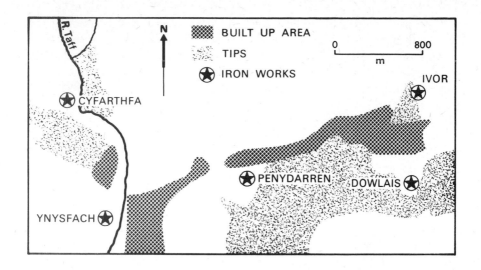

Fig. 4.1. Iron works and urban growth in the Merthyr area 1860. (After H. Carter, 'Urban Systems and Towns Morphology' in E. Bowen *et al* (eds.), *Geography at Aberystwyth*, University of Wales Press, 1968 p. 230)

(a) *The concentric zone model* suggests that the city is formed of a series of concentric rings and originated from the work of the Chicago ecologists of the 1920s. (See Fig. 4.2.) This geometrical view of the city is based on the view that CBD (Central Business District) users could outbid industrialists for the key, central city sites and depends for its validity on the idea that the central area, because of its supreme accessibility to all other parts of the city, is indeed the best place to locate. While unable to compete with offices for the central city sites, industrialists could outbid residential users for the first 'ring' and thus occupy what has become known as the 'transition zone'.

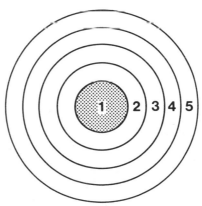

Fig. 4.2. Concentric Zone Model.

55

This idea is illustrated in Fig. 4.3 which shows three curves intersecting the X axis (distance from CBD) and Y axis (cost of land). It can be seen that, because offices need centrality more than industry, and are more intensive users of space, they are able to outbid industry for the prestige, high access sites. As the distance of locations increases from the CBD, however, offices find them less attractive and their 'bid rent curve' falls away rather steeply. The point where this curve intersects that for manufacturing industry marks the spatial limit of city offices and the beginning of the industrial belt. The same principle applies to the intersection of the curves for industry and residential land use.

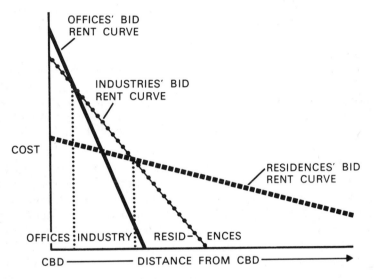

Fig. 4.3. Urban bid-rent curves producing zonation outwards from the Central Business District in a western city.

(b) *The sector model* is mainly based on the work of the land economist Homer Hoyt. Here (Fig. 4.4) the picture of the city looks more realistic with wedges of light industry sandwiched between areas of low class residential housing and factories strung out along transport arteries. This model, therefore, stresses that the city grows out along sectors, rather than in rings.

(c) *The multiple nuclei model* is the third of what have been called the 'classical models' of urban structure. Fig. 4.5 shows that this model, developed by Harris and Ullman, is rather more realistic than the previous two. The multiple nuclei approach recognizes that most cities grow up around several nodes, rather than around a single centre. Some of these centres may be of an industrial nature, as Fig. 4.1 illustrated. This model is also an improvement on the earlier ones from the viewpoint of the industrial geographer, but only inasmuch as it differentiates between light and heavy industries.

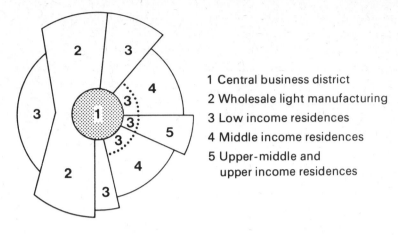

1 Central business district
2 Wholesale light manufacturing
3 Low income residences
4 Middle income residences
5 Upper-middle and
   upper income residences

Fig. 4.4. Sector or wedge model.

(d) *Criticisms of the classical models* From the standpoint of the industrial geographer the three classical models possess many inadequacies. This is hardly surprising, of course, since they were not formulated solely as an explanation of intra-urban industrial location. As these models have proved highly interesting to urban geographers, however, it may be worthwhile to comment on them from a different perspective.

(i) The models tend to assume that the CBD is the most accessible part of the city and that central sites are, therefore, highly desirable. It may be, however, that as we reach the late 1970s the CBD will finally become one of the least accessible points in the urban area as the centrally congested gluepot makes suburban sites more attractive both to offices and industry.

(ii) Concentric and sector models only contain one industrial area, whereas

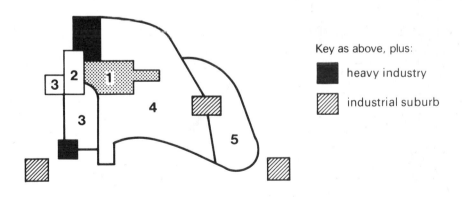

Key as above, plus:

■ heavy industry

▨ industrial suburb

Fig. 4.5. The multiple nuclei model.

57

C

the most casual of field observations would show that there are many industrial areas in most towns.

(iii) The concentric and sector models also present industry in a highly aggregated form and the multiple nuclei model only differentiates on the basis of 'light' and 'heavy' – terms which are not easy to define anyway.

(iv) These models concern themselves with individual *areas* of the city whereas the industrial geographer is interested in the location of individual *industries*. We need, therefore, to move towards a model which differentiates between industries, rather than areas.

(e) *The Isard model*, which we shall briefly consider, makes a start in differentiating between industries on a different basis from that adopted in the 'multiple nuclei' model. Isard modestly describes his urban land use model as 'one of many possible brews of (1) intuition, (2) logic and analytic principles relating to the interaction of general forces governing land use, and (3) facts. It is not a rigorous theoretical derivation.'[1] The urban area is pictured as containing four industrial districts differing greatly in size (see Fig. 4.6).

Each of the districts contains manufacturers who produce miscellaneous items or use materials that are found everywhere (i.e. the materials are ubiquitous). All producers of any other commodity are concentrated in one of the four industrial areas so that each may benefit from what are termed 'localization economies' – savings in costs from being located near firms in the

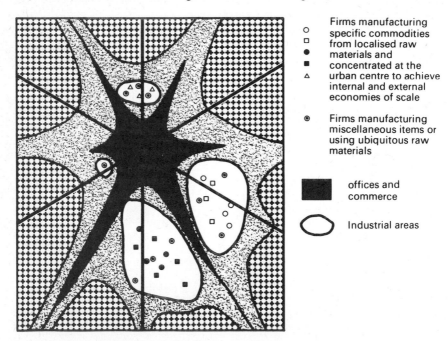

Firms manufacturing specific commodities from localised raw materials and concentrated at the urban centre to achieve internal and external economies of scale

Firms manufacturing miscellaneous items or using ubiquitous raw materials

offices and commerce

Industrial areas

Fig. 4.6. An urban land-use pattern as seen by Isard. (Source: W. Isard, *Location and Space Economy*, MIT Press, 1956, p. 279)

58

same industry. Isard thus introduces the useful concept of localization economies which distinguish some industries from those that are found all over the
place because of their use of ubiquitous raw materials. We will illustrate these
ideas later in this chapter. While helpful in some respects, the Isard approach
is lacking in others; for example, there is no industry included near the CBD.
In addition, the industries represented are shown to be located in discrete
wedges between areas of dense office and commercial development, whereas we
have already noted that in most towns industry is found interspersed with
other land uses. Finally, industries appear to be located in a single individual
district or are ubiquitous, with no intermediate pattern between these two
extremes.

ASSIGNMENTS

1. *Review the distinctive contribution made by each of the four models
   mentioned in the above section.*
2. *Given the assumptions of the bid-rent model shown in Fig. 4.3, draw a
   similar diagram based on the data in Table 4.1 concerning the different
   prices different users are prepared to pay for the same unit of land at
   different distances from the centre of a city.*
   (a) At what distance from the city centre is land used for industry?
   (b) How wide is the industrial belt?
3. *Which of the models is most applicable to the situation in two or three
   urban areas of your choice? Is it possible that all are partly applicable?*

Table 4.1. (Table for question 2)

Price willing to pay for one unit of floor space (p)			Distance from city centre (km)
Office	Industry	Residential	
300	200	150	0
200	175	137	0.5
90	150	125	1.0
0	125	117	1.5
0	100	100	2.0
0	75	87	2.5
0	50	75	3.0
0	25	63	3.5
0	0	50	4.0

B. Intra-Urban Industrial Location

Some of the inadequacies of the aforementioned models are highlighted in Fig. 4.7 and 4.8 which illustrate the location of industrial land use in two very different urban areas – London and Stafford. From both maps it is clear that industry is not *concentrated*, as the models would have us believe, in one or two areas, but is *dispersed* all over the urban area. It is true that in London, for example, a concentric belt of industry does encircle the CBD; but there are also sectors of industry as well as a vast number of other industrial districts which are not accommodated in our models. We will, therefore, turn to a different approach, one which seeks to classify intra-urban manufacturing locations on the basis of industrial type.

1. Centrally located industries

Industries which tend to be located near the centre of the urban area may be sub-divided into three main groups.

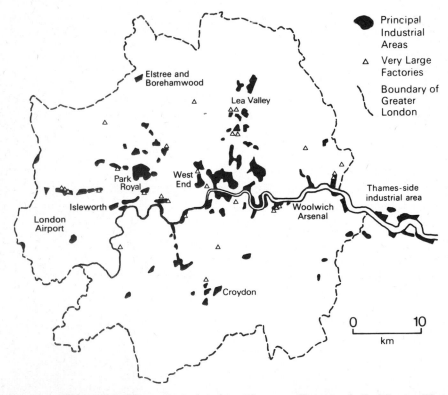

Fig. 4.7. Greater London – principal industrial areas. (Source: J. E. Martin, The industrial geography of Greater London', in R. Clayton (ed.), *The Geography of Greater London*, Philip, 1964, p. 122)

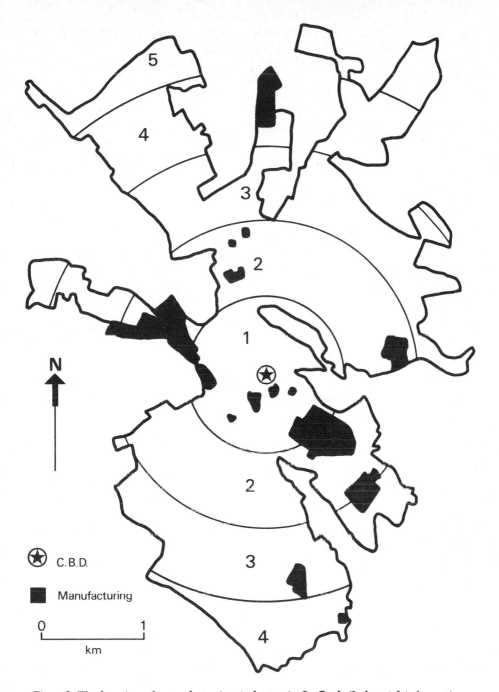

Fig. 4.8. The location of manufacturing industry in Stafford. (Industrial information derived from Sheet No. 515 of the Second Land Utilization Survey of Britain.) The concentric rings are numbered for the exercise on page 79.

(a) *Labour-oriented industries* need the best access to skilled labour from the whole urban area, to the Central Business District and to the whole urban market for distribution, thus offsetting the high cost of land near the city centre. Examples of these industries include instrument and jewellery making and the clothing trades. Often in central city locations distinctive industrial 'quarters' evolve, where industrialists needing close contact with each other 'swarm' in many small scale establishments. The origins of such quarters are frequently almost lost in history; they evolved at a time when place of work had, of necessity, to be easily accessible to place of residence, hence their location around what has traditionally been the most accessible part of the city – the CBD. Local industrial linkage (see Chapter 7) characterizes many of these quarters. The recognition that two linked industrialists serving the same city might as well occupy the same street led to many quarters being made up of workshops converted from houses.

Such industrial quarters are best exemplified, perhaps, by the clothing and furniture quarters of the East End of London and the gun and jewellery quarters of Birmingham. But smaller towns, too, possess quite specialized inner city areas. In the early twentieth century the plait and materials merchants and the hat manufacturers formed a distinct enclave in the Bute Street area of Luton in Bedfordshire. The inner Luton hat quarter remains to this day, though in a rather smaller form than earlier.

(b) *Market-oriented industries* are those whose market area is basically the city and its immediate hinterland. Allan Pred gives the term 'ubiquitous' to centrally oriented industries which are found in virtually every large city.[2] They are often linked with wholesaling functions and can best serve the urban areas from their central city sites. Bakeries and breweries exemplify this type of industry. Such factories are often much larger than other inner city work places.

(c) *CBD-oriented industries* form the third of the inner industrial groups. Pred has called these 'communication-economy' industries. Their locations are strongly influenced by the external economies which arise from close contact with the eventual purchasers of their products. A good example is printing and publishing where frequent demand comes from central city occupants and face-to-face contact is essential.

Similarly, the London bespoke tailoring industry has traditionally located in streets such as Savile Row with access to the centre of fashion and change of taste. Fig 4.9 shows that in some cases (e.g. San Francisco) some kinds of manufacturing industry are actually inside the CBD.

The location quotient

The location quotient (LQ) is a precise way of indicating the extent to which an industry is concentrated in a particular part of the urban area. The quotient is calculated by using the following formula:

Number employed in industry I in area X as a
percentage of the city total in that industry

Number employed in all industries in area X as a
percentage of the total city employment in all industries.

A quotient of 1.0 or more implies that the industry is more localized in the area of the city than is employment generally. Let us illustrate the calculation of the location quotient by substituting hypothetical figures which have been rounded off for arithmetic convenience. The area of Downtown in the city of Weberville has 100 workers employed in printing and the city as a whole has 1 000 employed in that trade. In all, 900 people are employed in Downtown and the city has a total workforce of 10 000. Using the formula:

$$\frac{\dfrac{100}{1\,000} \times 100}{\dfrac{900}{10\,000} \times 100} = \frac{10}{9}$$

Printing L.Q. $= 1.11$

Thus the printing industry is slightly more localized in Downtown than is industry as a whole.

Fig. 4.10 shows that for the square mile of the city of London the printing and publishing industry is highly concentrated in an area radiating west from St Paul's. The industry has a location quotient of 4.3 for the City compared with Central London and as high as 5.49 for Fleet Street compared with the City. The map thus shows that even within the City certain sub-areas of very small size have high L.Qs – many over 2.99.

A final general comment about inner city industrial establishments: with one or two notable exceptions, they are usually smaller than those in the suburbs. Why should this be so? We have already noted that small plants are often drawn together through localization economies. In addition, smaller plants can more readily make use of the small factory units in converted or multi-storey buildings which typify the central areas. Furthermore, higher land values near the CBD deter factories needing large amounts of space. The painstaking research of Dr J. E. Martin has revealed that in the mid-fifties employment location in London in small factories and workshops employing under 20 workers was highly concentrated in the West End and the East End around the City. Fig. 4.11 clearly illustrates this point. (The cartographic technique used is interesting in that grid squares have been adopted as the areal unit for depicting the employment density.)

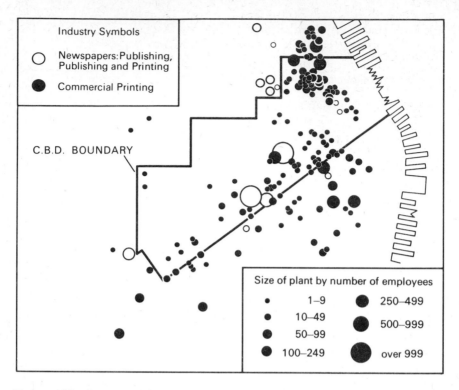

Industry Symbols

◯   Newspapers: Publishing, Publishing and Printing

●   Commercial Printing

C.B.D. BOUNDARY

Size of plant by number of employees

·	1–9	●	250–499
•	10–49	●	500–999
●	50–99	●	over 999
●	100–249		

Fig. 4.9. The location of letterpress printing, lithographic printing and newspaper plants in the Central Business District area of San Francisco, 1963. (After Paul A. Groves, 'Towards a typology of intra-metroplitan manufacturing location', *University of Hull Occasional Papers in Geography*, **16**, 1971, p. 34)

A second concluding comment about inner city industry is that it is unplanned, factories in the inner city 'just grew'. However, their future may be in jeopardy, since as central city areas are redeveloped, such industry is likely to be forced out to suburban sites. The importance of the central area for some industrialists is reflected, however, in the fact that some local authorities (e.g. in Birmingham and Inner London) have erected 'flatted factories' near the central area so that firms' contacts can be retained. (See Plate 4.1.)

The character of inner city industry is summarized in two concluding quotations. The first is about the inner city of Birmingham and was written by H. B. Rogers:

> The inner city is dominated by a very large number of tiny firms, largely concerned with rather traditional products and processes. . . . A pattern of industrial quarters with strong specializations has evolved from the middle of the nineteenth century; the gun and jewellery trades were dominant to the north of the city centre; the brass industry to the southwest and mixed metal trades to the southeast. An indescribable variety of light metal working has been

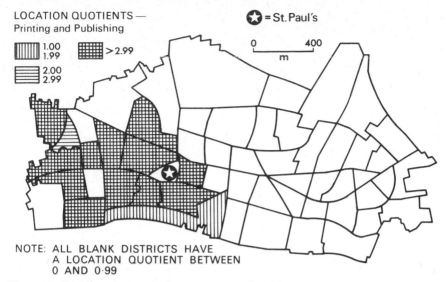

Fig. 4.10. Location quotients for printing and publishing in the City of London. Note (a) all blank districts have a location quotient between 0.0 and 0.99, (b) the scale of the map. (Source: J. H. Dunning & E. V. Morgan (eds.), *An Economic Study of the City of London*, Allen & Unwin, 1971, p. 370)

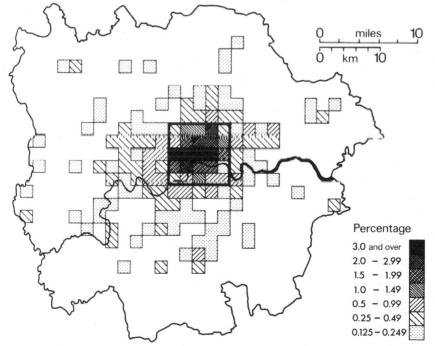

Fig. 4.11. Employment in small factories (less than 20 workers) in Greater London in 1954. (Source: J. E. Martin, 'Size of plant and location of industry in Greater London' *Tijdschrift voor Economische en Sociale Geografie*, 1969, p. 370).

added to these traditional interests. . . . This inner factory zone is today a form-less confusion of obsolescent industrial premises aligned along abandoned lines of communication. It is inextricably alloyed with grossly substandard housing and it closely encloses a city centre in an advanced stage of redevelopment.[3]

Plate 4.1. Flatted factory in London's East End. (*Photograph by Thomas Dalton*)

Peter Hall has brilliantly caught the flavour of industrial inner London :

This is a self-contained industrial world, where each firm finds just around a few corners a dozen suppliers, half a dozen skilled labourers, a score of markets, and connecting them all the omnipresent telephone and ubiquitous light van. In these circumstances the question to be asked is not, why is this industry here; but how could it conceivably be **anywhere else**?[4] (See **Plate 4.2.**)

Plate 4.2. Part of London's East End furniture 'quarter'. Chairs stacked outside a small workshop awaiting delivery to a nearby workshop for a further stage in the production process. (*Photograph by Thomas Dalton*)

ASSIGNMENTS

1. *Study Fig. 4.9 (page 64) and then answer the following questions:*
   (a) *Which of the inner city industries shown has the smallest size plants?*
   (b) *Which has the largest plants?*
2. *Explain Fig. 4.10 and the information on page 63 to someone who has no idea of what a location quotient is.*
3. *State five characteristics which summarize inner city industries.*

2. Waterfront or port industries

It should be emphasized initially that while firms may be located with access to water (in the form of rivers or sea), it does not necessarily mean that they use that water in any direct or indirect way. For example, at most ports there are several firms *serving* other firms which are typical of ports and which require or prefer port or waterfront locations.

(a) *Industries requiring a waterfront location* include shipbuilding and ship repairing, and manufacture of oil rigs. Because of the high costs involved it

67

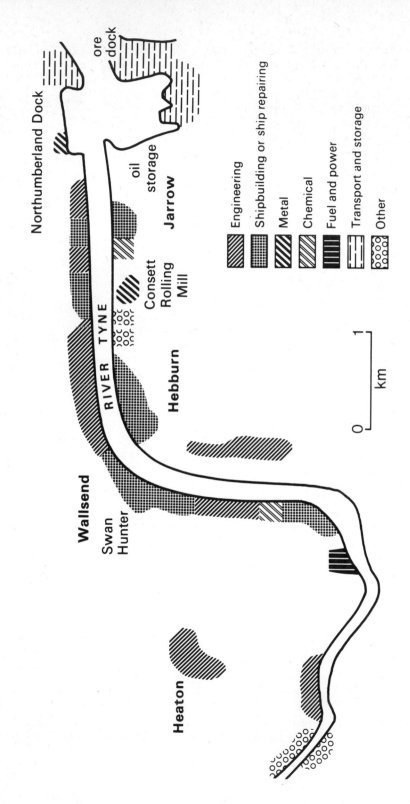

Fig. 4.12. Industrial land use on Lower Tyneside, 1971.

Northumberland Dock

ore dock

oil storage

Jarrow

Consett Rolling Mill

Hebburn

RIVER TYNE

Wallsend

Swan Hunter

Heaton

Engineering

Shipbuilding or ship repairing

Metal

Chemical

Fuel and power

Transport and storage

Other

0   km   1

would be virtually impossible to carry on industries such as these on inland sites.

(b) *Industries preferring a waterfront location* include such industries as oil refining, rope-making, steelworks using imported ores, fish curing and certain food processing plants (e.g. vegetable oils, flour milling, cane sugar refining) using raw materials brought in through the nearby port. Such locations as these are called 'break of bulk' locations because the bulkiness of the raw material is reduced to a more transportable form by processing at the waterfront.

Industries in both the above groups are exemplified by those shown in Fig. 4.12 illustrating industrial land use along the River Tyne. An even greater variety of industry might be observed along other rivers; for example, in the mid-sixties a short length of the Thames between the Rotherhithe and Blackwall Tunnels accommodated the following industries: (a) oil, asphalt and tar, (b) chemicals, soap and paint, (c) metals, foundry and engineering, (d) electric cables, (e) rubber and gutta percha, (f) miscellaneous food production, including animal foods, (g) sugar, (h) brewing and bottling, (i) timber, (j) flour milling, (k) miscellaneous small firms engaged in such activities as printing and glass making.

3. Suburban industries

We shall now consider those kinds of industries which may be located neither near the centre of the urban area nor at the waterfront. Such suburban industrial growth principally resulted from developments in the inter-war years, involving two main factors: (i) planned and voluntary suburbanization (i.e. movement to the suburbs of former inner city industry), a subject which is dealt with in detail in Chapter 9 (pages 204–206); (ii) the not inconsiderable growth of suburban industry *in situ*, composed of new firms in some cases or expanded branches in others. Suburban factories tend to be larger than those at the centre since they can benefit from lower land values and more expansive sites. We may sub-divide suburban industry into several categories.

(a) *Large basic processing industries*, many of which (e.g. chemical manufacture, metallurgical industries) are also noisy, noxious and pollute the atmosphere, desire suburban locations since they often take up large amounts of space. Tracts for such developments would be simply unavailable anywhere else in the urban area. Unlike many of the CBD-located industries, those in this group are not closely linked to the urban area and tend not to regard the urban area near which they are located as a major element in their total markets. The American geographer, Allan Pred, has interestingly suggested that such industries tend to be located on the side of the urban area which looks towards the regional or national markets,[5] but in a British context such a hypothesis remains untested.

While a suburban location for such industries may be desirable, some such industries may have originated nearer the CBD than is desirable today, but since there may be large amounts of investment in such sites they cannot easily be written off and the industries remain in their original locations through the forces of inertia. For example, in Ebbw Vale in South Wales, the steel works is located practically in the centre of the town, and nineteenth-century chemical industry is similarly located in St Helens and Widnes in Lancashire.

(b) *Communications-based industries* are characterized by clusters of industries strung out along lines of communication leaving the city. Such locations were commonly developed in the 1920s and 1930s at the time that road transport was increasing rapidly. Strip development along roads and railways leaving the city reflect the national markets which such industries tend to serve. For instance, the main industrial areas of northwest London are strung out along the Edgware Road, Western Avenue, Great West Road and North Circular Road.

In addition to the more obvious location factors such as cheaper land and road access, such areas were able to utilize cheaper, suburban female as well as male labour. Also, several sites were readily available for conversion into industrial estates (see below) such as, in London, Park Royal adjoining North Circular Road and Western Avenue which had originally been the grounds of the Royal Agricultural Society. At Wembley Park, the buildings for the great Empire Exhibition of the 'twenties were easily converted and let as factories once the exhibition was over. The kinds of industries occupying such factories are characterized by extreme diversity. In northwest London, for instance, such well known national firms as Guinness, Heinz, Walls, McVitie & Price and Hoover have major factories.

The kind of suburban industrial area described above has now often been submerged in the urban growth which has occurred since such factory development began and cannot literally be called suburban in location today.

(c) *Industrial estate* is a term which covers a multitude of variations and can be used by less than scrupulous property developers as a 'semantic gimmick' to promote an unlikely piece of industrial land. In general, however, an industrial estate, when complete, is an organized group of industrial establishments provided with certain common services and utilities laid down in advance of demand; it is established as a result of enterprise and planning by an organization independent of the firms which are on the site. As well as accommodating industry which has moved out from the central areas of cities, industrial estates are often attractive as 'industrial incubators' where the small businessman may hire or rent factory space provided by the estate developer and thus save himself time and money.

Industrial estates tend to house a great diversity of occupants, manufacturing industry often occupying a site beside other components of the 'manufacturing packet' such as warehouses or storage depots. As an example, Table 4.2 illustrates the diversity of industrial establishments found in the Ponty-

Table 4.2. Industrialists and activities on the Pontygwindy Industrial Estate, Caerphilly, 1971

Company name	Product/Activity
Admel International	Drawing office equipment
Allens Printers (Wales) Ltd.	Printing
A. C. Daniels & Co. Ltd.	Surgical instruments
Cardiff Music Strings	Guitar strings
Cantrell and Cochrane	Soft drinks
Catnic Components Ltd.	Prefabricated steel lintels
Contact Alarms Ltd.	Electronic burglar alarms
Delyn Cartons Ltd.	Cardboard cartons
Dialoy Ltd.	Non ferrous castings
Dragon Plastics Ltd.	Plastic injection moulding
E.H.S. Precision Engineering	Steel components
Electrical Raceways	Flexible conduits
Elka Electrics	Thermal controls
Firth Cleveland Ropes Ltd.	Steel wire ropes
*R. J. Bown	Truck specialist dealers
*Scottish and Newcastle Breweries	Distribution depot
Zinc Alloy Rustproofing Ltd.	Rustproofing
T. G. Beddoe and Son	General engineering
Castle Dairies (Caerphilly) Ltd.	Dairy products
Geoffrey C. Lloyd & Co. Ltd.	Structural engineering
Jig Tools (Pentyrch) Ltd.	Plastic components and tools
Hills Industries Ltd.	Rotary clothes lines
Gross Cash Registers Ltd.	Cash registers
*United Biscuits Ltd.	Storage depot

* indicates non-manufacturing activity.

gwindy Industrial Estate in Caerphilly, South Wales. Included on the estate are firms engaged in the manufacture of everything from musical instruments to surgical instruments and from steel components to rotary clothes lines.

The first industrial estates in Britain were developed towards the end of the nineteenth century. The most successful of these early estates was that at Trafford Park, Manchester (near Manchester United's football ground). Trafford Park did contain some heavy industry, however, and the prototype light industrial estate is generally thought to be that at Slough, set up following the First World War. The increase in mobility which characterized the inter-war years led to a proliferation of industrial estates at increasing distances from the city centre. We have already noted that such development occurred in suburban London in this period (page 70). The promotional literature from this period emphasized access to arterial roads; today such advertisements emphasize motorway access (see Fig. 4.15).

Most of the estate developers before 1936 were private companies but their success as agents of industrial growth stimulated the government to erect large estates at Hillington (Glasgow), Team Valley (Gateshead) and Treforest (Pontypridd) in attempts to lure industry to the distressed areas suffering from massive unemployment (see Chapter 8). At the same time more and more local authorities developed estates – early examples being Liverpool and Manchester. The post-war period has seen the proliferation of industrial estates by private developers, government and local authorities, and the total supply of industrial estates has been complemented by the activities of the New Town Development Corporations. Today almost every town has an industrial estate of some sort. The success of this form of development indicates that industrialists frequently want more than just a green field site. An estate developer, operating a 'package deal' can save the individual industrialist considerable inconvenience by supplying sites in a semi-finished form. The link between workplace and residence has finally been severed and today industrial estates can function equally well in ex-urban or rural environments.

While this section has stressed the suburban or peripheral nature of industrial estates, it is worth noting that as inner city and waterfront areas are re-developed vacant land may be taken over and developed as small industrial estates. This has been especially true in Glasgow where the provision of such developments has helped in limiting, to some extent, the suburbanward migration of manufacturing employment – a problem which we discuss in Chapter 9 on industrial movement (page 204).

4. Randomly located industries

Inevitably some firms or factories do not fit into the neat framework produced by the social scientist. Such industries may be described as randomly located though it is important to remember that randomness describes the distribution pattern of industry and not the cause. They tend to have non-local market orientations and produce high value goods which are non-bulky in nature such as electronic equipment. Contact with the CBD is not so important as for those industries discussed in Group 1 above.

The above discussion is depicted in Fig. 4.13, a diagram which represents the location of industry in a large (around 500 000) urban area. Some elements of the model would apply to smaller towns, but it is unlikely that small places would contain such a diversity of industries or industrial areas as the metropolis. Also, of course, waterfront industries would be missing from some towns though inland centres on rivers (e.g. Norwich) contain a surprisingly large amount of waterfront manufacturing.

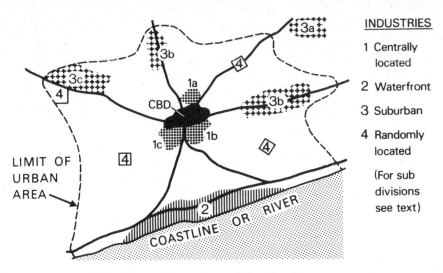

Fig. 4.13. A model of intra-urban industrial location in a western city.

INDUSTRIES

1 Centrally located

2 Waterfront

3 Suburban

4 Randomly located

(For sub divisions see text)

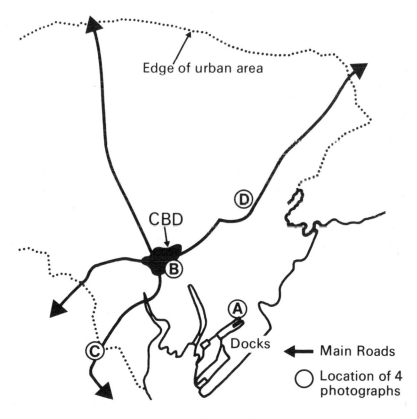

Fig. 4.14. Selected industrial areas in Cardiff (for assignment 2, page 74).

Edge of urban area

CBD

Docks

← Main Roads

◯ Location of 4 photographs

ASSIGNMENTS

1. Divide the industries shown on Fig. 4.12 (page 68) into those which (a) require waterfront locations and (b) prefer waterfront locations.
2. Consider the map of the city of Cardiff (Fig. 4.14). Four industrial areas are marked at A, B, C, and D. Match the photographs of the industrial areas shown in plates 4.3, 4.4, 4.5 and 4.6 with the appropriate locations on the map, giving reasons for your decisions.
3. Fig. 4.15 illustrates the promotional literature of a private industrial estate developer proposing to establish an industrial estate in Leicester. Study the diagram and then:
   (a) State how the advertisement tries to sell the estate.
   (b) Consider the factors which the development company may have taken into account in selecting Leicester as a location.
   (c) Write a 'pen-portrait' of the industrialist who might occupy this site (consider nature of product, trade area, previous location).

C. Industry in Towns; the future

As workplace and residence increasingly become separated what pattern might we expect to find in the intra-urban location of industry in the towns of the future? The New Towns provide some interesting pointers in this direction. Fig. 4.16 represents a generalized model of the evolving British urban area and the relationship between the location of industrial and residential land.

The traditional town (A) has its industrial area at its core with some more recent suburban development. After the Second World War, local authorities were involved much more than hitherto in the planning of industry (and other land uses) within urban areas. Just as on the national scale industrialists are not free to move where they like (Chapter 8), so too on a local scale they have been constrained by local planning regulations. Land within the urban area is 'zoned' for industry (or for other uses). The planning of intra-urban land use has been carried furthest in the New Towns which have evolved from the Garden Cities of Letchworth and Welwyn Garden City since the New Towns Act of 1946.

The first generation of new towns (B) possessed one large industrial estate on their peripheries. This produced a problem of traffic congestion at rush hours – the result of industry being concentrated in one part of the urban area.

The Cumbernauld pattern (C) has two industrial estates. This reduces the amount of traffic congestion at one point in the urban area and the idea was taken a stage further in the plan for Hook New Town (D).

In the final case of Runcorn (E) it is suggested that an even greater dispersal of industry is undertaken. Indeed, as industry becomes less noxious and

74

Plate 4.3. East Moors Steelworks. (*British Steel Corporation photograph*)

Plate 4.4. Colchester Factory Estate—the first privately developed industrial estate in Wales—set up in wartime buildings in 1948. (*Author's photograph*)

Plate 4.5. Speculative factory/warehouse units nearing completion on a privately developed industrial estate. Such units of about 200 sq m typify private industrial estate development in many British cities. (*Author's photograph*)

Plate 4.6. Redevelopment of this area has already commenced, small workshops awaiting demolition amid an area of nineteenth- and early twentieth-century industrial buildings. (*Photograph by Keith Bale*)

At the heart of the Midlands and minutes from the M1...

Already the Braunstone Industrial Estate numbers among its tenants some of the biggest names in British Industry.

Braunstone is sited on the edge of a large residential estate, is well served by public transport, and only 2½ miles from the centre of Leicester with its 285,000 inhabitants.

Mackenzie Hill have industrial units from 20,000 sq. ft. to let.

Mackenzie Hill
International property developers

1. British Shoe Corporation
2. Hiltons Shoes Ltd
3. Leicester Engineering Services Ltd
4. Leicester Co-op
5. Decca Radio & Television Ltd
6. Cadbury-Schweppes
7. English Glass Co
8. GEC-Elliot Process Automation Ltd
9. Marwin Hardmetals Ltd
10. Stibbes Ltd
11. Sylvan Fabrics Ltd
12. Milk Marketing Board
13. Olivers Shoes Ltd
14. Rowntree-Mackintosh Ltd
15. Budgen Cash & Carry
16. P. D. Visual Marketing Ltd
17. Crompton Parkinson Ltd
18. Eden Vale Dairy Food (Ski Yoghurt)
19. Nursery Units, mainly occupied by private companies
20. United Carriers Ltd
21. R.S.P.C.A.

Fig. 4.15. Mackenzie Hill come to Leicester.

offensive and as factory design standards improve, houses and workplaces may, once again, become intermingled. The wheel will then have turned full circle.

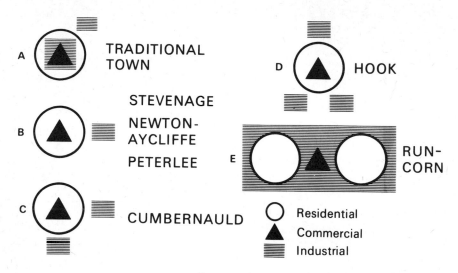

Fig. 4.16. Distribution of land uses in different forms of urban area. (Source: G. Jamieson *et al.*, 'Transportation and Land Use Structures', *Urban Studies*, IV, 1967)

Key Ideas

A. *Models of urban growth and manufacturing location* (pages 54–9)
1. Each of the 'classical models' (i.e. concentric, sector and multiple nuclei) includes industrial land use in concentrated locations within the urban area.
2. The classical models deal with industrial areas rather than with individual industries.
3. The Isard model includes the distinction between industries using ubiquitous raw materials and industries benefiting from localization economies.

B. *Intra-urban industrial location* (pages 60–78)
1. In most cities industrial land use is dispersed, rather than concentrated in a specific zone.
2. On the basis of industrial type, intra-urban industry may be divided into (a) centrally located industry, (b) waterfront industry, (c) suburban industry, and (d) randomly located industry.
3. The location quotient provides us with a precise measure of the extent to which an industry may be more concentrated in a given part of the urban area than is employment generally.

4. Small factories tend to be located near the central area of the city while larger plants are sited at the periphery – with notable exceptions.

Additional Activities

1. Why is a given hectare of land near the city centre more likely to be given over to offices than to industry? (Answer in a few sentences.)
2. Working individually or in pairs and using the maps of the Second Land Use Survey (see page 20), take as many towns as possible and on graph tracing paper:
   (a) mark in the limit of the built up area;
   (b) mark in the main Central Business District road intersection;
   (c) shade in all areas of manufacturing industry (red on the map);
   (d) using the CBD as your centre, draw a circle whose radius embraces the whole of the urban area;
   (e) divide the radius of the circle by five and mark in the four additional circles which will give you five concentric circles. (Your map should now look like the map of Stafford on page 61.)

You are now ready to calculate a precise measure of the degree to which industrial land use is centralized or dispersed within the urban area. Terms like 'concentrated' or 'dispersed' are rather vague and we thus replace these terms with an objective measure of intra-urban industrial land use. The formula for calculating the index of decentralization is:

$$I = \frac{(V \times 0) + (W \times 1) + (X \times 2) + (Y \times 3) + (Z \times 4)}{4}$$

where: I is the index of decentralization;
V is the percentage of total industry in the innermost circle;
W is the percentage of total industry in the first ring;
X is the percentage of total industry in the second ring;
Y is the percentage of total industry in the third ring;
Z is the percentage of total industry in the fourth ring.
The percentages are calculated by the use of graph tracing paper.

The index ranges from 0 indicating that industry is totally centralized (i.e. all industry in the urban area is in the inner circle), to 100 where industry is totally decentralized (i.e. all industry is in the fourth ring).

For the Stafford example you should be able to see how the index of industrial decentralization is calculated:

$$I = \frac{(13 \times 0) + (31 \times 1) + (32 \times 2) + (18 \times 3) + (6 \times 4)}{4}$$

79

$$I = \frac{0 + 31 + 64 + 54 + 24}{4}$$

$I = 43.25.$

How does this result, showing limited decentralization with a tendency for industry to be near the CBD, compare with those for the other towns you have selected?

3. Map the distribution of industrial land use in a city and try to account for its distribution, first testing hypotheses formulated from reading this chapter.

4. Draw four maps showing the changing location pattern of manufacturing industry for the hypothetical area shown in Fig. 4.17, which also indicates the limits of the built-up area for the years 1800, 1900, 1935 and 1976. Each of your maps should apply to one of these years.

5. On a 1:25 000 map of an urban area, locate places which appear to be potential industrial sites. What factors have you taken into account in selecting suitable sites?

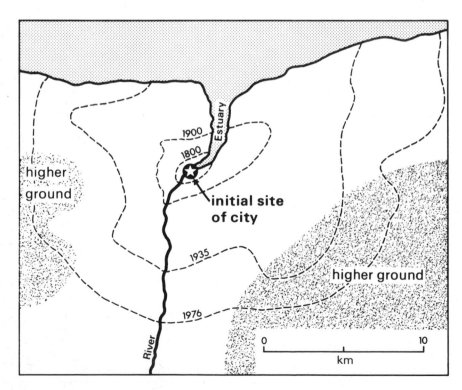

Fig. 4.17. (Base map for Additional Activity 4.)

Reading

A. Everson, J. A. & Fitzgerald, B. P., *Inside the City*, Longman, 1972, Chs. 2 and 3.
B. Carter, H., *The Study of Urban Geography*, Arnold, 1973, Ch. 13.
   Lewis, P. & Jones, P. N., *Industrial Britain: Humberside*, David & Charles 1970, pages 165–81.
   *Groves, P. A., *Towards a typology of intrametropolitan manufacturing location*, University of Hull Occasional Papers in Geography, 16, 1971.

The Weber model

This chapter will be concerned largely with an examination of the industrial location model of the German spatial economist, Alfred Weber.[1] This model, which dates from 1909, tries to explain and predict the locational pattern of industry at the macro-scale – that is to say, large scale industrial patterns – rather than the precise siting of factories within towns.

A. Assumptions of the Weber model

Weber's model was built on several simplifying assumptions about the real world, each of which must be reviewed if a full understanding and appreciation of the model is to be obtained.

(a) Many raw materials are *localized*, i.e. they are not found everywhere.

(b) Some raw materials may be *ubiquitous*, i.e. they are found everywhere (e.g. water, air).

(c) Markets for finished products are fixed at certain specific *points* and do not consist of continuous areas.

(d) Transport costs depend on the weight of the product and the distance which it has to be transported, i.e. the cost of transporting a raw material or finished product is *proportionate* to the distance transported.

(e) *Perfect competition* exists, meaning that there are a very large number of buyers and sellers in an industry and therefore no individual buyer or seller can influence the price of the product by his own actions (for instance, the average national price of sweets would be unlikely to be affected if one small producer, serving a local market, started lowering his prices). The concept of perfect competition also assumes that, because the price of a product is unaffected by individual firms in the industry and because all goods they produce will be sold at the same price, revenue (i.e. the price multiplied by quantity sold) for a given volume of sales will not vary from one location to another. Therefore, if revenue is everywhere the same, the 'best' location will be where costs of production are minimized. Thus the Weber model is called a 'least-cost model'.

(f) Man is rational and is in command of all knowledge of all information about the conditions of the industry in which he is engaged. Such a hypothetical animal is known as *'economic man'* who attempts to maximize his profits – in the case of the Weber model by seeking the location at which lowest costs are incurred.

ASSIGNMENT

Perfect competition is characterized by a large number of firms in an industry. The opposite situation, monopoly, exists when there is only one firm in an industry which is, therefore, able to dictate the price people pay for its product. Identify industries which approximate to (a) perfect competition and (b) monopoly.

B. Cost Factors influencing Industrial Location

We have seen so far that Weber postulated that industrialists would set up at the least cost location. This, for them, would be the optimum, or best, location. Weber believed that three factors would influence costs and thus location. These factors were: transport costs, labour costs, and the cost savings from agglomeration or deglomeration. We may deal with each of these in turn.

1. Transport costs

(a) *Some introductory working models* illustrate Weber's transport cost principle. Let us illustrate the principle of transport costs with a simple problem.

In Fig 5.1, C represents the market for 1 tonne of product X which needs 3 tonnes of the material from M_1 and 2 tonnes of the material from M_2. Assuming that all places within the triangle are equally accessible by transport, where would you place the point of production (P), assuming that you want to minimize transport costs? Would it be nearer M_1 than C and M_2?

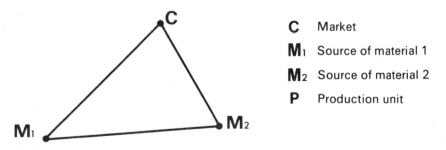

C	Market
M_1	Source of material 1
M_2	Source of material 2
P	Production unit

Fig. 5.1. A locational triangle. (The key also applies to Fig. 5.2)

Would it be at the centre of the triangle? Would it be nearer M_2 than C and M_1, or would it be nearer C than M_1 or M_2?

Given the assumptions of the model you should intuitively see that the 'pull' of M_1 (3 tonnes needed) will influence the least transport cost location and that the plant will gravitate towards the point M_1.

A hardware model can further illustrate this point. A string and pulley contraption called a *Varignon frame* (named after its inventor, Pierre Varignon, an eighteenth-century mathematician) consists of a triangle with pulleys in each corner through each of which runs a length of string. For the above example each piece of string will have one, two or three units of weight attached to it and will be passed through corners C, M_2 and M_1 respectively (Fig. 5.2).

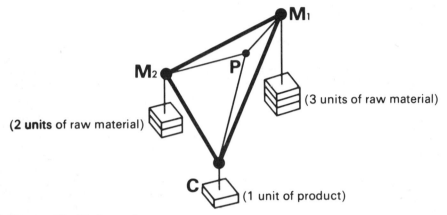

Fig. 5.2. The Varignon frame.

The pieces of string are then knotted together so that the length between the knot and the weight on each is the same. Where the knot comes to rest represents the optimum least transport cost location within the triangle. In this example, the production of the finished product is seen to be oriented towards M_1 – that is, the industry is raw material-oriented.

(b) *The material index* helps to determine whether an industry would be market-oriented or raw material-oriented. To avoid the cumbersome business of working out the orientation by use of the Varignon frame, Weber devised a material index which was calculated as follows:

$$\text{material index} = \frac{\text{weight of localised raw material inputs}}{\text{weight of finished product}}$$

If the index were more than 1 there would be a weight loss in the production process, and the industry would be oriented to the source of raw material. If the index were less than 1 the industry would be market-oriented and if the index were exactly 1 the industry would be located at either, or at an intermediate location. Thus, if for every tonne of pig iron produced at a blast furnace, about 4 tonnes of localized raw materials were used, the material index would be $\frac{4}{1} = 4$. Such an industry would clearly be raw material-oriented. The brewing industry, however, which uses a large amount of water as an input (i.e. a ubiquitous raw material), has a material index of only about 0.1, suggesting strong market orientation.

It is important to emphasize that not all raw materials are localized and that not all materials lose weight (like the iron ore above mentioned) in the production process. Some materials, such as air and water are found everywhere (i.e. they are ubiquitous). In addition Weber called materials with a heavy weight loss during the production process, gross materials, while those with little or no weight loss were called pure materials. Table 5.1 summarizes Weber's raw material classification.

Table 5.1. Gross, pure, sporadic and ubiquitous raw materials. (After: K. Cox, *Man, Location and Behavior*, Wiley, 1973, p. 225)

Localization	Weight change	
	Gross	Pure
Localized or sporadic	e.g. coal, iron ore	e.g. sand, gravel
Ubiquitous	e.g. water for cooling	e.g. water for brewing

In an attempt to test the value of the material index in predicting the location of industry, the late Professor Wilfred Smith[2] in the mid 1950s, examined the material indices for many British industries and their respective locational orientations. Were industries with a material index of more than 1 raw material-orientated and those with an index of less than 1 located independently of their raw materials? He noted that the processing of sugar had a material index of 8, the manufacture of dairy products 6, the making of pig iron between 3 and 4. In each of these cases the industry was raw material-oriented – the sugar factories being in areas of sugar beet cultivation (see Fig. 6.1), dairy produce (at the time of his study) was manufactured in the dairying districts, pig iron was produced on the ore fields. In fact, for all the industries which were located at their raw material sources, Smith found that they had an index of greater than 1. In addition, three-quarters of the industries located partly at materials had an index of between 1 and 2.

Furthermore, he discovered that those industries with an index of less than 1 were located either wholly or partly independently of raw materials (e.g.

bread baking or beer brewing). Thus, the Weber concept appeared to have some validity, with the material index of 1 as the watershed between raw material-oriented industries and those independent of raw materials in their locational orientation. There was, however, one snag in the analysis.

In looking at all the industries located away from raw materials, Smith was less successful in predicting their material indices. A large number of industries had indices of between 1 and 5 but were not located at materials as a literal interpretation of Weber would suggest. Because of this lack of precision. Professor Smith was led to conclude that the material index provided 'us with a tool of analysis but ... it is a blunt tool'.[3] He went on, therefore, to modify Weberian analysis by excluding the weight of coal (Weber includes this as a material) and then looking at the *weight of raw materials per operative* for each industry. In this latter examination he found a much sharper tool of analysis.

Where weight of materials per operative was high, Smith found that the industries were overwhelmingly oriented towards the raw materials (e.g. blast furnaces) whereas where the weight per operative was low the location of the industry was independent of the raw materials. Unlike the material index, there appeared to be no coincidence between the locations of industries at different stages in the production process of a particular product. Thus, in Table 5.2, and in Smith's own words, we observe that 'the more and more elaborately manufactured a material becomes the more completely do the mills or shops which manipulate it become divorced in location from the plants which handle the original raw material.'[4]

Table 5.2. Weight per operative and locational orientation for selected industries, *c.* 1948

Industry	Weight of material per operative	Location
Blast furnaces	1 447 tons	Tied to ore or coal, e.g. Scunthorpe
Steel mills	117 tons	Near blast furnaces e.g. any integrated steelworks
Tube mills	38 tons	Intermediate locations e.g. Sheffield
Chain, nail and screw mills	15 tons	Markets e.g. Midlands
Textile machines	5 tons	Markets i.e. textile districts
Motor vehicles*	7 tons	Market (e.g. the English Plain—Oxford, Luton)

* Motor vehicles had a higher weight per operative than textile machines because of mass production techniques.

(c) *Isodapanes*. Transport costs lie at the heart of the Weber model. It is not surprising, therefore, that Weber devised a useful technique not only for measuring but also for mapping the spatial variation in transport costs in order to find the least cost location. He constructed isodapanes – lines joining places of equal transport costs – in order to illustrate cost surfaces. The construction of isodapanes is illustrated in Fig. 5.3.

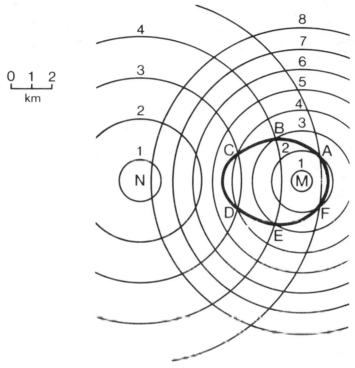

Fig. 5.3. Construction of isodapanes.

In Fig. 5.3, N represents market and M the material source for a simple industry with only one market and only one raw material. Let us assume that it costs one money unit to transport the raw material one kilometre and that it costs $\frac{1}{2}$ money unit to transport the finished product one kilometre. Thus, the concentric rings around N representing lines of equal cost are one money unit (or 2 kms) apart. Those around M, on the other hand, are closer together (the 'contour interval' is still only one money unit) indicating that costs rise more steeply away from M than from N. The isodapane is the line joining places of equal total transport costs and is shown by the thicker line joining points A–F. At A it is drawn where the 2 cost units line around M intersects the 5 unit line from N. Thus the total transport costs at A totals 7. Similarly, at B, the 3 and 4 unit lines intersect, again producing a total of 7.

1. For Fig. 5.1. (page 83), if one tonne of M1 and one tonne of M2 produced 2 tonnes of the finished product, what orientation would the plant logically possess?
2. For Fig. 5.3, draw in isodapanes for the values of 8 and 9 money units. What do they show?
3. Copper smelting has a material index of 2.8. What orientation would you expect it to have? Check your answer by referring to page 45 in the Oxford Economic Atlas of the World (fourth edition).

2. Labour Costs

While transport costs undoubtedly lie at the heart of the Weber model, Weber recognized that two other factors could exert major influences upon location. Although the Weber model is sometimes criticized for its over-emphasis on transport costs, it recognizes that the least transport cost location could be modified by the presence of a localized pool of cheaper labour. If the ratio of an industry's labour costs to the combined weight of its material inputs and product outputs were high, a pool of cheap labour would tend to attract that industry to a location different from the one resulting from calculations based on least transport costs *provided the savings from cheaper labour exceeded the extra transport costs incurred in marketing the finished product.*

In order to measure the significance of labour, Weber devised another index, the index of labour cost. For any industry this is the average cost of labour needed to produce one unit weight of output. The higher the index, the greater the likelihood of the industry's diversion from the least transport cost location. This measure may be compared with Smith's successful examination of the weight of raw materials per operative, which was discussed on p. 86.

3. Agglomeration and Deglomeration

Weber also pointed out that the least transport cost location could be deviated from if savings in costs could be achieved through the spatial association of industries. This 'coming together' of industrialists and industries is termed *agglomeration*. The kind of saving which can be achieved through agglomerating activities is illustrated in Fig. 5.4. (Further examples of the benefits of agglomeration have been noted in Chapter 4 – see pages 62–67 – and the subject is dealt with in other contexts in Chapters 3, 7 and 8 and is illustrated in Fig. 4.10.)

While agglomeration produces benefits such as a reduction of the time taken up, and thus costs incurred, in visiting linked activities, the establishment of a pool of skilled labour or the generation of co-operation between plants, it is possible for the nucleus to grow too big for its own good. Congestion could develop, land prices could rise if too many industrialists were jammed together, and firms might then benefit from the opposite of agglomeration – *deglomeration*. Thus, a critical size of nucleus could develop after which benefits would be replaced by disadvantages. Such benefits and disadvantages which derive simply from the *size* of the nucleus (e.g. town or industrial area) are called *economies* and *diseconomies of scale*. This is illustrated simply in Fig. 5.5.

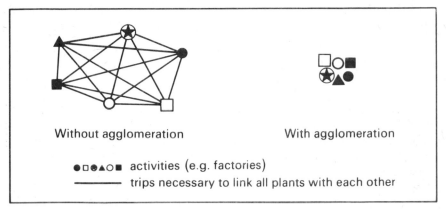

Fig. 5.4. Travel costs are reduced if linked activities are nucleated.

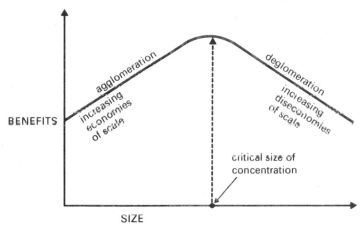

Fig. 5.5. Deglomeration replacing agglomeration after a critical size of nucleus is reached.

The most obvious examples of the benefits of agglomeration are the large cities of the world. The 'best' or optimal size for cities is a much debated academic point. There is probably no 'optimal city size', however, and it may be better to conceive of a range of sizes which are satisfactory, below which towns are insufficiently large to provide sufficient economies of scale, and

89

D

above which diseconomies rapidly set in. Also, different industries may possess different sized 'cities' as the optimum for their operations.

ASSIGNMENTS

1. *Study Table 5.3 carefully. It shows the details of nine industries and their orientations according to the principles of Alfred Weber. Inputs and other factors are included in columns 2 and 3.*

   Industry A, for example, requires one raw material which is ubiquitous. It obviously possesses a market orientation (M in column 4). Industry B needs one pure input which is located sporadically – in this case the industry can locate at the market, the source of raw material, or at an intermediate location since there is no weight loss in the production process.

   Having studied the table, complete column 4 for industries J, K, L and M. Justify your choice.

Table 5.3. Inputs, location factors and least cost locations for hypothetical industries according to Weber principles. (After an idea in F. E. I. Hamilton, 'Models of industrial location', in R. J. Chorley & P. Haggett (eds.) *Models in Geography*, Methuen, 1967, p. 371 and based on information in A. Weber, *Theory of the Location of Industries* (trans, C. Freidrich) Harvard University Press, 1926)

1 Industry	2 Inputs Ubiquitous	Sporadic pure	gross	3 Other factors Labour	Agglom	Deglom	4 Orientation
A	1						M
B		1					M, RM, or I
C			1				RM
D		2					M
E			2=				I
F			2≠+				M
G	2+	1					M, RM or I
H	unspecified			*			Labour
I	unspecified				*		Agglomeration
J	2+						
K	1+	1					
L	1+		1				
M	unspecified					*	

KEY

M – market
RM – raw material
I – intermediate location
* – definite location

+ – 'or more' materials
≠ – unequal weight losses for gross materials
= – equal weight loss for gross materials

2. *On the Fig. 5.6 diagrams mark the letter F where you would expect the factory to locate given the assumptions of the Weber model. Mention briefly why you chose the particular location(s) in each case. (Note that in some cases there is more than one possible location.)*

3. *How would you determine factory location if both raw materials were fixed and gross?*

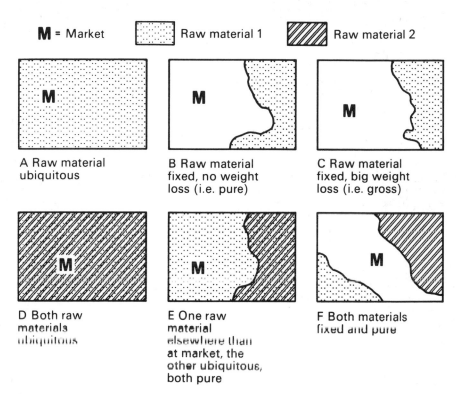

M = Market   ▢ Raw material 1   ▨ Raw material 2

A Raw material ubiquitous

B Raw material fixed, no weight loss (i.e. pure)

C Raw material fixed, big weight loss (i.e. gross)

D Both raw materials ubiquitous

E One raw material elsewhere than at market, the other ubiquitous, both pure

F Both materials fixed and pure

Fig. 5.6. (Fig. for Assignment 2)

C. Case Studies

1. Kennelley's Study of the Mexican Steel Industry

The American geographer, R. A. Kennelley, attempted to test the usefulness of the Varignon frame, the Weber model, and a reformulated Weber model, in predicting the location of the Mexican steel industry.[5]

The Mexican steel industry at the time of his study was centred on the city of Monterrey. The distribution and relative weights of supply inputs and the location of markets were known, so it was not difficult, by meticulous calculations, to locate the minimum transport cost point.

Would the Varignon frame predict that the industry was in Monterrey? Kennelley set up a contraption consisting of a board with a map of Mexico mounted on it. Holes were drilled through the map and board at the various supply and market points. Weights corresponding to the supply – market weights were suspended on strings of equal length running through the holes in the board and the strings joined in a knot above it. The knot was free to move in all directions, the friction being reduced by the use of glass bearings.

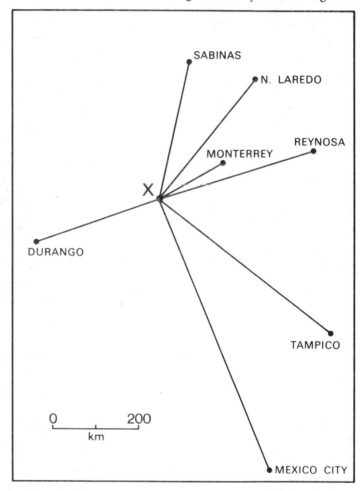

Fig. 5.7. Predicted location (X) of Mexican primary steel production using Varignon frame. Each point on the map represents an input source or market outlet for the Mexican steel industry. (After: R. A. Kennelley, 'The location of the Mexican steel industry', *Revista Geografica*, 1954/55)

Fig. 5.7 shows the result of the experiment with the hardware model. Note that the minimum transport cost point (X) (i.e. the position of the knot when the string had finally come to rest), does not exactly coincide with Monterrey, but is not very far from it.

Kennelley then decided to construct an isodapane map and thus test the theoretical position of the industry based on Weberian principles. The reader may recall that the isodapane values are based on weight and distance. Thus, Kennelley's isodapane map naturally produced the same result as the Varignon Frame and predicted that the industry would be located about 160 kilometres to the west of Monterrey, thus hinting that, like the Varignon prediction, Monterrey is close to, but not quite at, the optimum least cost location.

The lack of correspondence between the actual and predicted location is not difficult to explain. The Varignon and Weber models only took weight and distance into account, whereas freight rates also need to be considered (see page 99). In addition, the 'board' map of Mexico had no mountains or valleys – it was a completely smooth surface. Also, there was no transport network on the board to determine in exactly what direction and over what distances goods or products should be transported. Movement was by straight line distances without any form of constraint produced by relief or transport factors.

Kennelley went one step further in the use of isodapanes and constructed a second set, this time including not only weight and distance but also freight rates. The resulting map is shown in Fig. 5.8. Note that by this simple addition, the least cost location (X^1) is now almost spot on Monterrey. In other words, this slightly reformed Weber model has accurately *predicted* the location of the main steel producing centre. Now, just because the modified Weber model was able to predict the location of the Mexican steel industry, it does not follow that *all* steel industry locations can be similarly predicted. The author may have chosen his examples carefully to fit the model.

Nevertheless, we can see Weber at work on a general level if we consider the location of the production of pig iron which has a material index of between 3 and 4. Such locations do tend to be attracted to ore fields such as Lorraine, Duluth (Minnesota), the Jurassic Escarpment of Eastern England, or to coalfields such as Pittsburgh, the Ruhr, or South Wales. What is more, the lower quality the ore (i.e. more weight loss in the production process), the greater the tendency to attract iron making. This contrasts with the high grade ores (e.g. north Sweden) which can withstand transport costs because the ore loses less weight in the production process.

Over time, however, technology in the iron and steel industry has changed. Again, we may see overtones of the Weber model. Coal requirements are now one-third of what they were in 1908; there has also been a great increase in the use of scrap in the steel-making process and scrap is strongly located at markets. There has, at the same time, been an ever increasing demand from these markets, namely the great urban centres of the world. The market orientation of the steel industry has been especially marked in the USA, where

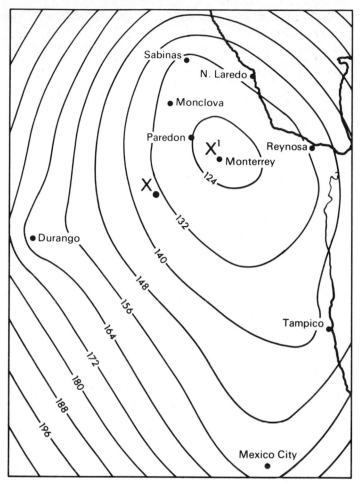

Fig. 5.8. Isodapanes based on weight, distance and freight rates (values in Pesos). (After R. A. Kennelley, *op. cit.*)

it has been relatively 'free' to adapt to market forces without the interference of government in the market-locational process which has been experienced in the British steel industry.

For Kennelley's Mexican study, the Weber model does appear to be a very useful aid to understanding the location pattern of the iron and steel industry. Nevertheless, the research for the study was undertaken in 1953 or earlier, and since then there has been a continuing trend for pig iron to be made at Monterrey and for steel-making to develop at Mexico City, close to supplies of scrap and the market for most finished steel.

Weber's model may be thought of has having specific, rather than general application. While it might still be applied at a macro-scale to other iron and steel industries, factors such as government aid and industrial inertia have led many steel works today to locate well away from the least cost location.

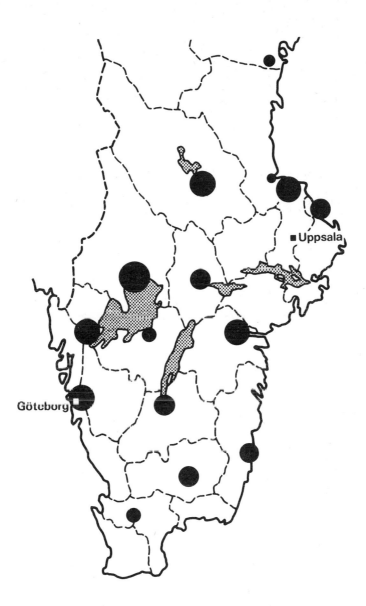

Fig. 5.9. Swedish paper production 1930–39. Circles are drawn proportionate to production of paper. (Source: O. Lindberg, 'An economic-geographical study of the localisation of the Swedish paper industry', *Geografiska Annaler*, **35**, 1953)

2. Lindberg's Study of the Swedish Paper Industry

Consider Fig. 5.9. It shows the value of Swedish paper production percentually for each county. To what extent are the major centres of production, in the Swedish Lakeland between Göteborg and Uppsala, at least transport cost locations?

Timber in Sweden may be regarded as a ubiquitous raw material and transport costs for the industry do not depend only on the raw material but also on coal, sulphur and limestone, as well as finished paper. The Swedish geographer, Olof Lindberg, calculated the total transport costs for some fifty paper mills in Sweden.[6] As costs are made up of inputs and outputs and because timber is ubiquitous and most Swedish paper is exported, it is not difficult to see intuitively that inland mills are often at a cost disadvantage compared with coastal mills. This is well illustrated by the isodapane map (Fig. 5.10) which shows lower values generally to be along the coastal areas.

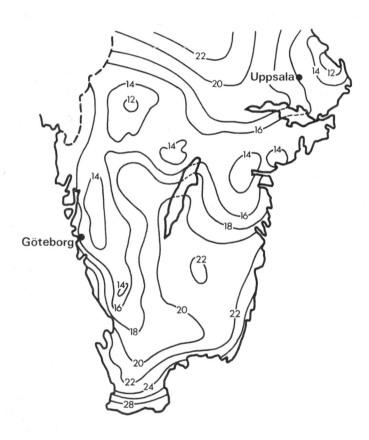

Fig. 5.10. Isodapane map for the Swedish paper industry. (After O. Lindberg, *op. cit.*)

The important thing to emphasize from Lindberg's study is that the raw material input – wood – is ubiquitous to the extent that it possesses virtually no localizing effect, and so market locations – or more precisely, port locations – are more important.

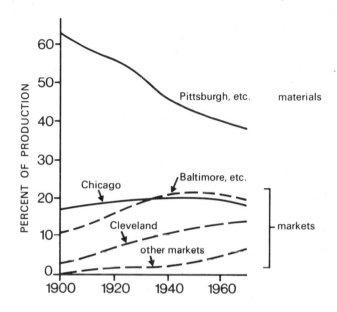

Fig. 5.11. Change in location of steel production. Locations near markets have become more important for steel production over time. (Source: R. Morrill, *The Spatial Organization of Society*, Duxbury Press – Ⓒ 1970 by Wadsworth Publishing Company, Inc.)

ASSIGNMENTS

1. The graph in Fig. 5.11 shows the changing significance of different steel-producing centres in USA since 1900.
   (a) Describe the trends shown for the location of American steel production.
   (b) Attempt to explain these trends.
   (c) In Weberian terms, what has happened to the value of the material index during the time period shown on the graph?
2. (a) For the Lindberg study of the Swedish paper industry, suggest why in Fig. 5.10 there are high isodapane values along the coast of Scania (i.e. the southern tip of Sweden).
   (b) While the Swedish paper industry is not, as commonly thought, raw material-oriented, you may be able to see if its locations minimize transport costs or not. This can be done by comparing the low cost locations on the isodapane map with the map (Fig. 5.9) of the major paper producing counties in Sweden.

97

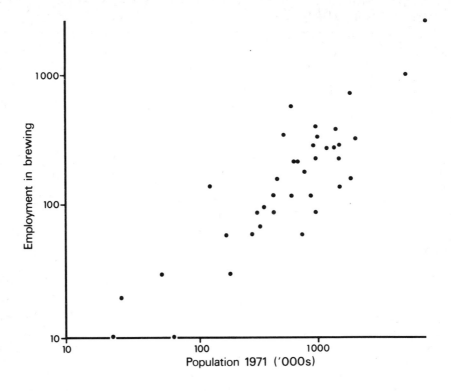

Fig. 5.12. Scatter diagram showing the relationship between the population of English counties and population employed in brewing.

3. *The above scatter diagram (drawn using logarithmic scales – see page 18) shows the relationship between employment in brewing and population for the English counties in 1966. Study the diagram, comment on the relationship shown, and in a paragraph attempt an explanation in Weberian terms.*

D. Arguments against Weber

It is easy to 'prove' that a literal interpretation of Weber's model does not fit the real world, but this would be a waste of time. Models are not meant to replicate reality – if they did they wouldn't be models. Theories and models are aids to our understanding of how the real world works. It is important, therefore, that we do not accept literally what the model states, and that we are aware of any drastic oversimplifications which might confuse, rather than enlighten us. Thus, it is important to heed the advice given in the introduction to Chorley and Haggett's seminal *Models in Geography*: 'the price of the employment of models is eternal vigilance'.[7]

In looking carefully at the Weber model, which points especially should we bear in mind?

1. Stepping of freight rates

One of the premises of Weber's model which has been most severely attacked as being unrealistic is that transport costs increase proportionately with distance and weight carried. What occurs, in fact, is that freight rates tend to be 'stepped' rather than increasing progressively with distance. An example of a stepped freight rate profile similar to those found in North America is shown in the hypothetical situation in Fig. 5.13.

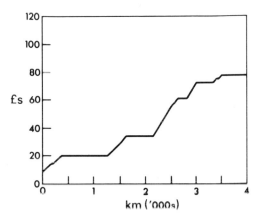

Fig. 5.13. A hypothetical example of stepped freight rates.

2. Variations in transport type used

In addition to stepped freight rates, the cost of transport between two points differs according to the type of transport used. Consider the costs in pence per tonne/km of moving containers along the Rhine Valley between Basle and Rotterdam by barge, rail, road and hovercraft. Fig. 5.14 clearly shows how the cost varies with mode of transport. In constructing isodapanes, therefore, the type of transport used would have to be specified.

3. Variations in transport networks and topography

Apart from the assumptions about transport costs increasing proportionately with distance, and the consistent use of one form of transport, Weber assumed

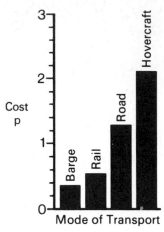

Fig. 5.14. Variations in transport costs between Basle and Amsterdam per tonne/km.

that movement was equally easy over all forms of surfaces. We have seen from Kennelley's Mexican study that transport networks and topography must obviously be taken into account in arriving at actual transport costs.

4. Existence of perfect competition

This assumption is perhaps the most unrealistic of all those made by Weber (refer back to page 82 for a definition of perfect competition). Perfect competition assumes that demand is constant spatially. With increased transport costs from the plant, however, demand must logically decline away from the plant as transport costs push up the price of the product. This assumes, of course, that it is the purchaser who pays the cost of transport incurred. Thus demand decreases as distance from the plant increases. Because of the unreality of perfect competition, it might be better to think of 'economic man' (see page 83) as a seeker of maximum profit, rather than of least cost, locations.

5. Market area approaches: Lösch

A further criticism often levelled against Weber is that he assumed demand came from only one point (i.e. the market) and all transactions were undertaken at this point. Likewise all sales would come from one production plant. We know full well that in reality demand is, in fact, spread over a rather wide area. The avoidance of any consideration of the demand factor was a major omission of Weber's model and it was left to another German economist, August Lösch, to correct the balance.[8] Lösch's main contribution is not in helping explain the location of production, which he takes as given, but in trying to formulate the optimum market areas for firms in competing industries in a given area. Lösch's ideas are more frequently reviewed in works on urban geography, since his 'economic regions' are akin to Christaller's hexagonal nets around central places.[9]

The approach of Lösch is best illustrated by considering the ideal supply area of a firm (something which Weber ignored). By 'ideal' we mean the area which will provide the maximum profit. Let us assume that farms are regularly spaced over a uniform surface. One farmer decides to manufacture beer. The basic question posed by Lösch is 'how large will his trade area eventually be?' In Fig. 5.15 P represents the point of production (i.e. the farm) and PQ is the price which the farmer will obtain for his product at P. As we move further away from P (i.e. along the axis PF) the price of beer will increase because of the costs of moving the beer away from the farm or because of the costs of travelling to the farm to collect. Either way, buyers will be paying more for it than if they lived at P. At F no beer will be sold because the price has become prohibitively high. Thus, QF represents the spatial demand curve for beer – sloping downward to the right showing that demand (but *not* price) declines with distance. PF is therefore the distance supplied from P. If we now rotate the demand curve through 360° we have what is known as a demand cone, enclosing the market area served from P.

Now if other farmers in the area start producing beer, they would be most profitably able to serve buyers outside the circular trade area centred on P (see Fig. 5.16) and thus a series of circular trade areas would grow up around the evenly distributed farms.

Over time the trade areas shown in Fig. 5.16 might grow in size since some parts of the diagram are clearly unserved by any of the distributors of beer. Thus, the stage might be reached as in Fig. 5.17 where circular trade areas touch each other with unserved areas in between.

Because circles either leave spaces unserved or overlap each other, the most efficient shape of trade area for the situation shown in Fig. 5.17 is that of the

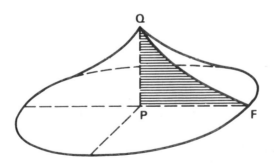

Fig. 5.15. A Löschian demand cone.

hexagon. In the case of Fig. 5.18 each brewer has a monopoly over his
hexagonal trade area.

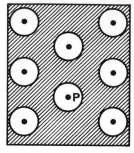

Fig. 5.16. Series of trade areas centred on points of production.

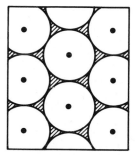

Fig. 5.17. Series of circular trade areas with unserved areas shaded.

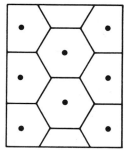

Fig. 5.18. Hexagons represent the most efficient shape of trade area.

While urban geographers have been hexagon-hunting for many years, there
have been relatively few attempts to identify hexagonal or any other kinds of
trade areas in industrial geography. This is because, in reality, competition
with other firms will exist within the trade area of any given plant, and so
spatial monopoly tends not to occur. This does not mean that trade area maps
for firms cannot be drawn, as Fig. 5.19 (page 103) shows, but it is most
unlikely that they would be hexagonal in shape.

The trade area concept of Lösch has been included here partly because of its
intrinsic interest and partly because it highlights one of the omissions of the

Weber model. While Weber may have over-stressed least cost locations, perhaps Lösch was preoccupied with maximum profits. One of the key ideas of this chapter is that both assumed an 'economic man' situation.

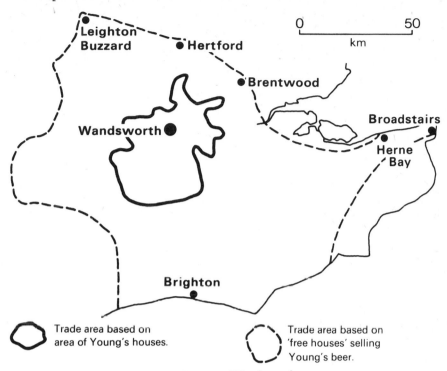

Fig. 5.19. Trade areas of Young's Brewery, Wandsworth.

ASSIGNMENTS

1. *Imagine that you are a manufacturer using timber as a major raw material input. What are the implications of stepped freight rate structures such as those shown in Fig. 5.13 for the choice of location for your plant?*

2. *Can you suggest why the costs of transport shown in Fig. 5.14 should differ? Would barge transport be cheaper than road over all distances? If not why not?*

3. *Fig. 5.19 shows two trade areas of Young's Brewery in Wandsworth, London. The company can be said to have two kinds of trade areas, one which is outlined by mapping the distribution of their own public houses and another made by delimiting the area of 'free houses' which sell their beer. Can you suggest why the trade area is not hexagonal in shape as Lösch's model suggests? In what other ways do the trade areas of brewing companies in Britain differ from the Lösch model? (You may need to read the reference under D(b) below to answer this in full.)*

103

E. Conclusion

Weber's work has been emphasized in this chapter for several reasons. First, he is often said to be the founder of modern industrial location theory and has undoubtedly had a tremendous influence on other workers in this field.

Secondly, he makes explicit the distinction between ubiquitous and localized raw materials and also distinguishes usefully between the various orientations of different industries. Given the time at which he was writing, it is not really surprising that there is a strong emphasis on the exploitation of place-specific raw materials and a lack of emphasis on footloose, modern light industry.

But perhaps Weber's greatest value is that, even today, he provides a useful conceptual instrument for understanding the broad locational patterns of industries such as those which we have described in this chapter. It is arguable whether the model is equally useful in understanding the location of say, a washing machine manufacturer or of a plant producing hi-fi equipment though, as we shall see from the chapters which follow, some geographers believe that modifications to the Weber model still make it a useful starting point in studies of industrial location.

We have noted that Weber has not been without his critics. The decline in the importance of transport costs and the fact that the persuasiveness of his philosophical underpinnings serve to 'straitjacket' the thinking of students may be additional reasons for suggesting that the model has outlived its usefulness. It is not surprising, therefore, that 70 years after Weber wrote his seminal work some geographers are beginning to think that there may be 'little to be gained from taking Weber as a starting point'.[10] Weber himself would not have been too unhappy with this since his work was, in his own words, 'expected to be a beginning, not an end'.[11] But if we knock down 'economic man', with whom are we going to replace him? We try to answer this question in the next chapter.

Key Ideas

A. *Assumptions of the Weber Model* (pages 82–83)
1. Raw materials may be localized or ubiquitous.
2. Markets for finished products are at fixed points.
3. Transport costs are determined by weight of material transported and distance moved.
4. Perfect competition exists so that the activities of one individual in the industry will not affect price and all goods produced can be sold.
5. Man is rational and locates at the locations which incur *least cost*.

B. *Cost Factors influencing Industrial Location* (pages 83–91)
1. As a result of the transport costs (the first of Weber's cost factors)

incurred, industries would be either raw material- or market-oriented or located at an intermediate position.

2. If an industry had a *material index* (weight of localized raw materials divided by weight of finished product) of over 1 it would be raw material-oriented, under 1 market-oriented, and of 1 it would be at an intermediate location or either of the above.

3. To determine least cost locations, *isodapanes* (lines joining places of equal transport costs) can be drawn.

4. Weber recognized that cheap *labour* costs could outweigh the significance of the least transport cost location.

5. Costs could also be reduced by *agglomeration* (the coming together of industries) or *deglomeration* (the splitting up of industrial concentrations).

C. *Case Studies of the Weber model* (pages 91–98)

1. The Kennelley study showed that the reformulated Weber model accurately predicted the location of the Mexican steel industry.

2. The Lindberg study of the Swedish paper industry took an example of an industry with a ubiquitous raw material and through the construction of isodapanes predicted the location of the timber-processing areas.

3. The Weber model seems useful for making broad predictions about the location of heavy industry.

D. *Arguments against Weber* (pages 98–103)

1. Transport costs do not increase proportionately with distance.

2. Costs of transportation over a given distance will vary according to the type of transport used.

3. Perfect competition does not exist.

4. Weber ignored the market area of firms and the demand for their products, a gap filled by the work of Lösch who argued that, given ideal conditions, a series of hexagonal trade areas would develop.

Additional Activities

1. In what ways does the model of Alfred Weber (i) illustrate the use of models in geography, (ii) adopt an 'economic man' standpoint?

2. Why did Wilfred Smith refer to the Weber model as a 'useful but blunt' tool of analysis?

3. If the assumptions of the Weber model are unrealistic, does this make the model valueless?

4. Identify industries which are 'market oriented' and suggest why this is the case in the light of ideas presented in this chapter.

Reading

A. HAMILTON, F. E. I., 'Models of Industrial Location', in CHORLEY, R. J. & HAGGETT, P., (eds.), *Models in Geography*, Methuen, 1968, pages 370–2.
B. SMITH, D. M., *Industrial Location*, Wiley, 1971, pages 112–9.
C. HAMILTON, F. E. I. *op. cit.*, pages 372–6, and 415–6.
D. (a) ELIOT HURST, M., *The Geography of Economic Behaviour*, Duxbury Press, 1972, pages 168–9.
   (b) RILEY, R. C., *Industrial Geography*, Chatto & Windus, 1973, chapter 5, especially pages 149–67.

6 Behavioural approaches to industrial location

A. Introducing non-economic man

1. Introduction

Sugar production is a material-oriented industry – you can see from the map (Fig. 6.1) that the factories are located in the main areas of sugar beet cultivation. You may recall that Wilfred Smith (see page 85) calculated its material index to be as high as 8. In fact over 70% of the total cost per unit of output was accounted for by sugar beet alone.

What is clear from a close look at Fig. 6.1 is that while *in general* the production of sugar in 1971 was oriented towards the raw materials, thus bearing out Weberian theory, the factories are quite dispersed over a wide area of sugar beet cultivation from Cupar in Scotland to Worcester in the English Midlands. We have seen that one of Weber's assumptions was that locational decision makers were rational, least-cost oriented, 'economic men'. Because they sought optimum locations, we may call them *optimisers*.

2. The satisficing principle

In real life it seems rather likely that many, if not most, businessmen do not aim at maximum profits or minimum costs (can they ever be sure what maximum profits could be, anyway?), but are quite happy with what they perceive to be satisfactory profits. Rather than search for the theoretically optimum location, they are pleased to employ the 'principle of least effort' and find a satisfactory location. In other words, they are *satisficers*, not optimisers. Such satisfactory locations will be those which continue to operate at a profit, though not the theoretically maximum profit.

B. Spatial Margins to Profitability

1. Explanation

Profit making locations are found within what can be termed spatial margins to profitability. Because of the conceptual and practical difficulties in arriving

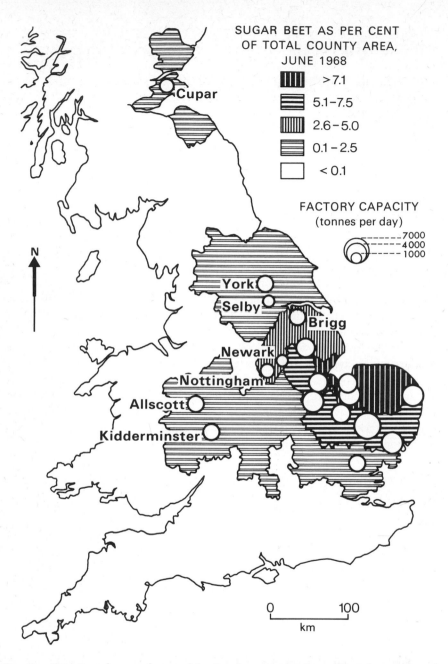

SUGAR BEET AS PER CENT
OF TOTAL COUNTY AREA,
JUNE 1968

▓	> 7.1
▬	5.1–7.5
▓	2.6–5.0
▬	0.1–2.5
☐	< 0.1

FACTORY CAPACITY
(tonnes per day)

7000
4000
1000

Cupar

York

Selby

Brigg

Newark

Nottingham

Allscott

Kidderminster

N

0   100
km

Fig. 6.1. Density of sugar beet cultivation by counties in 1968 and capacity of sugar beet factories in 1971. Circles refer to factory capacity. Names refer to towns with factories near spatial margins of profitability in 1971. (Source: H. D. Watts, 'Locational Adjustment in the British Sugar Beet Industry', *Geography*, **59**, 1974, p. 12)

at an optimum location, it might be better to think in terms of the spatial limits within which an enterprise can continue operating successfully. Thus the sugar factories which are named on the map (Fig. 6.1) were located close to the spatial margins of profitability,[1] while the remaining plants, mainly in East Anglia, were more optimally located. Indeed, in 1972 the Cupar factory was closed and four of the others named are likely to close in the near future.

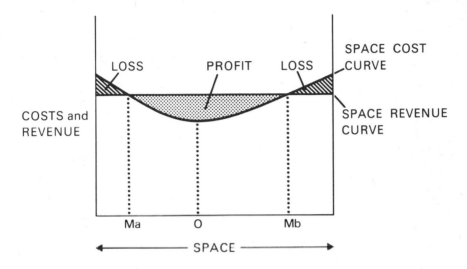

Fig. 6.2. Spatial margins with total revenue a spatial constant and total cost a spatial variable.

The spatial margins concept can be usefully summarized in Figs 6.2 and 6.3 in which costs and revenue are measured on the y axis and space (or distance) on the x axis. In Fig. 6.2 the *space cost curve* shows how costs for the firm vary over space, reaching a least cost location at O. The *space revenue curve* is depicted as a horizontal line, showing that in this case revenue does not vary spatially.

In Fig. 6.2 we can see that costs vary spatially while revenues remain the same, irrespective of location. The difference between costs and revenue is profit and it can be seen that profit is only being made if the firm locates between Ma and Mb. Outside Ma–Mb the plant would be operating at a loss. Thus, Ma–Mb represents the *spatial margins to profitability*.

Fig. 6.3 shows that the spatial margins concept can be illustrated equally well if the space revenue curve is the variable and the space cost curve the constant.

The diagrams we have seen so far are, of course, very greatly simplified versions of reality. In fact, the profitable area for an industry might well be

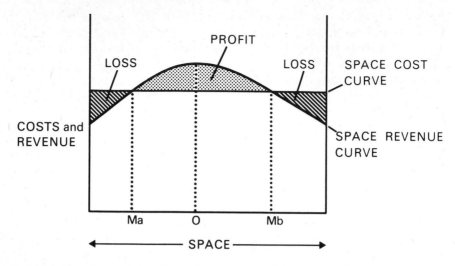

Fig. 6.3. Spatial margins with total cost a spatial constant and revenue a spatial variable.

interrupted by unprofitable areas. Each profitable zone would have its own optimum location for the profit-maximizing entrepreneur.

The idea of spatial margins to profitability was developed by two British geographers, E. M. Rawstron[2] and D. M. Smith,[3] the latter building on the ideas of the former. It is useful because it refines the concept of an optimum point location and makes allowance for sub-optimal behaviour. For example, the profit-maximizing location may not possess the boss's most important leisure facilities – a golf course or a night club – though these may exist somewhere within the spatial margins. If the businessman in question feels that the benefits gained from such sub-optimal locations compensate for the extra profits found at the optimum location, he will choose to locate there. By doing so, while not maximizing profits, he may be increasing his general level of satisfaction or utility.

Other common factors operating in the spatial margins which might make the industrialist locate away from the optimum location include:

the residence or birthplace of the founder of the industry;
the availability of a vacant factory or plot of land at the right time;
parental backing for the development of the enterprise;
imitation or gregariousness on the part of the entrepreneur;
the support of the local authority or the central government.[4]

2. Criticising spatial margins

Like most things, the spatial margins approach and the 'non-economic' man concept have not been without their critics. Irrationality, may not, in fact, be a characteristic of the present-day entrepreneur. It might be argued that economic decision making has never been so rational as it is today; that advanced business techniques, such as market research and advertising, aim at profit maximization.

Marxist geographers (who might assume that the monopoly position of the state was the most efficient form of organization) might argue that irrationality is more a description of the 'anarchy of competition' than of individuals making location decisions.[5]

Some geographers argue that the spatial margins approach simply represents a shift of scale – replacing a point (Weber) with an area. Within the 'area' sub-optimal man is allowed to locate where he likes but the gross locational boundaries are still determined by objective economic factors.[6] Furthermore, cost and revenue surfaces may be so irregular that it would be almost impossible to map the margins. Indeed, a firm would need to have so much information about market conditions, all sources and all costs of all inputs, all transport costs and all costs regarding the different technologies possible, that further difficulties in drawing the spatial margins would arise.

3. Drawing spatial margins—some case studies

An interesting problem encountered by more than one study is that for some industries it is impossible to draw spatial margins because the whole of the country is within them! For instance, in the context of the British iron foundry industry the West Midlands market for iron castings could be profitably served from any location in the UK.[7] In New Zealand the same result was found for industries such as leather and stationery whose Auckland market could be served profitably from anywhere within the country.[8] In such cases as this the spatial margins concept is clearly of little value in helping to explain the location of the industries in question. The manufacturer of the goods could, in each case, absorb transport costs for any location within the country and still serve his principal market at a profit.

For some industries, however, spatial margins can be drawn. In New Zealand, for example, the sheet metal and wire working industries' spatial margins more or less embrace the North Island – the extra cost of transport across Cook Strait eating into the industrialists' profits.

A further problem with the spatial margins approach is not only that different industries will have different margins, but that the margins for any one industry will change over time. Places once inside the margin may temporarily or permanently become unprofitable; those once outside the margin may become profitable. For example, the spatial profitability margins for the New Zealand basic metal industry differed greatly for the years 1963 and 1969. In 1963 margins extended well into the South Island whereas those for 1969 embraced only a small area around Auckland and Hamilton in the North Island (again taking Auckland as the market to be served).

Had the levels of profit which had occurred in the five years preceding 1969 been maintained in that year, however, the spatial margin to profitability would have embraced almost all of North Island. 1963 was a very profitable year for the entire industry so the spatial margin for that year extends well into the South Island.

Thus spatial margins can be drawn for some industries, although for the example quoted above there has been no attempt to locate the optimum location; instead the major national market for an industry was taken and the relevant spatial margins drawn. The concept of spatial margins to profitability is probably most useful as a conceptual refinement of Weber's model, since it is able to incorporate a very large number of 'non-economic' factors of a behavioural nature which can lead 'non-economic man' to locate at sub-optimal locations. Like Weber's model, the spatial margins concept should not be taken too literally; it is perhaps best thought of as a relaxation of some of Weber's rigid assumptions to incorporate some of the vagaries of human behaviour.

ASSIGNMENTS

1. *Having studied Figs. 6.2 and 6.3 (pages 109–10) attempt to construct a similar diagram showing both the space cost curve and the space revenue curve as spatial variables and with the least cost location and the maximum revenue points being at different locations. Mark in the optimum location and the spatial margins to profitability.*

2. *Review, with examples, the reasons why (a) it may be impossible to draw spatial margins for some industries, and (b) why movement may occur in the position of spatial margins.*

3. *Fig. 6.4 shows the actual space cost and space revenue curves drawn along the railway line from Rio to the region called Itabiro (check these locations on your atlas if necessary) for a steel plant serving the Rio de Janeiro market in Brazil around 1905. Copy Fig. 6.4 and (a) mark in the spatial margins, and (b) mark in the optimum location. The steel plant was located at Itabirito. Was it optimally located? If not, how far was it from the optimum location? Could it have operated at a profit at Rio, the major market for its products?*

C. The Behavioural Matrix

1. Explanation

We have seen that the spatial margins approach is able to include the vagaries of 'man the satisficer'. Much of the variety associated with the choice of location derives from the different ways decisions are made and the varying level of ability of the decision makers.

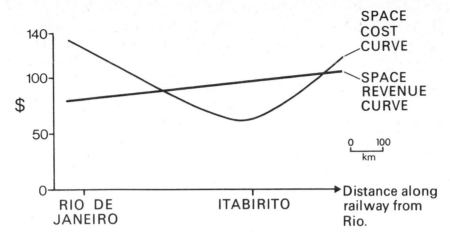

Fig. 6.4. Space cost curve and space revenue curve for the steel mill at Itabirito, 1905. (Based on P. R. Haddad & J. Schwartzman, 'A space cost curve of industrial location', *Economic Geography*, 1974, p. 142)

This section focuses on how sites are found within the spatial margins to profitability. Location decision making is important to the geographer because any location pattern is the result of numerous individual decisions taken over varying periods of time. An understanding of how location decisions are made is therefore necessary.

If you were faced with making a decision about where to locate a factory, it would not be too unfair to suggest that you would possess little *information* about how to do so and, because of your inexperience in such matters, would have little *ability* in locating factories. In an attempt to replace 'economic man' with something nearer the real thing, Allan Pred[9] has suggested that the degree to which optimal decisions are made depends on: (a) the amount of information available to the decision maker; and (b) the decision maker's ability.

He conceives of a 'behavioural matrix' into which all decision makers can be theoretically slotted. The two axes of this matrix (Fig. 6.5) thus measure 'amount of information' and 'ability to use'. In Fig. 6.5 decision maker Y is located in the top left hand corner of the matrix. His matrix position shows that he possesses little or no locational information, and, poor fellow, he is totally inept as a decision taker. It seems hardly likely that he will select the optimum location for his plant. Decision maker Z on the other hand, possesses perfect knowledge and is perfectly rational. Not surprisingly, he is able to locate at the optimum location.

We may also envisage Mr Average on the matrix, who is shown on Fig. 6.5 as X. He is sub-optimal man, locating within the spatial margins to profitability but not possessing enough information or ability to locate at the optimum. Decision maker A in Fig. 6.5 is seen from his matrix position to

113

possess limited information and ability. He is able to make a viable locational choice because of 'chance factors' or 'good luck', in spite of his relatively poor matrix position.

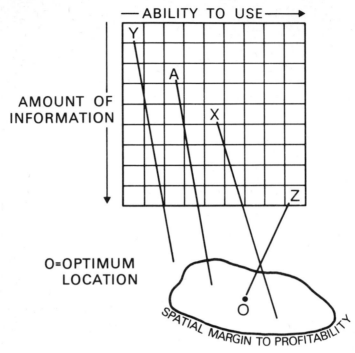

Fig. 6.5. The behavioural matrix and the spatial margins to profitability.

Fig. 6.5 also shows that the behavioural matrix idea is easily amalgamated with the spatial margins model. However, in studying this diagram it should be remembered that an improvement in entrepreneurial skill may not only provide the potential to move the decision maker closer to the theoretically optimum location; it may also produce the potential for the spatial margins to profitability to be expanded. This is because entrepreneurial skill could theoretically have the effect of lowering costs, thus pushing spatial margins to profitability further away from the optimum location (see Fig. 6.6).

2. Adding the time element to the behavioural matrix

We saw earlier in this chapter that the spatial margins to profitability can change over time. Let us now add the time element to the behavioural matrix. We may hypothesize that over time decision makers not only get more experienced but that they also imitate others. New firms copy the successful location decisions of others until ultimately widespread entrenched behaviour

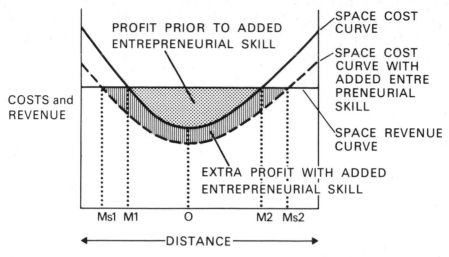

Fig. 6.6. The effect of added entrepreneurial skill on the spatial margins to profitability. The spatial margins expand from M1 – M2 to Ms1- – Ms2.

becomes the norm. Over time, more information about 'best locations' accumulates and businessmen learn from earlier mistakes. These changes are represented by the letters A–D in Fig. 6.7 where it is shown how, from time period t_x to time period t_x+2, there has been a shift in the average position of decision makers in the behavioural matrix downwards to the right. The spatial counterpart of the behavioural matrix, the industrial landscape or region, becomes more orderly and more rational.

A major technological 'shock' (see bottom of Fig. 6.7), such as a new form of transportation, a newly developed technique or newly acquired knowledge, makes what was once a satisfactory or even optimal location no longer so. This produces a backward shift in the matrix in time period t_x+q. Looked at in another way, major changes in information or ability mean that the scale of the matrix expands; when further knowledge is acquired and ability to use it learnt, the centre of gravity of the occupied cells starts moving again, downwards to the right.

It is not easy to find examples of the behavioural matrix in reality for reasons which will be discussed below. What is observable, however, is a growing orderliness and logic in the industrial location pattern of particular industries. A good example is that of the American car industry. Since about 1914 the industry has gradually concentrated in the most profitable locations; the almost random distribution of the industry in the early days[10] (every state in the USA except Hawaii, Arizona, Alaska and Montana at some time in its history possessed a motor vehicle manufacturing plant!) has been replaced by the highly concentrated industrial location pattern to be found around the Detroit area today.

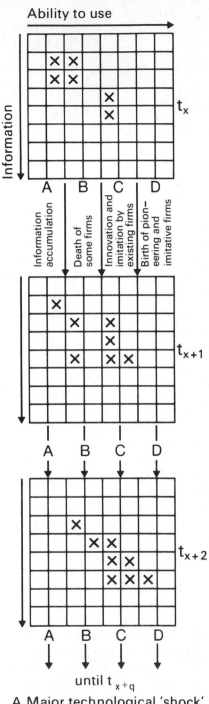

Fig. 6.7. Temporal changes in the behavioural matrix. (After: A. Pred, *Behavior and Location*, Gleerup, 1969, p. 11)

3. The behavioural matrix—a critique

Let us now review the idea of the behavioural matrix just as we have reviewed the Weberian and spatial margins approaches. The essence of the behavioural matrix is that whereas the spatial margins approach sets up the locational stage, the matrix tries to account for the locational behaviour of the actors. Pred replaces 'economic man' with 'behavioural man' so that deviations from the optimum location can be explained by the locational 'actor's' position in the behavioural matrix. The matrix is an attractive idea in that it accommodates complex locational processes, changing locational choice over time, with information accumulation and the births and deaths of firms in the economic landscape. What is debateable, however, and as yet unresolved, is whether the matrix can actually be applied. It might be argued that it is *too* oversimplified for real situations, and that it is this which needs to be attacked, not 'economic man'. Is it possible to define perfect knowledge and optimal user ability so that the matrix can be tested? Can the extremely complex ideas of behaviour be collapsed into two concepts – ability and information? Can the matrix be used as an analytical tool? These questions have yet to be satisfactorily answered.

In any consideration of the matrix it is important to emphasize that, while a decision maker may not possess perfect information and can therefore only make an objective optimal locational choice if he is lucky, it does not mean that he is not *trying* to optimize on the basis of what information is available.[11] Furthermore, sub-optimal or personal factors may influence a location decision on one level of scale (e.g. the intra-regional location) although the regional location might be selected on economic grounds. In fact, what might appear to be sub-optimal factors (e.g. personal reasons, such as proximity to a golf course) might in fact be very profit-oriented.

We have also seen from the changing internal arrangement of the matrix over time (see Fig. 6.7) that through learning and imitation industrialists become more rational and move to the bottom right hand corner. But, we may ask, why should businessmen do this if one of the corner-stones of the behavioural matrix is that many businessmen are not, in fact, profit maximizers/risk minimizers at all?[12]

ASSIGNMENT

Simulating locational behaviour

Fig. 6.8 illustrates a region at three different time periods (t_x, t_{x+1} and t_{x+2}). The region possesses one large urban area and one major transport artery. In the initial time period we note that 11 firms are 'born' – they are set up for the first time on the hypothetical economic landscape. By the second time period (diagram B) some of the firms have 'died', others have survived and some new ones have been 'born'. Using the assumptions of Pred's behavioural matrix, how might you expect the spatial arrangement of plants to be in t_{x+2}? Mark in the pattern of plants in this period, explaining the location of each. This simple exercise should test your understanding of the Pred model.

The more thoughtful or adventurous reader may like to take this model to time period t_{x+q} (see Fig. 6.7) and introduce a major technological shock into the system (perhaps the railway becomes defunct and a new form of transport replaces it running east-west out of the region – e.g. a motorway).

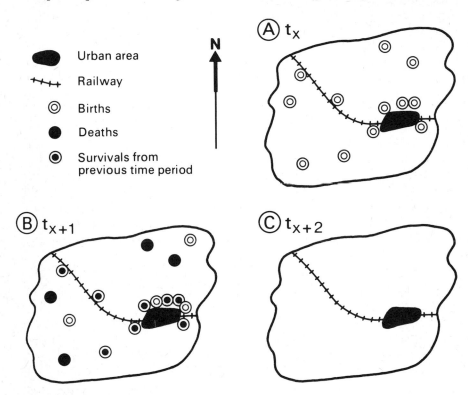

Fig. 6.8. Simulating locational behaviour.

D. Decision making

1. Pressures to (re)locate

Much of the preceding theoretical discussion has aided (it is hoped) an understanding of the location problem. In reality, however, it may be that most initial location decisions are non-events. The first decision for an industrialist starting up is *what* to produce rather than *where* to produce it. Unless insurmountable problems exist the beginning industrialist will locate in his home town. It is only when he comes to move, probably as a result of a desire to expand, that he faces the question, where do I locate?

118

In this section we look at how industrialists go about looking for locations and some of the pressures which are upon them to move. Consider the attitude of the following hypothetical businessman:

I am all right where I am. I am making a living. The home trade suits me. I don't like to move to a new location, it might be worse there. More income means higher taxes. Moving is a bother. Here I know where I am – suppliers, customers, workpeople, council officials, transport agents. If I move I might be richer, but I might be poorer. I know of a chap who went bankrupt after he moved. I am too old to think of expanding very much. We've got all we need. If I move out of reach of toolmakers, repairers, suppliers ... I might have to pre-plan production. They might make me adopt stock control, progress chasing, introducing computing or accounting staff.[13]

Such a reaction is not uncommon among 'small' industrialists. Here is yet another example of satisficing behaviour – an industrialist clearly happy with 'income' of a psychic rather than a monetary nature.

For industrialists faced with the problem of relocating, however, it is worth bearing in mind that there seem to be two sets of factors operating upon them, *pushes* from their existing location, and *pulls* to other areas.

2. Pushes

Because the location decision is far less frequently undertaken than other investment decisions, it is a rather risky business and ideally many firms would prefer not to have to make this decision at all. As about 85% of all relocation can be attributed to expansion of the firm[14] it follows that a large number of industrialists have been prevented in some way from expanding *in situ* – an arrangement which would suit most of them best of all. Why may such *in situ* expansion be difficult or impossible? We may identify several *ceilings* on local expansion, the first being that for many firms there is simply not enough room, especially for those located in inner city areas.

If a short distance move is then contemplated a second ceiling in the form of high land prices on the city cost surface may be encountered. If inter-regional movement is the next possibility the firm may find itself up against another ceiling in the form of government refusal to grant permission (see page 170). Thus the alternatives may be to move out of the region altogether or not move at all. If the latter course is adopted then the government might unwittingly have been guilty of putting the brakes on the expansion of industry. If space is available for expansion *in situ* the government must decide on the *potential mobility* of the firm – that is, can it justify expanding in its present location because a move might reduce its efficiency through the severence of essential linkages?

3. Deciding to relocate

From Fig. 6.9 we see that while space requirements for expansion may be the most important factor pushing a firm to seek a new location, several other factors may act as pressures for a new site. For instance, a contraction of space requirements means that existing plant is being underused, thus increasing overhead costs. On the other hand, existing locational costs may increase (e.g. local labour cost may rise) or existing locational receipts may fall through increased competition or increased taxes. Other external pressures (that is, pressures from *outside* the organization of the firm) include things like planning requirements which result in the factory being razed to the ground as redevelopment of inner city areas takes place or the factory has to make way for an urban motorway. Other external pressures may originate from an even higher authority – the factory may be struck by lightning and burnt down!

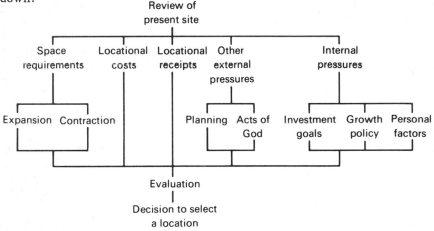

Fig. 6.9. Some pressures to select a new location.

Finally, there may be important internal pressures to seek a new location. These originate from *inside* the firm. If the plant is a branch factory, pressures may originate from the parent plant. In other cases, policies of the management may induce movement and sometimes personal interpretations of the economic climate may stimulate the search for a new location.

4. Pulls

Having decided to move (Fig. 6.9), which location and which site will be chosen? A key element in pulling a firm to a particular location will be that area's accessibility to a variety of location factors such as those shown in Fig. 6.10. These include labour, raw material inputs, external economies such as the presence of linked firms and services, and the market. All these may be

120

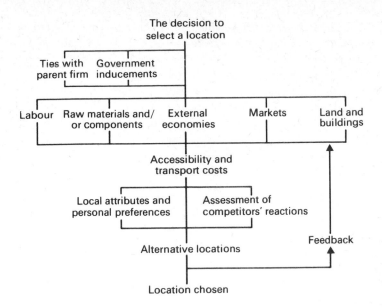

Fig. 6.10. The search for a new site.

outweighed, however, by the influence of the government (see Chapter 8) or of the parent firm. Likewise, while each locational pull may be evaluated as a potential cost to be incurred, local attributes such as good scenery and personal preferences (see pages 126–9) may count for something too.

Having weighed up a short list of possible alternatives, the location decision will be made, following a final re-assessment of the factors considered important. Generally speaking, firms do not short-list many locations. Again, as a general rule, the larger the firm the more alternatives are investigated. Thus, when Richard Thomas and Baldwin decided to open a new steel plant in the early sixties, no fewer than ten sites throughout Britain were selected.[15] A smaller plant employing fewer workers and having a more restricted market area might only look at three or four locations, all within a relatively small area. For the small firm the final choice may be the result of personal preferences rather than rational economic factors, especially if on economic grounds there is little to choose between selected sites.

5. Spheres of influence of locational pulls

While various pulls may be exerted upon the firm, it is not easy to measure *how important* each pull is. It is also difficult to know *how distant* from a location factor an enterprise must be before efficiency decreases.

Let us take four location factors and assume that we can identify the firms which do benefit materially from their proximity to the location factor in

E

question, as distinct from firms which do not. How concentrated are such firms around the location factor which they claim is important to them? Do their numbers decrease rapidly or only slowly away from the location factor? Just as in urban geography we talk of a town's sphere of influence, so we can talk in industrial geography of a location factor's sphere of influence.

The spatial extent of such spheres of influence will be determined by assessing the percentage of firms known to benefit from the factor and clustered close to it. This assumes, of course, that the location factor in question is a *point* in space (e.g. an airport or docks), rather than a more general pull like access to labour or availability of government grants.

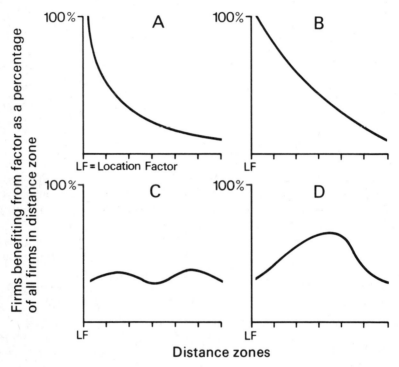

Fig. 6.11. Spheres of influence of four location factors. (After: A. G. Hoare, 'The spheres of influence of industrial location factors', *Regional Studies*, **7**, 1973, pp. 301–14)

In Fig. 6.11 we see four different graphs representing the distribution of firms around four hypothetical location factors. In A we see that the location factor (LF) requires close proximity of firms valuing their access to it, almost 100% of the firms in the distance zone nearest to the factor benefiting from its presence. This location factor has a relatively limited sphere of influence and this is shown by the steepness of the curve. Such a curve is said to present a strong *distance decay* effect – as distance increases the impact of the location factor rapidly decreases. The London Stock Exchange is an example of this sort of factor.

In B the advantage is less localized and the distance decay curve less steep. Here a relatively large number of firms in the first two distance zones benefit from the factor, and the sphere of influence of B is, therefore, greater than that in the case of A. London Docks are an example of factor B.

In C (an eighteen-hole golf course, for instance) no concentration is found within the area under consideration, and high percentages of nearby firms claiming the factor to be important are absent. In D we see that a composite picture exists. Here a location factor may act as a local deterrent but is also an advantage on a larger scale. London Airport typifies this sort of location factor.

In concluding this section it should be emphasized that we know very little about how far firms utilizing particular location factors have to be from those factors before efficiency declines. The strength of attraction of a locational pull is usefully illustrated, however, by adopting a sphere of influence approach.

ASSIGNMENTS

1. Distinguish between, giving examples, locational pulls which might be thought of as 'points' and those which might be interpreted as 'areal' in extent.
2. Which of the diagrams in Fig. 6.11 (page 122) would you apply to the following location factors: (a) access to rail termini; (b) access to hotels and entertainment?

E. Spatial Perception and Decision making: Mental Maps

INTRODUCTORY ASSIGNMENT

Table 6.1 lists 50 British towns. It also gives a desirability scale ranging from 1 (for towns which you, as a potentially mobile industrialist, would feel highly desirable as a place of residence) to 5 (which you would regard as highly undesirable places to live). Ranges of desirability are found between these two extremes. Each member of your class may be taken to represent a firm which could operate equally efficiently from each of the 50 towns. Each member should score each town between 1 and 5 on the desirability scale (for instance, if you are indifferent to town X then score it 3; if you think town Y is very undesirable score it 5).

When all towns have been scored, add up the scores for each town recorded by each member of the class. The lower the total score, the more desirable the town in your class's mental map.

Table 6.1. (Table for introductory assignment)

	Ind	G			Ind	G
1 Sheffield			26 Southampton			
2 Brighton			27 Bedford			
3 Carlisle			28 Leicester			
4 Lincoln			29 Liverpool			
5 Nottingham			30 Worcester			
6 Bristol			31 Aylesbury			
7 Bath			32 Manchester			
8 Bradford			33 Gloucester			
9 London			34 Colchester			
10 Lampeter			35 Birmingham			
11 Exeter			36 Plymouth			
12 Shrewsbury			37 Cardiff			
13 Cambridge			38 Northampton			
14 Swindon			39 Hull			
15 Leeds			40 York			
16 Canterbury			41 Dorchester			
17 Salford			42 Swansea			
18 Reading			43 Taunton			
19 Norwich			44 Hertford			
20 Oxford			45 Coventry			
21 Newcastle-upon-Tyne			46 Stoke-on-Trent			
22 Lancaster			47 Durham			
23 Aberystwyth			48 Merthyr			
24 Bangor			49 Ipswich			
25 Guildford			50 Hereford			

RATING
1 = Highly desirable
2 = Desirable
3 = Indifferent

4 = Undesirable
5 = Highly undesirable
Ind = Individual rating
G = Group Rating

You may have time to map your results. Locate each place on an outline map of the UK and put a different coloured dot for each of the four groups of scores (for instance, green for 20–40 – if there are 20 in your class, 20 will be the minimum score possible – blue for 41–60, brown for 61–80; red for scores over 80. You will need to vary the range of scores depending on the size of your group). Another way of mapping your results is shown in Fig. 6.13 (page 127).

Is there any pattern on your map? Do undesirable places cluster in particular parts of the country?

Is there a neighbourhood effect – places closest to the area in which you live being more desirable than those some distance away?

1. Behavioural and objective environments

We have already noted that personal factors may influence industrialists' locational choices. Among the personal factors which may affect a locational decision maker is his perception of a place – what he thinks it is like rather than what it actually is like. We may thus compare the world inside our heads with the real world; the former being termed the *behavioural environment* and the latter the *objective environment*.

The way we perceive the world is important because it affects the way we behave. The way we behave influences the objective environment (the real world) and therefore the link between perception, behaviour and reality is quite strong. This link is illustrated in Fig. 6.12. Here we see that information is obtained from reality which forms an image of that reality in our minds.

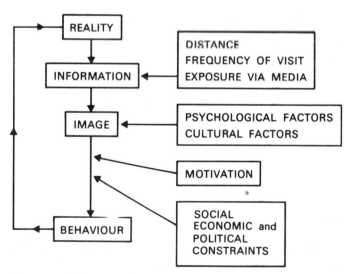

Fig. 6.12. Elements of behavioural geography.

125

(For instance, Wigan possesses some real characteristics, but the image of Wigan in the reader's mind may be different from that in reality as a result of the partial information obtained about that town.)

The reader may be able to see examples of the distortion of images from the introductory assignment. There seems no reason to believe that industrialists behave any differently from your class in favouring some places rather than others solely on the basis of spatial perception.

2. Influences on our mental maps

What influences our images of places? Fig. 6.12 suggests that the amount of information we obtain about a place is going to have some effect on our image of it. The amount of information on a place may be hypothesized as being dependent on things like the distance we live away from it, the frequency of our visits to it, the degree of exposure it gets in the media and, perhaps, its size. Other factors working upon the image we receive include those of a psychological and cultural nature (for instance, we may have a certain class prejudice against any place west of Offa's Dyke or north of Hadrian's Wall). As a result of our image we undertake behaviour (such as whether to locate or not in a particular place) which, of course, influences reality – the feedback loop in Fig. 6.12.

Man is located in an intimate personal space, a mental map of which becomes very well known as a result of continuous contact with, say, house and home. His perception of these places will be very clear. Cultural factors such as racial prejudice or social factors like class prejudice are less likely to influence his image of personal space than his image of far places with which he will have had contact only via TV, radio, newspapers, or from talking to other people. Between the relatively hazy images of distant places and the intimate knowledge of personal space, man possesses a variety of images about places resulting from acquaintance through work, shopping or from visiting friends. The various images people have of different places lead them to prefer some places more than others.

Interestingly there have been attempts to discover the locational preferences of people from a variety of areas of Britain. For example, when sixth formers from 23 locations in the UK were asked to rank the counties of Britain in order of preference, some remarkable regularities emerged. For example, the students living in Stornoway and those living in Bournemouth preferred the local area – the neighbourhood effect being well emphasized. Nevertheless, the collective view of all students at the 23 locations was that, in general, certain parts of Britain were preferred to others.[16] For example, the south coast scored consistently as a desirable place to live, as did East Anglia. London tended to be relatively undesirable, while the peripheries of the country – Wales and Scotland – were also generally low on people's order of preferences.

Fig. 6.13 shows the collective space preference map of 16 college students at

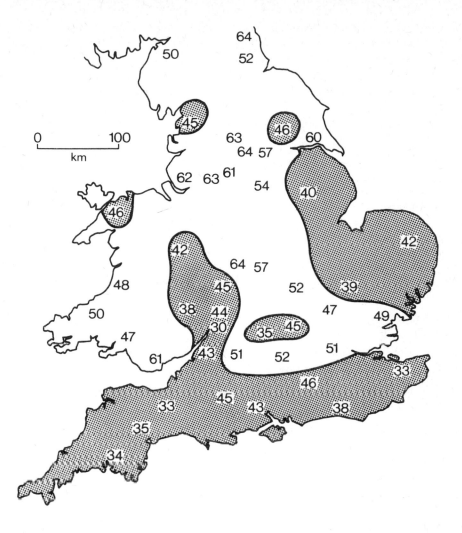

Fig. 6.13. Space preference map of 16 geography students at Avery Hill College of Education, London. Scores below the median are in the shaded areas. The results of the exercise described on page 123 should be compared with this map. Numbers refer to scores obtained by each town.

Avery Hill College of Education in London. The home locations of the students were scattered throughout England and Wales. The map illustrates the result of an exercise similar to the one on page 123, and confirms the general preference for places in the south and in East Anglia and, apart from some 'islands of preference', the relative dislike of places towards the periphery.

As only a very small proportion of firms employ professional location analysts to investigate the problems of a location, it is very unlikely that subjective factors fail to enter into the locational decision making process.

Certain areas may be dismissed because of prejudice or emotion, because they are far away or small places or places visited only rarely. The managing director may associate a particular place with the memory of his mother-in-law – worse still, his mother-in-law may live there!

Consider the following example of how one member of senior management of a branch plant of a metal components firm responded to Peter Townroe's survey of industrial location decision making of some firms in the North East:

> We are trying to get away from the labour difficulties we have here. Although some of our raw material comes from South Lancashire and we have a few customers there, we had heard the labour was bad there from friends and customers. The word gets round. Also with Scotland. We never really looked at them closely. South Wales was not considered because, well, you understand, they're not English. They're different. They might resent an intruder. Distribution was also bad from there. Northern Ireland was looked at but was ruled out on transport grounds. We did think of Redditch but there are no incentives and we would have the same sort of labour problems there as here. And Dawley New Town? Well, that never really got off the ground did it?[17]

Notice how the respondent immediately dismisses South Wales without a thought and how hearsay evidence resulted in South Lancashire not being considered even though the firm possessed some trade links with that area. It is also interesting to note protests from civil servants when decentralization is mooted.

3. A Potter's Bar effect?

It is clear from Fig. 6.13 that the South of England appears to be the most favoured area. As this is the case, areas in other parts of Britain have to sell themselves either by promoting their own image (Figs 6.14 and 6.15) or by attempting to denigrate the image of the South (see Fig. 6.16).

Gould and White[18] talk passionately about the 'spatial bias of the decision makers and, literally, the capitalists, who are mainly Southerners, [which] is reflected in the national perception surface of Britain'. They go on to argue that 'planning in a humane economy, that puts people first, must surely consider the mental images of places as a crucial input to policy decisions which affect in such deep ways the patterns and satisfactions of individual lives'.

Clearly mental maps exist. They make up the world inside our heads and we should not be surprised if they influence our locational decisions. Our mental images of places also contribute to industrial inertia and the whole concept of 'perception geography' fits in very neatly with the sub-optimal location models we discussed earlier in this chapter. At the same time, industrialists' mental images of the peripheral areas of Britain may well have retarded economic growth in those regions. If space preferences can be identified consistently among decision takers in industry, the government may be able to act upon the information provided by their mental maps. After all, government policy is all about improving the images of the regions concerned.

Potters Bar a 'false barrier'

They were not thickheads, blockheads, and bumpkins, who were born north of the Thames, **Mr Kenneth Lomas** (Lab, Huddesfield W) told the Commons yesterday. He called for an end to that "London-based mentality" about the North. Nothing could be further from the truth.

Mr Lomas, who was opening a debate on the needs and problems of Yorkshire and Humberside, said tourists should go North to see the real England. He praised the work of the Yorkshire and Humberside Development Association.

"I agree entirely with what they are seeking to do to protect the region as part of modern Britain, and do away with the image that Yorkshire is an area of cloth caps, fish and chips, and Coronation Street."

Mr Lomas also called for recognition that in Yorkshire the tourist industry was of vital importance to the economy. It ranked with Yorkshire's top six industries, and in 1973 expected to have a turnover of £135 millions. He would like the Government to look again at the Development of Tourism Act because it splits Yorkshire in two.

Mr Lomas said the Government should forget about building a third London airport, and instead concentrate on regional airports, particularly the Leeds-Bradford airport.

Mr Roy Mason, Opposition spokesman on Trade and Industry, said: "Our country is plagued with this problem of the Potters Bar barrier. Investors, developers, and speculators are tumbling over themselves in one-tenth of the country below Potters Bar, while nine-tenths of the nation is struggling to live and expand.

The attractions of Yorkshire were now becoming evident. There was some evidence that the Government's policies were working through, and the region was at last on the move.

Mr Christopher Chataway, Minister for Industrial Development, said he believed that the Government could claim to have pursued a more forward regional policy than its predecessor. "I do not think the charge stands up against this Government that we are interested solely in the South-east of England," he said.

The debate ended.

Fig. 6.14. From 'In Parliament Yesterday'. *The Guardian*, 3 November, 1973. This newspaper report clearly illustrates the problem of overcoming the 'Potters Bar Effect'.

ASSIGNMENT

We conclude this section with a role-playing game which attempts to synthesize much of what has been said so far in this book. The game invites you to find a location for the Texonic Electrics company in the UK. The game puts YOU in the place of someone faced with the problem of finding a location for a relatively 'footloose' kind of factory.

NORTH WEST ENGLAND

South America & Australasia

U.S.A. and Canada

NORTH WEST

E.E.C.

Scandinavia

Logical Centre for expansion

WHICHEVER WAY YOU LOOK AT IT, North-West England is the physical, industrial and commercial centre of the U.K. With major seaports at Liverpool and Manchester and a major international airport at Manchester, it provides a natural stepping stone from Continental Europe to the Americas. Excellent motorways and inter-city train services exist throughout the region.

Labour is skilled and adaptable and there is no lack of existing accommodation for industry and commerce. There is a wide variety of sites available for new premises too.

This major industrial centre of Europe is the logical centre for expansion and that is why numerous British firms and companies from all parts of the World are already taking advantage of its excellent facilities. Why not join them? It makes sense in any language.

Consult:
Clifford F. Chapman, Director,
NORTH WEST INDUSTRIAL DEVELOPMENT ASSOCIATION
Brazennose House, Brazennose Street, Manchester, M2 5AZ. Tel: 061-834 6778.

Fig. 6.15. How the North West Industrial Development Association would like industrialists to see Britain.

Texonic comes to Britain

Texonic Electrics of Dallas, Texas, plan to open a factory in the UK which will make a new form of dictating machine, selling mainly in Britain. Texonic are hoping for market penetration into Europe in the 1980s. They have decided to locate in Britain because the radio and telecommunications industries have shown

130

Fig. 6.16. Doncaster and the South East. How Doncaster tries to help attract industrialists 'up north'.

rapid growth in recent years – employment in these industries growing by 59.8% between 1959 and 1969.

You are part of a management team of Texonic. Your job will be to find a suitable location for your firm in the UK. Before sending four senior members of management to Britain to seek out a location, your company has drawn up a check-list of conditions that it needs to have satisfied for its plant.

1. An adequate supply of labour must be available – much of it can be female since this is a light industry. About 200 workers living within 10 kilometres of the factory would be required, though the 30 or so members of senior and supervisory grades might want to live further away.

2. Texonic will have a national market, but its products will sell mainly in the most populated areas and in those regions with a high proportion of offices. Thus access to the Axial Belt between Lancashire and Kent is important.

3. The electronics industry is relatively 'footloose'. Texonic's analysts have cal-

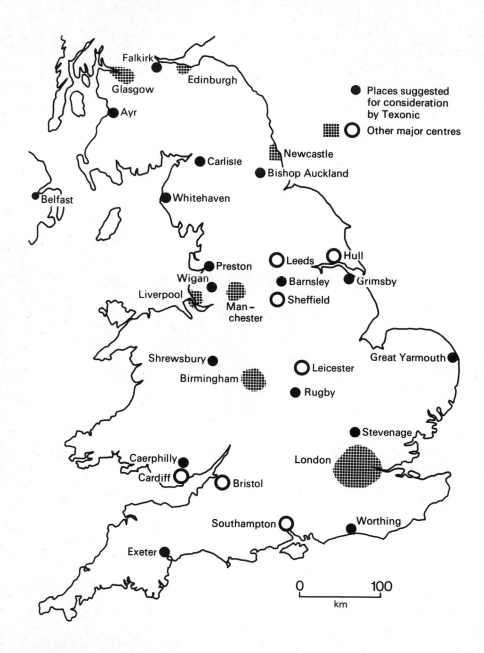

Fig. 6.17. (Map for Texonic game.)

culated from American experience that it has a value/weight ratio of 155 cents/lb. (This should be contrasted with a product like cement which has a low value/weight ratio of 2 cents/lb.) As well as not depending greatly on transport costs, the industry is not strongly linked to other industries.

4. Location near an airport with international services would be helpful since Texonic will need quick and frequent contact with headquarters in Dallas. In addition, some components for the firm could be flown in by air freight if necessary.

5. Future exports and some imported components will probably be shipped by sea — port access should, therefore, be available.

6. Management would like the factory to be located in a place which is pleasant environmentally. Good schools for workers' children, a golf course for senior management and some 'night life' should be within easy travelling distance.

7. It would be helpful if a readily available factory were at the chosen location, but this could be quite a small building and it would not be a major consideration.

8. Government help would be acceptable but not at the expense of a good location.

Texonic have provided the four members of senior management who are going to make the locational choice with a short list of potential locations which are shown on Fig. 6.17. But the visitors to Britain do not *have* to select one of these places.

It is suggested that your class divides itself up into groups of four, working out this problem as a role-playing game. It should show you how location decisions are the result of behavioural factors — the individuals within each group may differ in their final recommendations and so may each group too. Before starting to play, you may find it useful to have the following items available for consultation :

(i) *The Stateman's Year Book, Whittaker's Almanac* or the AA or RAC members' handbook in order to obtain population information for towns and counties;

(ii) road maps, especially an Ordnance Survey Route Planning map (1 : 250 000 or 10 miles to the inch) for distances and locations;

(iii) recent issues of the *Department of Employment Gazette* for unemployment numbers and percentages;

(iv) information about what the development areas have to offer — i.e. pages 171–6 in this book, noting especially pages 174 and 175.

Playing the Game

Step 1

Allocate the four roles shown below to a member of each group, either by agreement or by drawing lots. (A role profile is provided for each member. To make the simulation even more realistic, you might wish to identify with the role profile when making your decisions. The identification with role profiles is optional, however, as the human element in decision making is likely to be felt anyway.)

Member 1 Bill Morrison — a long standing Texonic employee; you want the best for the company but know little about Britain and would ideally have liked a team of consultants to have made the decision for you. *Your main task is to investigate the labour supply position and the nature and availability of government assistance.*

133

Hints – which of the towns are located in development areas? Which are in areas of heavy industry and coal mining? These places may have a female labour surplus. Which regions have the highest proportion out of work? Is it advantageous to be sited in a big city where it should not be too difficult to find 200 people to work for Texonic anyway?

Member 2 William Bagshawe-Smythe – expatriate Englishman working for Texonic; because of your Eton, Oxford and Mayfair background you are strongly prejudiced in favour of a location south-east of the Tees–Exe line, especially as you may have to visit the plant in Britain from time to time. *Your main task is to consider the position of the factory in relation to the national market of Britain.* Here you may be aided by the map in Fig. 6.18. This is an economic potential map. Economic potential for any point in the country may be thought of as a measure of the proximity of that point to all other points in the country. It is an aggregate measure of all distant places on that point.[19] Thus, the higher the economic potential, the higher the power to attract economic activity.
Hints – where would you think the national market for dictating machines is? Do affluent areas spend more on electronic equipment? Where is the best place from which to reach this market? Is the centre of the country best? How would the products be delivered? Road transport is more expensive but quicker. Would it be better to develop a fleet of vans?

Member 3 Joe Domanski – a Texan by birth, you possess the stereotype image of Britain; when Britain is mentioned the first things that come into your mind are 'The Queen', 'Fog', 'Accent' and 'Old World'. *Your key job is to consider questions of availability of airports, seaport environment, and the presence of reasonable shopping and entertainment facilities, not too far away.*
Hints – from which places do airlines make regular flights to the USA? Obviously, London (Heathrow), but also Luton (near Stevenage). Manchester and Prestwick (Glasgow) Airports are the next best. Locate these and other airports. Where are the main seaports of Britain? Packaging is important – note availability of paper etc. Which areas are scenically attractive and which are polluted and congested?

Member 4 Herman Grundy – graduate of the Harvard Business School, you are the 'young dynamo' of the Texonic organization. You have a reputation for undertaking thorough research before the making of very shrewd business decisions. *Your task is to co-ordinate the views of the other three and to think up any other difficulties.*
Hints – try to ensure the availability of good shops within about 40 km of the factory location. Look for any extra advantages which places possess which might benefit senior management – but don't overstress the golf-course effect! Assess carefully the advantages and disadvantages of development area location.

Step 2

Spend up to thirty minutes deciding on *your short list* of five places. These may be taken from the seventeen shown on the map or can contain some you have selected yourself.

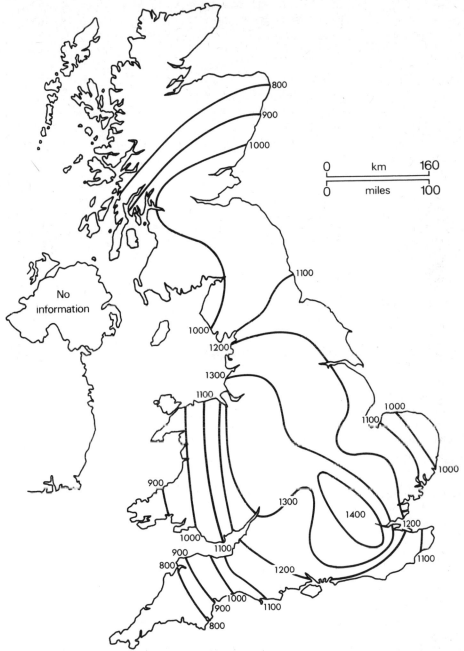

Fig. 6.18. Economic potential map of Britain (Source: C. Clark. 'Industrial location and economic potential', *Lloyds Bank Review*, 1966, pp. 1–17)

Step 3

At the end of thirty minutes the four members of each group should get together, compare choices and finally decide on the five places most highly recommended.

Step 4

Under the chairmanship of their Herman Grundy each group then puts the five final short-listed locations in order of preference. This is the list which will be sent to Texonic headquarters.

Step 5

The member nominated to be Herman Grundy for each group should now write the five short-listed towns, in order of preference, on the blackboard. As spokesman for the group, he now reports to the rest of the class on WHY the five places were chosen and why others were rejected. The lists of places should be compared to see if there is much agreement. A lively discussion could bring this lesson to a close.

What did you learn from this game?

Postscript

Having undertaken this simulation you may be wondering how American firms *actually* set about locating a plant in the UK. A survey of the factors considered in selecting a region or city of operation revealed that labour pool, labour costs and access to market were the primary considerations. Local communications, services, industrial structure and social factors were also considered (though rarely rated decisive) by many respondents. Surprisingly, grants from both local and national governments were ignored by over half the companies investigated.[20]

To what extent did your decision making with Texonic agree with the findings of the survey quoted above?

Key Ideas

A. *Non-economic man* (page 107)
1. The Weber model (Chapter 5) assumes that man is rational, and that he locates at the *least cost point location*.
2. In reality it seems that many businessmen aim for *satisfactory* rather than optimum locations. Such decision makers are termed *satisficers*.

B. *Spatial margins to profitability* (pages 107–112)
1. The spatial margins approach extends the Weber model to include *satisficing* behaviour.

136

2. Spatial margins delimit the *area within which it is profitable* to the firm to locate.
3. Drawing spatial margins involves constructing *space cost curves* and *space revenue curves*.
4. It is possible for some countries to be entirely within the spatial margins to profitability of some industries.

C. *The behavioural matrix* (pages 112–18)
1. The matrix consists of two axes, one indicating *ability to use* information and the other *amount* of information.
2. The matrix suggests that the degree of optimal decision making depends on the position of the location decision maker within the matrix.
3. As information accumulates, and as imitation and learning occur over time, the decision maker becomes more adept at making location decisions. The *average position* of the 'locational actors' within the matrix thus moves downward to the right, that is they become more 'rational'.

D. *Actual decision making* (pages 118–23)
1. For most firms a choice between different locations is only made when the plant faces a move to a new location.
2. Pressures to relocate include *pushes* from the present location and *pulls* from potentially new locations.
3. In reviewing the selection of a new location, pressures may be both *internal* and *external*.
4. Locational pulls possess *spheres of influence* which are measured by noting the percentage of firms in a given distance zone from the local location factor which refer to it as significant.

E. *Spatial perception* (pages 123–30)
1. We may distinguish between an *objective environment* and a *behavioural environment* – the latter being that which is perceived.
2. The way businessmen *perceive* particular places may influence their location decisions.
3. Our image of places seems to depend on factors such as their size, the number of times we have visited them, how far they are from us and the coverage they are given in the media.

Additional Activities

1. Consider the factors which might influence the southerner's mental map of Wigan and the northerner's mental map of Dorking?
2. If you were faced with making a decision about a factory location, what non-economic factors might influence your final choice?

3. Why is the study of the way industrialists make decisions of interest to the industrial geographer?
4. Draw up a strategy (to include advertisements) as a local P.R.O. to change the southerner's mental map of say, Manchester, Newcastle or Glasgow.

Reading

A. SMITH, D. M., *Industrial Location: an Economic-Geographical Analysis*, Wiley, 1971, pages 181–7.
*SMITH, D. M., *op. cit.*, pages 181–206.
B. PRED, A. & KIBEL, B., 'An application of gaming simulation to a general model of locational processes', *Economic Geography*, **46**, 1970, pages 130–56.
*PRED, A., *Behavior and Location*, Gleerup, 2 vols., 1967 and 1969.
C. TOWNROE, P., 'Locational choice and the individual firm', *Regional Studies*, **3**, 1969, pages 15–24.
D. GOULD, P. & WHITE, R., *Mental Maps*, Penguin, 1974.

7 Industrial linkage

A. Towards a Definition of Linkage

All firms have some links with other firms. Such links may, or may not, be with the final consumer of their product. In the motor car industry, for example, the output of many firms passes into the assembly stage of the motor vehicle industry. The products of firms such as Lucas, Triplex, Goodyear or Britax all link up with the products of Fords, British Leyland or General Motors. Apart from these obvious and well known linkages, however, firms possess other kinds of links which may be equally important. Fig. 7.1 illustrates the kinds of linkages which all firms possess.

In order to simplify a very complex situation, Fig. 7.1 adopts a simple systems approach to linkage. A series of elements are seen to be linked in various ways to the production unit (the factory). Some links are input, others

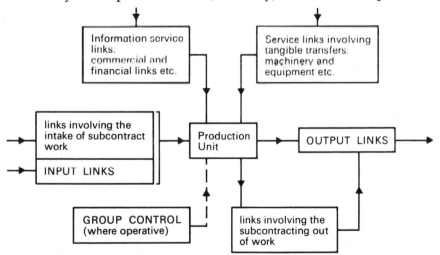

Fig. 7.1. Types of 'linkage' displayed by any manufacturing enterprise. (Source M. J. Taylor, ' "Industrial linkage", "seed bed" growth, and the location of firms', *Occasional Papers*, 3, University College London, Department of Geography, 1969, p. 2)

output links, and in their simplest form are like those we were introduced to in Chapter 3. But some of the factory's other links may involve things like sub-contracting out particular jobs, or taking in sub-contract work itself. It may have ties with financial institutions or commercial services from whom it obtains information rather than a tangible good. Other services may take the form of machinery or equipment supplies, while for some firms which are part of a complex manufacturing 'packet' (see page 26) group control may apply with linkages to head office or administration.

Thus industrial linkage may be defined as 'all the operational contacts, including flows of materials and exchanges of information, between the separate functional elements of the manufacturing system.[1] These 'elements' can be thought of as whole industries, sectors of the economy, or individual plants, depending on the scale at which one is considering the system. Not all geographers consider the final sale of the firm's product to the consumer as a link and there is considerable debate as to what exactly the concept means. What is important, however, is the way in which some geographers have seen in linkage an alternative approach towards the explanation of industrial location. This is because it focuses upon the actual transactions and exchanges of firms within a systems framework. It thus replaces the 'economic man' approach of Weber and the 'behavioural' approach of Pred, with a material-istic basis of enquiry.[2]

Though all firms possess linkages, some are more important in the locational choice for the firm than others. Geographers seek to discover, therefore, how important linkage is in the locational choice of firms and in their continuing operation at given locations. Another important question, the extent to which linkage acts as a constraint on movement, is dealt with in Chapter 9.

B. Variations in the Complexity of Linkages

1. Linkages as chains

Linkages vary in their complexity from the simple movement of a single product from one plant to another, to a series of inputs from a large number of origins converging on one plant. We can conceive of linkages as chains binding the manufacturing system together. Some of these chains are of considerable complexity, as Fig. 7.2 shows.

The concepts shown diagrammatically in Fig. 7.2 may be illustrated by actual examples. In A, for instance, a firm might be sending all its products to one warehouse or retailer; in B primary metals might be going to various second stage mills; the motor vehicle industry represents a classic example of the situation shown in C (as many as 17 000 different factories supply one US car plant with parts); D – a simple chain – is illustrated by the sequence: logging, sawmill, furniture.

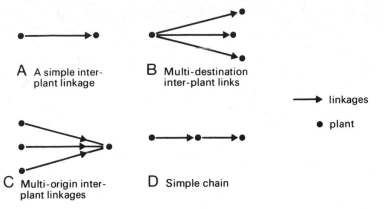

Fig. 7.2. Linkages as chains. (After: C. W. Moore, 'Industrial linkage development paths in growth poles: a research methodology', *Environment and Planning*, **4**, 3, 1972, p. 251–71)

2. The scale of linkages

A second dimension of complexity is the scale at which linkages are studied. Linkage may be studied from the street scale, where sub-contract work or particular processes in the manufacture of a product can be undertaken in the workshop next door (see Plate 4.1), to the industry scale where we might think of linkages between, say, the different elements in the iron and steel industry. We must be quite certain, therefore, about the scale at which we are studying industrial linkage. Early writers on industrial linkage stressed the spatial proximity of interfirm contacts, the juxtaposition of firms reducing transport costs on semi-finished materials, products or components. Such linkages provide external economies to the firm; they led to the development of the West Midlands metal trades, for example. But some West Midlands firms will sell their products to London firms. Should this be regarded as industrial linkage? Given the definition adopted on page 140, there seems no logical reason for imposing any kind of spatial limit on the study of linkage. We can distinguish, therefore, between localized linkages and links with firms further away. Logically it seems likely that firms will use the local area for certain links (such as sub-contract work), while sales of their finished product may be nationwide. But the question of deciding which linkages are important remains.

3. Distance decay effects

The previous section has distinguished between local and nationally oriented linkages. If a firm's local linkages are numerous, we may infer that local external economies are available in the form of agglomerated related activities.[3]

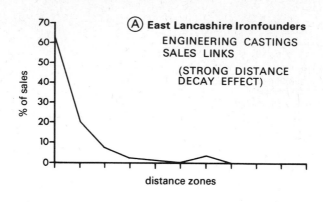

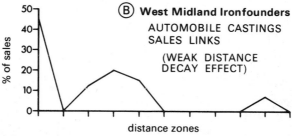

Fig. 7.3. Sales decay curves for East Lancashire ironfounders of engineering castings and for West Midlands ironfounders of automobile castings. Distance zones shown at 40 mile intervals. (After: M. J. Taylor, 'Local linkage, external economies and the ironfoundry industry of West Midlands and East Lancashire conurbations', *Regional Studies*, **7**, 4, 1973, p. 397)

A pervasive concept in geography is that of *distance-decay*, the effect that distance imposes on the movement of a given phenomenon (for example, people to work – see page 208, supporters of a football team, inputs to a factory). As the distance away from a point increases, the amount of movement to that point decreases. The term *friction of distance* is sometimes applied to such a process. In the context of industrial linkage we can ascertain the importance of local agglomeration economies of scale by considering sales and purchases decay patterns for individual industries in particular areas. Fig. 7.3 for example, shows how in the East Lancashire iron foundry industry, sales of engineering castings show evidence of strong links with the local area. For the West Midlands sale of automobile castings, however, local links are much less well marked and the distant decay pattern less apparent. This indicates the relatively weaker local linkages in the British car industry because of its relative dispersal throughout the country.

4. Spatial association or functional linkage?

Because industries are found together in the same region (they are spatially associated), it by no means indicates that they are linked functionally. Cheap or skilled pools of labour may attract a variety of firms which, though clustered in a given region round a common labour pool, are not linked themselves. In other cases, firms may be attracted to common facilities such as a port or, on a micro-scale, an industrial estate. In such areas links among the constituent firms may be very weak and unimportant to their operations. Thus spatial association and functional linkage need to be differentiated.

At the national level of scale the presence of spatial association and functional linkage can be illustrated by examples of such industries as soap production, paint manufacture, furniture making, grain milling and the production of sugar from imported cane. Such industries tend to be spatially associated because of their need for tidewater locations. But only in one or two cases – grain milling and sugar, and paint and furniture – can they be said to be functionally linked. Other traditional British industries which are both spatially associated and functionally linked include coal mining and coke production, cotton manufacture and textile finishing, and leather production and footwear.

In some of Britain's 'newer' industries there is a correspondence between industrial linkage and spatial association (such as in the engineering and metal trades), but a relative lack of linkage in the spatially associated 'metropolitan' science-based industries. We should note that spatial association and, indeed, linkage may result from decisions made a long time ago in the historic past and thus reflect what was convenient at the time of the decision and not necessarily the best possible solution or location today. The force of industrial inertia is clearly felt in the concept of industrial linkage just as it is in the analysis of industrial location in general.

C. A Typology of Industrial Linkages

1. Material and information exchanges

We may first of all distinguish between those links which are of a tangible nature and those which are informational. Material linkages may be of four kinds:

(a) *process links* where goods are moved between firms at different stages of the production process. An example of such a link would be that involving the movement of a windscreen wiper from the plant manufacturing them to the car assembly plant;

(b) *sub-contract links* where work is undertaken by one firm for another (e.g. if the demand for windscreen wipers suddenly increased and the usual producer's capacity could not meet that demand, the work might be sub-contracted out to a neighbouring firm);

(c) *service links* involving the supply of machinery, equipment or ancillary parts and the maintenance of a firm's plant and equipment;

(d) *marketing links* involving the movement of goods to another plant or establishment for purposes of marketing and distribution.

Non-tangible (informational) linkages include ties with such establishments as banks, stockbrokers or insurance agents. Similarly, information exchanges are frequently made between firms engaged in the various forms of tangible exchanges described above. The medium by which such contacts are made is frequently the telephone, though face-to-face contacts are also common.

2. Variations in the strength and complexity of linkages

We have noted that linkages may exist between firms but that they may be insignificant in their operations. A basic problem is deciding which links are important or essential for the location of the plant. These may be termed strong linkages. We can initially distinguish, therefore, between (a) weak and strong links of both a material and informational nature, and (b) relatively simple and complex links, also of a material and an informational kind.

In Fig. 7.4 some real-world examples are used to illustrate the varying types of linkage. Thus, material linkages which are weak and simple are typified by footloose industries – they are not constrained by links from moving within very wide limits. Linkages which are individually weak but when taken together form a complex series of interconnections are exemplified by the

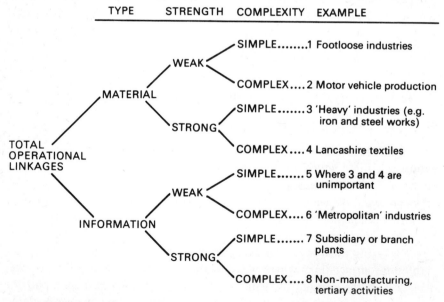

Fig. 7.4. A typology of industrial linkages. (After P. A. Wood, 'Industrial location and linkage', *Area*, 1969, p. 32–9)

144

motor car industry, in which vast numbers of component parts are assembled to form the finished product. Links which are simple but very strong make movement difficult if not impossible, a case in point being the heavy industries such as iron and steel manufacture. In other industries, such as textiles, material linkages are not only very strong – they are also very complex. Information linkages can also be subdivided as in Fig. 7.4 and we will return to these later in this chapter.

3. Measuring linkage strength

Perhaps the most significant kind of division between the many kinds of linkages would be those links which are absolutely vital for the operation of the firm in its present location and those which are unimportant locationally. One way of attempting to measure the importance of the different kinds of linkage is to establish their percentage of the total value of purchases made. This approach is illustrated in Table 7.1 which illustrates the purchase links of a London mechanical engineering firm.

In the case of the firm in Table 7.1 we might expect the suppliers of components and the sub-contractors to be located nearby since they form a major proportion of the firm's total inputs.

Table 7.1. Purchases of a London mechanical engineering firm. (Source: *Strategic plan for the South East, Studies Vol. 5*, Report of Economic Consultants Ltd., HMSO, 1971, p. 88)

Type of purchase	% of total value of purchases
Raw materials (mainly stainless steel)	15
Components	39
Sub-contract work:	
(a) complete machines (e.g. presses)	15
(b) part processes (e.g. machining)	13
(c) civil engineering	4
Other purchases (e.g. stationery)	14
	100

4. Measuring information exchanges

Information exchanges may be of sufficient importance to influence location, but are far less studied than the material links described in the previous section of this chapter. Personal contacts with other producers, customers, financial institutions and local government departments can obviously have a locational impact if their presence leads to faster deliveries of goods, easier contact with special requirements, the possibility of holding smaller stocks, better knowledge of the habits or special tastes of the local populace, mutual understanding through frequent visits and fewer misunderstandings. Such links seem more likely to be developed between the headquarters of manufacturing firms than the actual production plants, but how can such contacts be studied, let alone analysed?

For office locations (perhaps headquarters of manufacturing firms) person-to-person and telephone contacts have been analysed by asking businessmen to keep records of all meetings and telephone calls they have had or made over a given period of time.

Research such as this has been most significantly developed by Swedish geographers who have revealed that top-level personnel in some firms spend upwards of 40 hours per week in face-to-face contacts.[4] This suggests that the extra time that would be involved in travelling would preclude decentralization of these top-level functions from their existing locations – which are often at the city centre. By keeping 'contact diaries' and 'time-space budgets' geographers are able to monitor executives' time-space behaviour and thus add to our knowledge of information exchanges.

ASSIGNMENTS

1. For a firm to which a member of your group has access, or a firm visited during fieldwork, draw histograms to show its purchase and sales decay patterns. Bars can be drawn to show percentages of purchases and sales in (a) the local town, (b) the rest of the county, (c) the rest of the country, (d) the rest of the world. Alternatively, draw diagrams for hypothetical firms with (a) strong and (b) weak, local purchase and sales decay curves.
2. Fig. 7.5 shows the destinations of outgoing telephone calls from one manufacturing firm in Malmö, Sweden, in one week. Each dot represents the destination of one percent of the total telephone calls going out from the firm in one week. What would be the implications of the information shown on the map for the firm, if the government tried to make it relocate in Norrland?
3. From a regional text on the British Isles, locate the traditional areas where functional linkage between such industries as those mentioned in Section 4 (Spatial association and functional linkage, page 143) may be found,

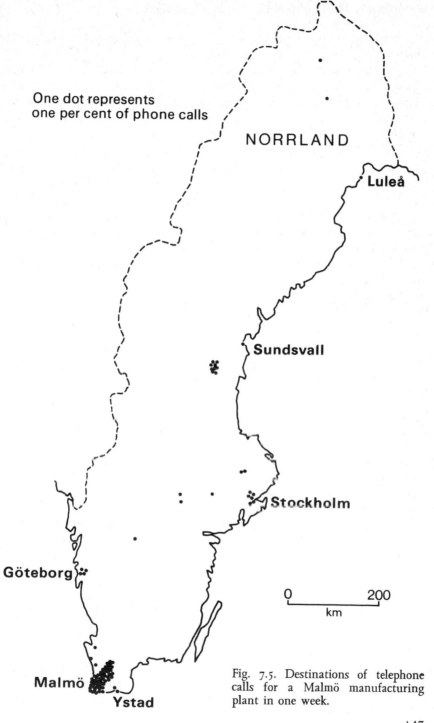

One dot represents
one per cent of phone calls

NORRLAND

Luleå

Sundsvall

Stockholm

Göteborg

Malmö

Ystad

Fig. 7.5. Destinations of telephone calls for a Malmö manufacturing plant in one week.

0   200
km

147

D. Intra-urban Variations in Linkage

It is important to relate the idea of linkage to some of the ideas discussed in Chapter 4 on the location of industry in cities.

The metropolitan area provides a variety of advantages for many firms which can be catalogued under the general heading of urbanization economies. Firms find other firms which can supply them with services, components or just advice. Industrialists in all kinds and sizes of plant benefit from these economies but logic and some empirical evidence suggest that some manufacturers benefit from metropolitan linkages more than others. Small firms, for example, might be expected to make use of the array of services provided by a large city, to a greater extent than large firms. Such latter firms are able to *internalize* the economies for which the smaller plant is dependent on others in the metropolitan community. Another generalization which we might make about linkage and the metropolis is that firms at the edge of the city have fewer links with the city than those at the centre.

Not only does the metropolis provide links of the various kinds discussed in this chapter. It also provides a vast market for the finished products of many firms. Thus the ready availability in the city of input and output links makes it an attractive location for industry, a location which can partly at least be explained by industrial linkage.

ASSIGNMENTS

Consider the following hypotheses and then look at Table 7.2 which shows percentages of total linkages (in terms of purchases and sales) to the Montreal metropolitan area of sample firms of different sizes located at the centre, the suburbs and at the periphery of the city region.

Hypotheses
(a) The strength of linkage with the metropolis varies inversely with the size of the industrial establishment;
(b) industrial establishments nearer the centre are more dependent on metropolitan linkages than those at the periphery;
(c) for each increase in size category there is a constant diminution of the strength of total linkages with the metropolitan economy.

Are these hypotheses verified by the data in Table 7.2?

It is very important to remember that the evidence for one city is insufficient for either the acceptance or the utter rejection of a hypothesis. Only more research will push the hypothesis towards the status of a model.

Having studied the table and considered the appropriateness of the hypotheses, attempt an explanation of the spatial variations in the linkages illustrated in Table 7.2.

E. Conclusion

Essentially industrial linkages are cost-reducing factors and as such their spatial variations could theoretically be treated in the same way as any other cost items. If this is so, a reformulated Weber model with each input source and each output destination making up a corner of the locational polygon[5] (a much more complicated figure than Fig. 5.1 on page 83) seems theoretically possible. However, the problem of replacing a locational triangle (Fig. 5.1) with a figure with as many corners as there are input sources and output destinations, seems formidable in the extreme. Also, many components play little part in the total cost structure and are, therefore, of no significance locationally.

We have come a long way from the conceptual framework of Alfred Weber to that of Allan Pred, and an equally long way from the study of industry by using the material index to the study of information exchanges through the use of contact diaries. Some geographers believe, however, that the Weber model still serves as a useful conceptual starting point since we only need to stretch the optimum least cost point location to a spatial margin of profitability to include a behavioural component in our studies. In addition, Weber includes agglomeration benefits in his theory and, because linkage is one important facet of agglomeration and can be theoretically conceived as savings of transport costs (as can information exchanges), this, too, can be said to be within the scope of a reformulated Weber model.

Table 7.2. Total linkages with Metropolitan Montreal (by size of establishment and location). (Source: S. Brooks, J. Gilmour & K. Murricane, 'The spatial linkages of manufacturing in Montreal and its surroundings, *Cahiers de géographie de Québec*, **17**, 40, 1973, pp. 107 22)

Size of establishment (employees)	Location of establishment	% of total linkages with Metropolitan Montreal
1–25	centre	49.6
1–25	periphery	39.4
1–25	suburbs	43.1
26–100	centre	35.9
26–100	periphery	34.1
26–100	suburbs	44.3
101+	centre	27.2
101+	periphery	28.6
101+	suburbs	29.2

Key Ideas

A. *Linkages between firms* (pages 139–40)
1. All firms possess links with other firms.
2. In their simplest form links may be inputs or outputs.
3. Linkages may be tangible or may be of an informational nature.

B. *Variations in the complexity of linkages* (pages 140–43)
1. Linkages may be conceived as 'chains' of varying degrees of complexity.
2. Linkages can be considered at different scale levels, ranging from the street scale to the national scale.
3. The linkage pattern of a firm will exhibit different degrees of 'distance decay' effect. Strong distance decay effects will indicate strong local linkages, weak distance decay effects illustrating weak local linkages.
4. Linkage should be distinguished from spatial association. Firms may be located close together to share common facilities but may not be linked themselves.

C. *A Typology of Industrial Linkages* (pages 143–6)
1. Material linkages may be divided into process, sub-contract and service links.
2. Information exchanges also take place between firms, either by 'phone or by face-to-face contact.
3. Linkages may also be differentiated on the basis of their strength and complexity.
4. Both material and information links may be weak or strong and at the same time simple or complex in nature.

D. *Intra-urban Variations in Linkages* (page 148)
1. Small firms tend to rely on links with the **metropoli**tan area more than large firms.
2. Large firms are able to *internalize* many of the services which small firms obtain from the urban/industrial agglomeration.
3. Central city firms tend to have stronger links with the metropolis than those located at its periphery.

Additional Activities

1. Review the distinction between firms which are spatially associated and those which are functionally linked. Provide examples.
2. How can a geographer justify an interest in telephone calls between offices? Quote contrasts between different types of firms.

Reading

A. WOOD, P. J., 'Industrial location and linkage', *Area*, 1969, pp. 32–9.
B. ESTALL, R. & BUCHANAN, R. O., *Industrial Activity and Economic Geography*, Hutchinson, 1964, pp. 108–11.
   *GODDARD, J. B., *Office Location in Urban and Regional Planning*, Oxford, 1975.
C. SMITH, D. M., 'On throwing Weber out with the bathwater', *Area*, 1970, pp. 15–18.

Government regional policy

Central government is an omnipresent element in present-day industrial location. It is all very well talking about Weber and contact diaries but for many firms the overriding influence on their location has been government activity.

We will not refer here to the all powerful role of the state in countries of the Communist bloc. In such states, government direction is the norm, and the state is able to locate industry according to political as well as geographical ideals. In the so-called mixed economies which constitute the rest of the world, however, a remarkable degree of government intervention into industrial location does occur – even in the largely private enterprise economy of the USA. General ideas about the impact of government are illustrated in this chapter with examples from the British experience. We are not concerned here, however, with individual government enactments but with the reasons why government should help industry to locate in places which it might otherwise avoid. In addition, we look at some of the theoretical mechanisms by which government policy is thought to work and in doing so consider some further models of industrial location.

The chapter also outlines some more simple quantitative measures which industrial geographers use. These are based on data sources already outlined in Chapter 2 (pages 19–22) and supplement the techniques suggested in Chapters 2 and 4.

A. Problem Regions

1. Youth, maturity and old age

The Davisian adage about 'youth, maturity and old age' may have more relevance to regions than to rivers. Let us trace the life cycle of a hypothetical region with the help of Fig. 8.1.

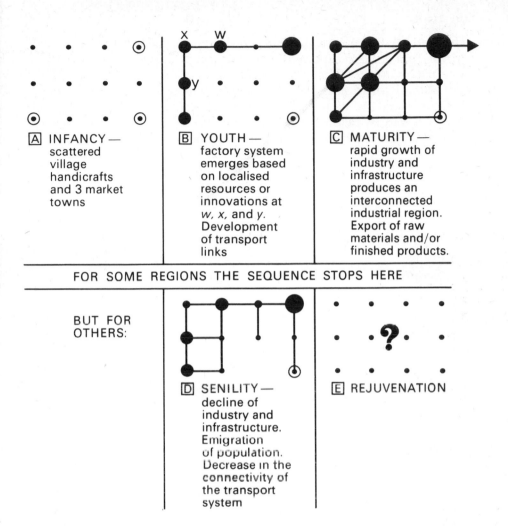

A INFANCY —
scattered
village
handicrafts
and 3 market
towns

B YOUTH —
factory system
emerges based
on localised
resources or
innovations at
w, x, and y.
Development
of transport
links

C MATURITY —
rapid growth of
industry and
infrastructure
produces an
interconnected
industrial region.
Export of raw
materials and/or
finished products.

FOR SOME REGIONS THE SEQUENCE STOPS HERE

BUT FOR
OTHERS:

D SENILITY —
decline of
industry and
infrastructure.
Emigration
of population.
Decrease in the
connectivity of
the transport
system

E REJUVENATION

Fig. 8.1. The cycle of erosion – industry style. (Based on an idea in F. E. I. Hamilton, 'Models of industrial location', in R. J. Chorley & P. Haggett (eds.) *Models in Geography*, Methuen, 1967, p. 399)

(a) *Infancy*

In this stage the region is given over mainly to primary industry or to manufacturing on a domestic scale, a situation which existed in many parts of Britain before the Industrial Revolution. Hardly any industrial towns existed at this time, urban centres primarily performing a market function and only secondarily acting as processing centres. Indeed, much manufacturing actually took place in the countryside as Fig. 3.6 (page 39) and Plate 8.1 illustrate.

153

F

(b) Youth

The youthful stage starts with the development of manufacturing in a factory system. Such development can either be initiated by an innovation transforming domestic industry or the discovery of a technique for converting localized raw materials which have high weight-loss ratios for industries with a high materials index (see pages 84–5). Such development represents what John H. Thompson has called 'the industrial frontier', that is the contemporary limit of industrial development in a given country.[1] This initial industrialization is, of necessity, followed by a growing infrastructure – houses for workers, allied industries supplying or being supplied by the pioneer factory, canals, roads, railways, service trades and so on. Clearly the initial factory has produced wealth and employment in the region far in excess of the wealth generated by the factory alone. An example of this 'youthful' stage would be the Lancashire cotton industry of the early nineteenth century.

(c) Maturity

The arrival of the mature stage implies that the region has experienced large-scale development of manufacturing industry and economic development over many decades, usually for well over a century. It has evolved a deep-rooted and highly complex system of industries and services, many of which are inter-related in a variety of important ways, and it depends for its survival on the outside sale of its manufactured products[2] (such as in the twentieth-century Lancashire cotton industry). But the mature stage involves more than this. Derelict buildings in inner cities, slum conditions and dated infrastructure are all found in mature industrial regions such as the London and West Midland conurbations. The landscapes of mature regions are exemplified by Plate 8.2, showing the area around St Helens in Lancashire.

(d) Old age

The old age stage starts when areas begin to exhibit the well known features of the 'problem region'; growth is slow, the industrial structure is not diversified, extractive industries like coal mining are relatively important, unemployment is relatively high, large numbers of people leave the region for other areas, the region exhibits decrepit infrastructure, the region's population is often depressed by the seeming impossibility of bringing back the prosperity which it once knew. The closure of a local coal mine or factory means that spending power in the local community is reduced and that service traders such as shopkeepers also suffer as a result. Human despondency is inevitable when regions face levels of unemployment like those illustrated in Table 8.1.

The figures in Table 8.1 have been deliberately chosen because they illustrate the extremely high levels of unemployment which existed in Britain before the

Plate 8.1. The infancy stage of the industrial cycle. Rhaeadr Tannery, an eighteenth-century tannery from Radnorshire, Wales. This example of rural industry was concerned with the production of heavy leathers for boots and horse harness. (Now re-erected at St. Fagans Folk Museum, near Cardiff. *National Museum of Wales – Welsh Folk Museum – photograph*)

Table 8.1. The five highest rates of unemployment for employment exchange areas in three depressed areas in mid-1934. (Source: *Reports of Investigations into the Industrial Conditions in Certain Depressed Areas*, Cmd. 4788, HMSO, 1934)

Area	Employment exchange areas	Unemployment (%)
West Cumberland and Haltwhistle	Maryport	61.2
	Haltwhistle	57.3
	Cleator Moor	52.8
	Cockermouth	45.3
	Alston	41.4
Durham and Tyneside	Jarrow	56.8
	Bishop Auckland	50.4
	Shildon	47.4
	Hartlepool	44.5
	Sunderland	41.0
South Wales	Brynmawr	74.1
	Dowlais	73.4
	Blaina	71.7
	Merthyr	69.1
	Ferndale	65.7

Plate 8.2. A mature industrial landscape – St. Helens, Lancashire. (*Aerofilms*)

Second World War. The national rate of unemployment in April 1934 was 16.1%, compared with a present day figure of around 4% – 5%. In the problem areas of the 1930s it was not simply high numbers of unemployed workers which characterized the problem. For example, in Bishop Auckland in April 1934, 80% of those unemployed had been out of work for over one year. Individual industries suffered as well as individual towns and regions; in the South Wales iron and steel industry, for example, 40% of the workforce was out of work. Such were the problems in a largely free-market economy that the government felt duty-bound to step in and help.

Some regions are seemingly able to offset permanently the old age stage of the industrial cycle. They possess diversified economic bases and over time have been able to adjust to changing economic circumstances. Classic examples are London and Birmingham, both centres of industry from before the Industrial Revolution up to the present day.

(e) *Rejuvenation*

If the cycle of industrial erosion really is a cycle, youth should follow on from

Plate 8.3. Rejuvenation. This government factory is at Ystradgynlais in the Swansea Valley and illustrates the way in which governments attempt to inject new industry into declining regions. The factory, producing light industrial tools, contrasts with the nineteenth-century terraced houses in the background. Thus diversification of industry manifests itself in changing landscapes. (*Author's photograph*)

old age. We can borrow the Davisian concept of rejuvenation to carry our analogy between rivers and regions a stage further. What does rejuvenation mean in terms of a senile region? Does it mean injecting brand new industries into it? Should it be 'converted' into a 'dormitory zone', simply supplying workers to 'growth points' around its periphery? Why not let the region die and thus save government money? How can the government help? These are the kinds of questions which this chapter tries to answer.

ASSIGNMENTS

1. Relate the model in Fig. 8.1 (page 153) to a region of interest to you. Attempt to reconstruct the industrial geography of the region based on sketch maps related to each of the 4 (or 5) stages of the model.
2. Relate the nature of the industry carried out in the factory in Plate 8.1 (page 155) to the environment in which it was originally found.
3. Comment on the various ways in which industry has moulded the landscape of the area of St Helens shown in Plate 8.2 (page 156). In what ways is it diagnostic of (a) maturity and (b) old age? What evidence of these does it not show?

2. Regional Disparities

(a) Wealth and poverty

Governments of most countries recognize that a 'regional problem' exists if regional variations in opportunity and affluence persist. Britain and many other nations, therefore, continue to follow government policies aiming to equalize the extremes of wealth and poverty, employment and unemployment, and the many less tangible measures of what one might broadly term *economic health*. While unemployment is usually taken as the indicator of regional well-being, a vast number of other variables can be used. Eric Rawstron and Bryan Coates[3] have charted the face of Britain in the sixties to show the regional variations which exist today. Two of their maps are illustrated in Figs 8.2 and 8.3.

Fig. 8.2 shows which counties of Britain possessed net incomes above the 1964 average of £1 004 (index number 100 in the key to the map). The poorer parts of Britain are towards the edge of the country; the high income locations stretch in a black belt from the South Midlands to Sussex.

Fig. 8.3 shows the location of what might best be called 'the establishment'. The pattern of residences listed in Who's Who differs greatly from the distribution of the population as a whole and suggests that power is vested in those who live in the area showing the densest concentration of dots in Fig. 8.3. Rawstron and Coates suggest that 'these powerful people will tend to give preference to their regions by their decisions. Regional imbalance can never be

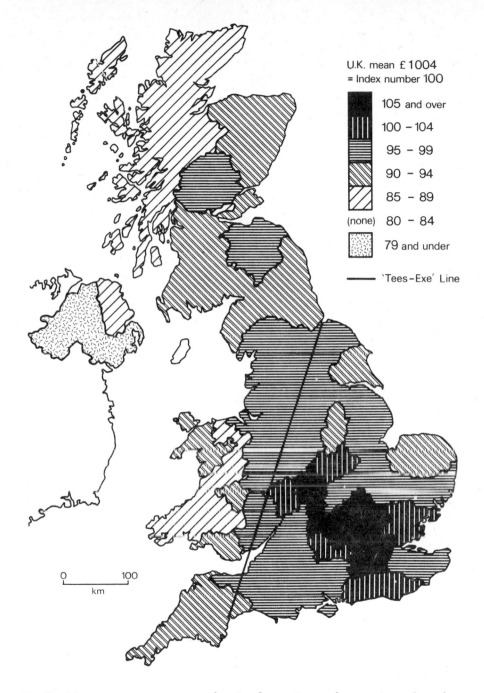

U.K. mean £1004
= Index number 100

105 and over

100 – 104

95 – 99

90 – 94

85 – 89

(none)   80 – 84

79 and under

——— 'Tees–Exe' Line

0   100
        km

Fig. 8.2. Net income as a percentage of national mean income by counties, 1964–1965. (Source: E. Rawstron & B. Coates, *Regional Variations in Britain*, Batsford, London, 1971)

159

Each dot represents
one sample entry.

Entries listed under
London postal addresses
are shown in the square.

——— 'Tees – Exe' line

Fig. 8.3. A residential Who's Who. The map is based on a sample of entries in Who's Who, 1964. (Source: As Fig. 8.2.)

solved if such is the accepted wish, until the creators of the magnetism of the South East redistribute themselves to find and create outlets for their energies and interests more evenly over the United Kingdom'.[4]

In other words, despite the identification of a regional problem in the UK before 1940, strong regional imbalance persists in Britain and in other countries. Government policy, mainly with regard to manufacturing industry, has attempted to redress this imbalance in economic health, but before looking at the role of the government let us look a little more carefully at some of the characteristics which the 'problem areas' possess.

ASSIGNMENTS

1. *The Tees–Exe line – one of the most famous of geography's imaginary lines – is drawn on Figs. 8.2 and 8.3 Consider the view that the Tees–Exe line not only separates Paleozoic rocks from Tertiary rocks, and not only highland from lowland Britain, but acts as a significant economic and social division as well.*

2. *How do the maps referred to above correlate spatially with Fig. 8.6 (p. 171) which shows the present extent of the areas of Britain eligible for government assistance.*

(b) Unemployment

Being out of work is not a bad thing in itself. Men may be in the process of changing jobs; they may be ill; they may be unemployable; women may feel that their place is in the home; the dispassionate economic theorist might argue that unemployment is a good thing because it is deflationary.

Nevertheless, for the unemployed worker it is undoubtedly a serious problem – especially if he lives in an area where there is little hope of finding a new job. We thus devote a few lines to a deeper consideration of what is meant by unemployment.

For statistical purposes unemployment is defined as the number of persons registered as unemployed expressed as a percentage of the total number of economically active persons. It is important to stress that unemployment is generally regarded as a percentage. In fact, many of our more prosperous areas frequently have large *numbers* out of work though this figure may represent a small *percentage* of that area's total work-force. Similarly, many sparsely populated areas may have high unemployment rates though numerically the numbers may be very small. For instance, in February 1974 Greater London had over 60 000 people registered as unemployed although this amounted to only a 1.5% unemployment rate, while the whole of Northern Ireland had 29 600 unemployed – a percentage figure of 5.8.

Unemployment data are collected by the Department of Employment and Productivity and are based on the number of persons registered as unemployed

Table 8.2. Unemployment and activity rates in the British economic planning regions. (Source: *Barclays Bank Review*, November 1973)

Region	Unemployment†	Activity rate*
Scotland	4.3	70.9
North	4.4	70.2
Yorks—Humberside	2.6	71.6
North West	3.3	73.3
Wales	3.3	67.2
West Midlands	2.0	74.1
East Midlands	2.0	72.8
East Anglia	1.7	70.0
South West	2.2	69.0
South East	1.3	73.1
Great Britain	2.4	72.0

* Based on 1971 census (when the school-leaving age was still 15)   †June 1973

at the local labour exchange. There is strong evidence to suggest that these official figures understate the real labour reserves of a given area since there is no obligation to register as unemployed – especially for married women who are not eligible for unemployment benefits if they opt out of the National Insurance scheme. Activity rates (the proportion of the population above the age of 16 which is available for work) are associated with unemployment percentages. They are often low in problem regions, just as unemployment rates are high. (See Table 8.2.)

If the understatement of unemployment is higher in Britain's problem regions than in her prosperous zones, the regional problem is greater than it seems.

Obtaining data on unemployment for a given area is not as easy as it might seem. The obvious places to obtain these data – the local offices of the Department of Employment – are not obliged to provide them. The *Department of Employment Gazette* is probably the most readily available source for rates of unemployment. At the *regional* level this source is useful, though not all local employment exchange areas are included in each edition.

(c) A *measure of economic health?*

So far we have seen that 'problem regions' are characterized by (a) higher than average levels of poverty and (b) higher levels of unemployment. There are many other spatial variables which could be used to delineate regions of distress as the maps from Rawstron and Coates's work illustrate. Table 8.3 shows several other possible measures which the student may be able to obtain if undertaking work in the area we have been discussing.

Table 8.3. Ten criteria for measuring regional economic health

1. Index of unemployment variability (highest month ÷ lowest month)
2. Change in industrial employment over a given period
3. Change in service employment over a given period
4. Change in total employment over a given period
5. Females employed in industry (% of all employment)
6. Industrial employees (% of all employment)
7. Industrial floor space built in a given period
8. Number of houses without bathrooms (% of total houses)
9. Percentage of local authority area consisting of derelict land
10. Net migration from region over a given period

At the beginning of this chapter we talked of unemployment as being the most used variable for designating those areas requiring government help. Indeed, as we shall see in Table 8.6, at one stage in the 1960s an unemployment rate of 4½% was a prerequisite of government assistance. In fact, unemployment is not a particularly good indicator of an area's general industrial well-being. If it were, values for other measures of well-being would increase (or decrease) more or less regularly in the same way as unemployment (that is they would correlate strongly with it). It has been shown by D. M. Smith, however, that for 12 indicators of economic health for North West England, the degree of correlation is surprisingly low.[5] (If you have not been introduced to statistics note that a value of $+1$ or -1 means perfect correlation and that as the value tends towards 0 the strength of the relationship between the two variables becomes weaker. In Smith's study many correlation coefficients hovered around the 0.3 mark, with several around 0.) In the case of North West England, the old textile towns often possess remarkably low levels of unemployment yet when considered against almost any other indicator of economic prosperity they emerge very badly indeed. Low levels of unemployment may, therefore, hide a large number of other problems and in order to establish a general picture of economic health an advanced technique called factor analysis is used whereby a large number of variables are correlated, rather than just two as with simple correlation.

(d) Diversification

The regional problem is not just an unemployment problem. As we have seen from our simple model (Fig. 8.1, page 153), a region can have problems if most of its workers are employed in a narrow range of declining industries. Indeed, it is no coincidence that the regions which in the nineteenth century developed a high degree of regional specialization are today those which are in our development areas and in need of help from outside.

'Regional diversification was seen to be the logical consequence of getting new kinds of employment into the depressed areas and a desirable goal in its own right, as a means of reducing the risks of future unemployment heavily concentrated in a few unfortunate areas.'[6] Some consideration of what is meant by diversification, therefore, and how it is measured would seem appropriate at this point, since it is generally thought that diversification 'spreads the risk' and also enhances the prospects of economic growth.

(e) Measuring diversification

In Chapter 2 (pages 19–22) several sources of data were suggested for students wishing to compare the industrial structure of one area with that of another. We now introduce some simple quantitative measures which show how diversified or how specialized the economic structure of given regions may be.

In calculating the various indices considered in the pages which follow, it should be decided initially whether all orders of the Standard Industrial Classification (see page 12) are being considered, or whether it is only manufacturing industry which is being analysed. Having decided on this, several techniques are available to you.

(i) *The specialization index* This is calculated by means of the following formula:

$$I = \sqrt{P_1{}^2 + P_2{}^2 + P_3{}^2 + \ldots\ldots\ldots P_n{}^2}$$

where: I is the index of specialization and P_1, P_2, P_3 etc., are individual industry percentage shares of the total employment under consideration. Consider the manufacturing data for the employment exchange areas of Keswick and Whitehaven in Cumbria (Table 8.4). From this example we can see immediately that both towns are rather specialized but that Whitehaven is very specialized with over 95% of its workforce employed in only three industries. The Specialization Index provides a precise measure to replace vague terms like 'rather' and 'very specialized'. The calculation of the index for Keswick proceeds as follows:

$$I = \sqrt{0.3^2 + 0.3^2 + 0.3^2 + 0.3^2 + 0.3^2 + 0.6^2 + 5.9^2 + 32.9^2 + 12.3^2 + 47.0^2}$$

$$I = \sqrt{0.09 + 0.09 + 0.09 + 0.09 + 0.09 + \overline{0.36 + 34.8 + 1082.4 + 151.3 + 2209}}$$

$$I = \sqrt{3478.3}$$

$$I = 58.9$$

The corresponding figure for Whitehaven is 86.5. These indices are very high when they are compared with the kinds of figures found in areas of South East England, for example, where few areas have indices of over 56.0 and many are under 36.0.

164

Table 8.4. Manufacturing data for Keswick and Whitehaven

Main Order Heading	Employment Keswick		Employment Whitehaven	
	Nos	%	Nos	%
III	1	0.3	144	1.9
V and VI	1	0.3	49	0.6
VII	1	0.3	62	0.8
VIII	1	0.3	2	0.02
IX	1	0.3	9	0.1
X	0	0	3	0.04
XI	2	0.6	3	0.04
XII	20	5.9	2	0.02
XIII	0	0	8	0.1
XIV	0	0	7	0.1
XV	0	0	9	0.1
XVI	112	32.9	0	0
XVII	42	12.3	0	0
XVIII	0	0	756	10.1
XIX and IV	160	47.0	6452	85.9
Total	340	100.0	7477	100.0

(ii) *Diversification indices and Lorenz curves.* We may utilize the data in Table 2.1 (pages 12–13) to show the degree of diversification in a chosen region in graphic form. By drawing a *Diversification Curve* we are able to see how the manufacturing structure of a given region compares with the maximum degree of diversification theoretically possible. It will become clear that the technique is also useful for comparing diversification in the same region over time, or for the comparison of diversification in different regions. The steps in the construction of a diversification curve are as follows:

(1) calculate percentages of total employment in each Main Order Heading of the Standard Industrial Classification for the region under consideration (again, decide whether you are going to study diversification of employment generally, or only manufacturing employment);
(2) rank the percentages in ascending order;
(3) cumulate the percentages;
(4) plot the cumulated percentages on a graph, the y axis of which is 'percent of manufacturing labour force' and the x axis is 'percent of industrial groups'.

Let us work this out step by step from the data for Wales shown in Table 2.1.

(1) The ranked percentages of each MOH of manufacturing industries and

the cumulated percentages for manufacturing industries, are shown in the left and right hand columns respectively of Table 8.5.

(2) We now plot the cumulated percentages (right hand column, Table 8.5) against percentages of industrial groups. (There are 17 MOHs for manufacturing industry; therefore each MOH represents about 5.8 percent of the total.)

Table 8.5. (Table for constructing diversification curve for Wales)

0.6	0.6
0.6	1.2
1.1	2.3
2.3	4.6
2.6	7.2
3.1	10.3
4.0	14.3
4.8	19.1
5.1	24.2
5.6	29.8
5.6	35.4
6.5	41.9
7.1	49.0
7.4	56.4
8.8	65.2
9.4	74.6
25.4	100.0

Having plotted the points on the graph, they should be joined up to form a curve, as in the curved line on Fig. 8.4.

In Fig. 8.4 the 45° line represents the maximum possible diversification, and such a line could only be drawn if exactly the same number of people were employed in each of the industry groups (i.e. 1% of the labour force were in 1% of the industry groups, 10% were in 10%, 30% in 30%, and so on). Complete specialization, on the other hand, would be represented on Fig. 8.4 by the line OXP. The diversification curve for Wales is seen to lie somewhere between the lines showing maximum possible and zero diversification. The nearer the diversification curve is to the 45° line, the more diversified is the employment structure represented.

From Fig. 8.5 we can see how diversification curves can be used to show the decreasing degree of specialization in a hypothetical region's economy. Diversification like that illustrated in Fig. 8.5 has occurred in regions such as Central Scotland, the North East and South Wales.

In addition to its graphic qualities, the technique can also provide us with yet another objective measure of a region's degree of diversification. Using the diversification curve diagram we can easily calculate (using graph paper) a *diversification index* by measuring the area beneath the curve and expressing it as a percentage of total possible diversification (that is the whole area

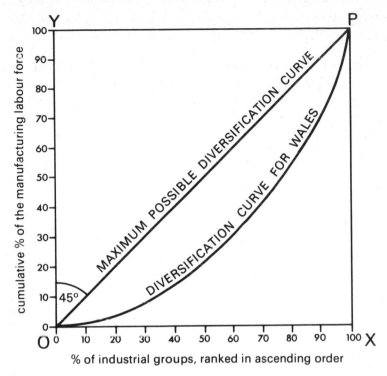

Fig. 8.4. Diversification curve for manufacturing industry in Wales, 1971.

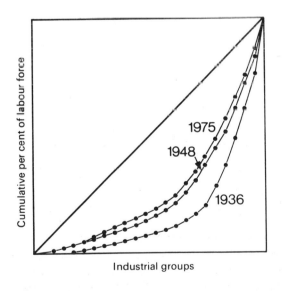

Fig. 8.5. Diversification curves for a hypothetical region.

underneath the 45° line). For instance, the diversification indices for South Wales have gradually increased from 35.0 in 1931 to 48.4 in 1949 and to 51.9 in 1959.

(iii) *Location Quotients* We have seen on page 63 that the location quotient is a useful technique, not for illustrating the degree of diversification as such, but for showing to what extent one industry is localized within a given area. In our earlier example we used the technique to show how certain areas within cities possessed a high proportion of employment in certain trades – if the location quotient is 1.0 or more, an industry is more highly localized in the area than is employment generally. In our last example the 'areas' were in the City of London. We only need to change the scale of our thinking to make the technique applicable at the regional level. Thus, the formula might now appear as follows:

$$\frac{\text{Number employed in industry I in region J as a percentage of the national total in that industry}}{\text{Number employed in all industries in region J as a percentage of the national total employment in all industries.}}$$

There are several other techniques available for use by students of industrial geography which might be discussed but for which space is unavailable. Perhaps among the most useful is combination analysis. For details of this technique, the reader is referred to pages 27–31 of *Quantitative Techniques in Geography* by Hammond and McCullagh (Oxford University Press).

ASSIGNMENTS

Using the data provided in Table 2.1. (pages 12–13), construct diversification curves for manufacturing employment for Scotland and for Great Britain. What are the respective diversification indices? What do they signify? (Use graph paper for calculating the diversification indices.)

B. Government Intervention

1. Rationale of government intervention

Although we tend to take regional policy for granted in the UK, it was only in the 1930s that the British government started to take an active interest in regional imbalance. At that time the means of countering the regional problem consisted mainly of encouraging workers to leave their local areas (and in some cases to leave the country for the colonies) to establish public amenity schemes in the so-called Depressed Areas; and to try and place government contracts with firms in those areas. Little attempt was actually made to take work to the unemployed workers. World War II temporarily cured the unemployment problem although, as we have seen, we still possess a regional problem, albeit in a less serious form than in the 1930s. We should, therefore, consider why the government feels it should help and whether it would be better to let the problem regions run down and die.

(a) Political factors

No political party would enter an election pledged to increasing unemployment, but in Britain where a regional policy has operated for many years, recent successes of the Welsh and Scottish Nationalists suggest that such a policy has not been as successful in those areas as the government might have hoped. In order to reduce potential separatist movements, it is in the interests of the government to have low unemployment figures in the regions where the potential for high levels of unemployment is greatest.

(b) Social factors

Social problems, which arise from the lack of employment opportunities for school leavers on the one hand and the uncontrolled growth of booming cities on the other, are both relevant to the question of regional policy. There is, therefore, a social case both for providing work in areas of high unemployment and for constraining the extent of growth in areas of 'over full' employment. If a region declines a whole range of social institutions – indeed, a way of life – decline with it. Quality of life is difficult to measure but it frequently contains a cultural element which centralized bureaucrats often find hard to appreciate until it is too late. Aid to lagging regions is, therefore, justified in that societies are prevented from breaking up.

(c) Economic factors

(i) Free market forces cannot be relied upon to operate satisfactorily in industrial location decisions since this assumes that businessmen know best where to locate. We have already seen in Chapter 6, however, that optimum locations are often not sought by industrialists. Indeed, the great success of many firms which, on the face of it, appear to be in eccentric locations, shows that government assistance can work (see page 174).

(ii) If the country is to experience economic growth, it is important that spare resources are as fully utilized as possible. Without government aid to senile regions, land, labour, and capital would be wasted. Labour *could* move elsewhere, but we have seen that land and capital are fixed spatially and would, therefore, be wasted if some form of assistance were not provided. We should include *social capital* such as schools, roads and hospitals as well as fixed industrial capital.

(iii) Concentration of economic activity can produce diseconomies of scale. Thus the increase in air pollution, congestion, house prices and mental illness are just some of the increased costs society might have to bear if uncontrolled growth of metropolises continued. Regional policy can be seen, therefore, as a two edged sword, *controlling* growth in certain areas and offering *incentives* for industry to go to others.

2. The nature of government intervention in Britain

(a) *Development controls*

Should a firm wish to establish a new plant in certain parts of Britain, it is not necessarily free to do so. Since 1947 Industrial Development Certificates (IDCs) have been required from the Department of Trade and Industry (and its predecessor, the Board of Trade), and their availability has depended on the size of the plant and the location selected. Certain areas of Britain have been designated eligible for government aid and it is for these areas that IDCs are not required. Any new plant of over 3 000 sq. ft. requires an IDC if it is not in an assisted area.

(b) *Financial incentives*

Just as controls (IDCs) have been enforced over some areas, incentives have been available in others. The nature of incentives has varied considerably from time to time, but basically they have consisted of loans, grants and premiums. The details of such incentives are spelled out in Tables 8.6 and 8.7.

(c) *Other features*

Apart from the controls and incentives, the government has operated a variety of other policies. Perhaps the most successful of these has been the establishment of government industrial estates and advance factories – factories built in locations where the government anticipates industrial growth but which at the time of their erection have no definite occupant. They are built in advance of demand. Because fixed capital is an important input to the firm, such inducements are very attractive to many industrialists wishing to get into a new factory quickly and avoid the trouble of building their own.

(d) *Areas designated*

We now look at the geography of assistance and control. Fig. 8.6 shows which areas were eligible for aid in early 1975. As Table 8.6 shows, however, there has been considerable chopping and changing of regions eligible for aid, as well as of the incentives provided. A constant feature since 1934, however, is that most of the regions benefiting from government aid have been north-west of the Tees-Exe line.

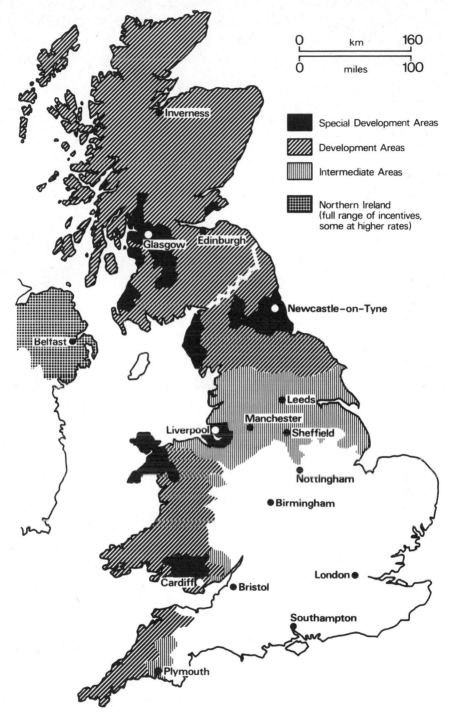

■	Special Development Areas
▨	Development Areas
▥	Intermediate Areas
▦	Northern Ireland (full range of incentives, some at higher rates)

Fig. 8.6. The regional incentives; the areas which qualify for help.

Table 8.6. Chopping and changing: the main British regional measures since 1934. (Source: *The Economist*, 21 April 1973, p. 60)

Legislation	Areas designated	Financial incentives	Development controls	Other features
Special Areas Acts, 1934, 36, 37	North-east England, west Cumberland, south Wales, Clydeside	Loans to firms moving to SAs Contributions to rent, rates and tax Exemption from national defence contributions	None	Policy run by two commissioners Trading estates formed to provide industrial sites and premises Funds for physical rehabilitation
Distribution of Industry Act, 1945	South Lancashire (1946), Merseyside (1948), part of Scottish highlands (1949) and north-east Lancashire (1950) were added to the SAs	Loans for sites, buildings Treasury loans and grants on 'lender of last resort' basis for approved projects	None (though building licences favoured DAs)	Board of Trade (now DTI)** takes over supervision Industrial estates. Advance factories until 1948
Town and Country Planning Act, 1947			IDCs* needed for over 5000 sq ft and favoured DAs	Stick to complement the carrot of the 1945 Act
Distribution of Industry Act, 1958	Concentrated on areas, in or out of DAs where unemployment more than 4½%	Extended Treasury loans and grants	None	With low unemployment in most of the DAs, 1945 Act powers allowed to lapse
Local Employment Act, 1960	Replaced DAs with Development Districts—areas with over 4½%	Loans and grants without 'lender of last resort' restrictions. Building	IDCs to favour DDs	Industrial estates re-organized

172

			None	Advance factories programme stepped up
Local Employment and Finance Acts, 1963	As 1960 Act	25% building grant, 10% plant and machinery grant. Accelerated depreciation		Advance factories programme stepped up
Industrial Development Act, 1966	Back to DAs: most of Scotland and Wales, Merseyside, Cornwall, north Devon and north of England	40% investment grants replace all investment tax allowances	IDC limit lowered and ODP§ started	
Further Labour action, 1967	Special DAs added: Northumberland, Durham, Cumberland and Scottish and Welsh coalfields	REP† introduced for DAs and SDAs 35% building grants in SDAs Investment grants raised to 45%, 1967–8 only		Extra help for hard-hit areas in SDAs, eg collieries
Local Employment Act, 1970	Creation of intermediate areas: Leith, north-east Lancashire, Yorkshire coalfield, north Humberside, Notts/Derby coalfield, south-east Wales and Plymouth	25% building grant: training grants		Advance factories
Conservative action, 1970-71	SDAs extended to include: Clydeside, Tyneside, north-west England, and south Wales	Investment grants replaced by 'free depreciation'. Larger building grants 30% operational grants in SDAs		£160m allocated to 'public works' in DAs and SDAs
The Industry Act, 1972	DAs and SDAs remain the same	Back to investment grants: 20% in DAs, 22% in SDAs; free depreciation to remain		Regional executive created with power to give additional grants and loans; budget of £250m

* IDCs = Industrial Development Certificates   **DTI = Department of Trade and Industry
† REP = Regional Employment Premium   § ODP = Office Development Permit

Table 8.7. Summary of incentives for industry in the assisted areas (as at January 1975). (Source: Department of Trade and Industry, *Incentives for Industry in the Areas of Expansion*, 1974, as amended January 1975)

Incentive	Special Development Areas	Development Areas	Intermediate Areas	Northern Ireland
Regional development grants:				Capital and industrial development grants
New machinery, plant and mining works	22%	20%	Nil	⎫
Buildings and works (other than mining works)	22%	20%	20%	⎬ 30% to 40%* ⎭
Selective assistance loans	On favourable terms for general capital purposes for projects which provide additional employment;* on non-preferential terms for other projects that maintain or safeguard employment if the finance required cannot reasonably be obtained from commercial sources.			On favourable terms for general purposes; loan guarantees may also be negotiated.*
or interest relief grants*	As an alternative to loans on favourable terms, grants towards the interest costs of finance provided from non-public sources for projects which provide additional employment.			As in SDAs, DAs, IAs.
Removal grants*	Grants of up to 80% of certain costs incurred in moving an undertaking into a Special Development, Development, or Intermediate Area.			Up to 100% of costs of transfer from place of origin.
Service industry removal assistance	For offices, research and development units, and other service industry undertakings moving into the assisted areas, a fixed grant of £800 for each employee moving with his work, up to a 50% limit, and a grant to cover the cost of approved rent of premises in the new location for up to 5 years in a Special Development or Development Area and up to 3 years in an Intermediate Area. (Projects helped under this scheme are not eligible for help under the key workers scheme.)			Flexible range of assistance under the Industries Development Acts (Northern Ireland) 1966 and 1971.
Government factories for rent or sale: rent-free period possible for certain new undertakings	Two-year rent-free period*			Rent-free period of 3 years and concessionary rent for further 2 years.*
Employment grants	Nil			A substantial contribution paid during the initial build-up period to companies establishing attractive male-employing projects

174

Incentive	Special Development Areas	Development Areas	Intermediate Areas	Northern Ireland
Tax allowances: (a) Machinery and plant (b) Industrial buildings	100% first-year allowance on capital expenditure incurred on machinery and plant (other than private passenger cars). 54% of the construction costs can be written off in the first year and subsequently 4% per year. Note: These tax allowances apply to the country as a whole. Regional development grants in Great Britain for machinery and plant and buildings are not treated as reducing the capital expenditure in computing tax allowances; neither are the corresponding grants in Northern Ireland.			
Finance from European Community funds	Loans may be available on favourable terms from the European Investment Bank (EIB) and the European Coal and Steel Community (ECSC).			
Regional employment premium payable to manufacturers	£3.00 weekly for every male adult employee; lower rates for other employees.	Nil		As in SDAs and DAs.
Training assistance	Free training services operated by the Training Services Agency.			Free training courses at Government Training Centres; grants of £15 per male (£12 per female) per week for training on employers' premises
Help for transferred workers	Free fares, lodging allowances and help with removal expenses			Full fares (inc. preliminary visit) and household removal costs (inc. legal fees) or lodging allowance plus substantial settling-in grants for key-workers from anywhere outside Northern Ireland.
Contracts preference schemes	Benefits from contracts placed by government departments and nationalized industries.	Nil		As in SDAs and DAs.

Note: Incentives marked * are subject to the provision of sufficient additional employment to justify the assistance sought.

1. *What do you think would have happened if the government in, say, 1800 had operated a regional policy offering incentives to industry to locate in depressed areas and deterrents to locate in booming areas?*
2. *From Table 8.6 (page 172) and Fig. 8.6 consider whether the British regional policies have been successful in removing from the areas eligible for assistance those areas originally designated under the 1934 Special Areas Act.*

3. Effects of government intervention

Having described briefly the nature of British regional policy, let us now try to develop some theoretical underpinnings about how government policy works. In this way we use some further models in order to shed light on the functioning of regional policies.

(a) *Extending spatial margins*

One way of thinking of government policy is to incorporate the idea of government subsidies (that is investment grants) into the Smithian space-cost curve discussed in Chapter 6. This can easily be included in the spatial margins approach since subsidies can be interpreted as attempts to make profitable those locations which businessmen might otherwise avoid on the grounds of unprofitability. In other words, the spatial margins to profitability are artificially extended, as shown in Fig. 8.7.

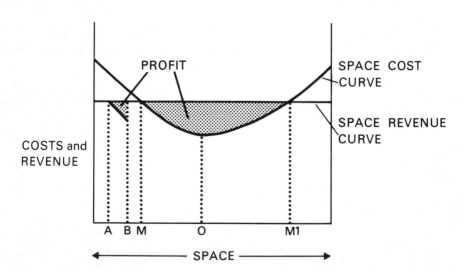

Fig. 8.7. Government subsidies and spatial margins to profitability.

In this diagram the effect of government subsidies has been to reduce total costs in relation to total revenue in development area AB by pushing down the space cost curve below the space revenue curve. Thus with the subsidies AB becomes a profitable location whereas without them it was beyond the spatial margins to profitability.

(b) The regional multiplier

Government regional policy may also be thought of in terms of what is called the *regional multiplier*. The multiplier concept is a very basic idea from the social science of economics, but we need modify it only slightly in order to give it a spatial slant. The basic theme of the multiplier is that if a given amount of money is injected into a region, the income of that region increases, not by the value of the injection, but by some multiple of it. Let us make two simple assumptions in order to illustrate this idea of the multiplier: (a) the region is a closed system – it has no imports or exports; (b) every person spends 50% of any addition to his or her income and saves the other 50% (the proportion of an increment of income that is saved is called the marginal propensity to save (MPS) – in this example the MPS is 0.5). In order to find the value of the multiplier let us now imagine that the government builds a factory in a development area which creates additional income for the region's workforce of £1 000. If each worker's MPS is 0.5 this means that £500 will be spent on, say, beer, thus increasing the incomes of beer producers, who spend 0.5 of their additional income (0.5 of £500=£250) on, say, clothes, thus increasing the income of the clothes producers by £250. They in turn spend 50% of their extra income somewhere else – and so on, and so on until the multiplier has worked itself out.

The value of the multiplier (and thus the cumulative wealth created by the initial investment) can be calculated for a closed system by using the following simple formula:

$$K = \frac{1}{MPS}$$

where K is the multiplier
and MPS is the marginal propensity to save.

In our above example:

$$K = \frac{1}{0.5}$$

$$K = 2.$$

Thus, in this case an initial increase of income of £1 000 has, when multiplied by 2, produced an increase in income in the region of £2 000 (i.e. £1 000 +

£500 + £250 + £125 . . . . + £n = £2 000). You should be able to see the importance of the multiplier from this absurdly simple example.

So far we have assumed a closed system, but in real life people living in the region into which investment is injected are unlikely to be able to spend it solely in that region. They will purchase goods made outside the region; they will travel out of the area to buy goods; they will purchase imports from overseas; they will pay taxes to the national government. Clearly, the initial investment will do the region less good if a high proportion of people's spending is on items produced outside the region; it will create wealth for someone else and not add directly to the region's wealth. Such expenditures are called *leakages*, and need to be incorporated into our multiplier model to make it more realistic. Thus, a regional multiplier formula can now be written as:

$$K = \frac{1}{MPS + p}$$

where K is the regional multiplier,
MPS is the marginal propensity to save,
p is the percentage of additional income spent on leakages.

While the multiplier model is an exceptionally useful and important conceptual aid, it has been found that actual regional multipliers can be calculated for real places. For example, when various leakages have been taken into account, the Scottish regional multiplier has been estimated at around 1.4 – a very low figure indeed, which 'makes the resolution of regional problems more difficult than would otherwise be the case because of the high leaks which go with a low multiplier. A low regional multiplier means that attempts to resolve a regional problem are likely to be a long process. It is rather like trying to fill a bath with the plug out.'[7]

(c) *Cumulative Causation*

A slightly more complex way of thinking of the multiplier concept is in terms of an initial investment by the government (that is a new factory) having a multiplier effect on the region in which it is located by creating, in itself, the impetus for even more investment, more jobs, and more infrastructure (the basic requirements of a modern industrial society – roads, railways, schools and so on) which would in turn induce more factories.

Fig. 8.8 illustrates the model of cumulative causation (that is, one thing leading to another) developed originally by the Swedish economist, Gunnar Myrdal, in discussing the whole problem of economic development. The idea can be applied at the regional level as well as at the national level, for which it seems originally to have been intended.

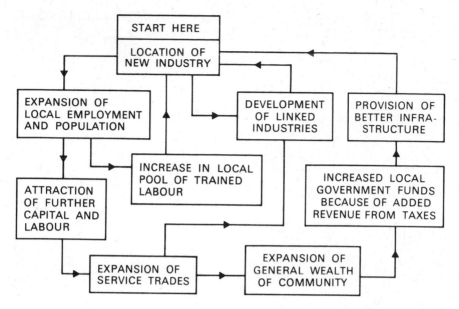

Fig. 8.8. The location of new industry leads to an expansion in the local work-force which, in turn, produces other effects inducing more new industry to locate in the region. (After: D. Keeble, 'Models of economic development', in R. Chorley & P. Haggett (eds.). *Models in Geography*, Methuen, 1967, p. 258)

Fig. 8.8 shows how the location of a new industry in a given region leads to, first, an expansion in local employment and population, and an increase in the local pool of skilled labour which will then lead to further industry coming to the region. This is represented by the small loop at the top left of the diagram. You will be able to see how the location of a new industry has further implications by studying the diagram. Once started, this cumulative process is self-sustaining – it does not need outside help.

Thus, by establishing a new industry in a given region, the government, through the multiplier process illustrated in Fig. 8.8, has produced more employment in the region than that provided by the initial industry. Service trades, transport employment and linked industries have all been attracted.

Of course, the multiplier works backwards as well. If a large employer such as the steelworks in Plate 8.4 were forced to close down, more people than those formerly employed at the works would eventually be out of work. Because former steelworkers would have to cut down on their expenditures, shopkeepers would suffer as their trade declined as a result of the reduced spending power. Such a catastrophe could be averted, of course, if alternative employment opportunities were made available in the local area.

Plate 8.4. The Ebbw Vale Steelworks, South Wales. If the plant closes down, the profound multiplier effects will be felt throughout the region in which it is located. (*British Steel Corporation photograph*)

(d) *Firms' catchment areas for labour*

We may finally conceive of the multiplier in a more explicitly spatial sense by noting that government investment often produces benefits which spread away from the precise point at which the investment is located. One factory, for example, may provide employment for quite a large area. An actual example illustrates this. In 1945 Smiths Industries chose to locate in a government factory built at Ystradgynlais in the Swansea Valley in South Wales. By 1973 the factory had a workforce of 1 191 employees but only about 11% lived in Ystradgynlais itself. Fig. 8.9 shows how the catchment area for the factory's workforce provided jobs for people within a radius of 23 km of the factory. The days of mass car-ownership have meant that people can travel relatively long distances to work; the spatial impact of investment may therefore spread over an area much greater than that of the site of the investment.

The regional multiplier is an important concept in understanding how government policy works. Of course, the same effects are felt if the investment which triggers off the multiplier is generated privately instead of by the government. But in the peripheral areas of Britain (see Fig. 8.6) it has been the

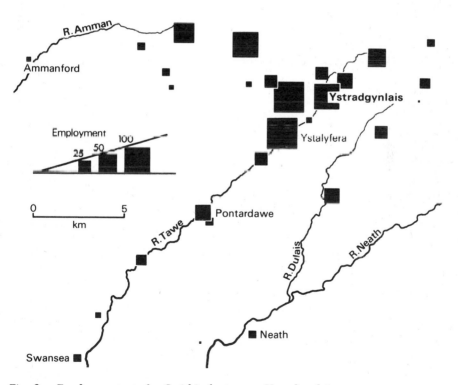

Fig. 8.9. Employment at the Smith's factory at Ystradgynlais.

government which has undertaken to provide much new employment. Indeed, for South Wales it has been said that 'virtually everyone who is employed in South Wales is now in a new job, either a job which did not exist in 1945 or which did exist but in a different location.'[8] This region is also described as 'the closest to a nationalized region' that exists in Britain.

(e) Has government policy worked?

You might easily assume from the above quotations that government policy in Britain has been a rousing success. Some industrialists, however, have not been happy with their moves to development areas. Consider the view of a manager of a branch plant of a vehicle components firm:

> How would I do it again? Well, I wouldn't go to a development area. You have to be very big and you must take your key men. The workers are ruined to death by the unions. There are no ancillary services there: you need a large tool room and maintenance is difficult. This area is only suitable for the indigenous industry.'[9]

On the other hand, the response to the development area might be quite different:

> 'Do it again? Well, we should have gone earlier. We are a very satisfied customer for the development areas. The golden rule is never to take anyone with you on a move. The training grants are good and the labour force will buckle to for a full day's work for a full day's pay. We can pay them all by cheque. Three shifts are no problem and absenteeism is low. Productivity is high, there is no incentive scheme which cuts down administrative costs, and there is no demarcation. There are only five rates of pay instead of one hundred and five and the rates are 10% lower. The unions don't want parity: they are for a quiet life too.'[10]

For every satisfied customer we may find an industrialist who has had difficulties since choosing to locate in the development areas. Looking at individuals in this way is not likely to provide us with an overall appraisal of the success or otherwise of regional policy. We need more aggregated approaches.

Although Britain can be said to have had a regional policy since the 1930s, it is really only since 1963 (note the change of the nature of the financial incentives since that date in Table 8.6) that that policy has been really strong. Yet after ten years of strong regional policy, unemployment in all development areas was higher than before it was introduced. Using these criteria, regional policy can hardly be called successful although, of course, such an argument is rather misleading since it does not show what would have happened if there had been no regional policy at all. Nevertheless, many of our declining areas still suffer from the possession of a large share of declining industries and a small share of growth industries.

4. Regions grow when the nation grows

Fig. 8.10 shows the unemployment in North East England compared with Great Britain as a whole for the years between 1946 and 1962 (one dot on the scatter diagram represents one year).

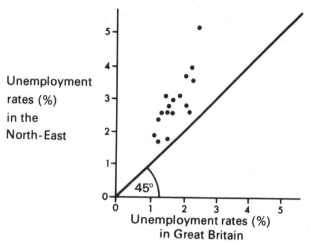

Fig. 8.10. The relationship between unemployment levels in Great Britain and unemployment levels in the North East, 1946–1962. Each dot represents one year.

Clearly, there is a positive relationship between the unemployment situation in the country and unemployment in the region. In other words, when the country is doing relatively well so, too, are the regions. But from Fig. 8.10 it will be seen that in all years between 1946 and 1962 unemployment in the North East was higher than in Great Britain as a whole (and would have been higher still had there not been a continuous migration from the region). Similar comments could be made about other development areas illustrated in Fig. 8.6. The irony of the situation is that it has been at times when the regions and the country are doing poorly that government aid to the regions has been most vigorous. Yet these are times when it is least likely that businessmen can be persuaded to move there.

A further problem with British regional policy is that two government agencies have, for much of the post-war period, been pulling in different directions. In the immediate post-war period the 1946 New Towns Act and the 1947 Town and Country Planning Act (see Table 8.6) not only introduced the stick of IDCs to complement the carrot of development area incentives, but also gave the green light to the creation of New Towns – mainly in South East England – the very region where IDCs were supposed to be the most difficult to obtain. Similarly, on Merseyside, where industry was being encouraged to locate by the Board of Trade (the area having full development area status), large numbers of workers were being rehoused at the same time in overspill towns (see page 202) which were outside the development area and thus less able to get IDCs.

Another interesting anomaly of regional policy has been that some capital intensive industries, which do not soak up unemployed labour, are eligible for the same grants as those industries which do. Likewise, firms locating just outside a development area but perhaps employing large numbers of workers who live in it are not eligible for grants.

Even if the factory which has been steered to the peripheral area does employ large numbers, it does not necessarily mean that large pools of unemployed workers will be accommodated therein. For example, when the Ford motor company located at Swansea in 1965, the majority of the 1 000 workers employed there made voluntary job changes from 208 local firms.[11] Thus, in the short term, the movement of a major employer into a development area could have an adverse effect upon local firms and produce some disorganization in the labour market.

5. Unemployment ancient and modern

It is worth noting that many of Britain's current problems are found in regions which are not in any kind of development area but in places like London, Folkestone and Torbay. Such places possess surprisingly high *numbers* of unemployed workers and in some cases high *percentages* of unemployed, too. Thus 'unemployment ancient and modern' contrasts such present-day unemployment black-spots with those which have been experiencing variations on the same problem since the 1930s.

'Mine closures, shipbuilding, and textiles continue to provide the ancient core of unemployment while newer industries, such as engineering and vehicle manufacture, provide an increasingly significant proportion of the jobless.'[12] Today it can no longer be said that unemployment is confined to certain well-defined senile industrial regions. Mergers of companies, such as that between GEC-AEI-EE – often lead to large numbers of redundancies, by no means all within development areas. In this example, large numbers were laid off in Birmingham, London and Manchester. It may be, therefore, that the policies of taking work to the workers, which have been traditionally adopted, need to be supplemented by providing greater aid to those workers willing to travel to work, and greater help in retraining workers for whom change may be a normal state of affairs in years to come.

ASSIGNMENTS

1. *Draw a diagram similar to Fig. 8.7 (page 177) to show how congestion costs within a profitable area (M–M1) may produce diseconomies leading to an unprofitable enclave.*

184

What's so different about the New Cumberland?

If your factory is sited in an area where...	You should move to the New Cumberland...
1 sq. ft. of land costs £2	1 sq. ft. of land costs 11p
1 sq. ft. of rented factory space costs £1.25 p.a.	1 sq. ft. of rented factory space costs 50p p.a.
labour is costly and scarce	workers are available and willing to work
traffic is heavily congested	transport moves freely
expansion is blocked	industrial development certificates are unnecessary
countryside is an hour's drive away	countryside is on your doorstep
air is dangerously polluted . . .	air is clean and healthy . . .

Add to these plus points the keen co-operation of local authorities at all levels, the solid benefit of maximum financial aid from the Government and Cumberland County Council, and you will begin to realise just how different the New Cumberland is – and the difference it can make to your business.

For further details please write or ring
Geoffrey Burrows, Industrial Development Officer,
The County of Cumberland, The Courts, Carlisle. Tel: 23456.

The New Cumberland
-where the grass is greener.

Fig. 8.11. How Cumberland projected itself in 1972.

2. *The government decides to undertake a road-building programme in the closed economy of South West England costing £250 million. Workers engaged in the project and all other southwesterners will spend 80% of their additional income. What regional income will result from the initial investment of £250 million? (You will need to read pages 176–8 before answering this.)*
3. *Using the same information concerning government investment, and the same 80% consumption of additional income created but now including in the problem the fact that 10% of additional income is spent on imports from outside the South West, calculate the value of the regional multiplier. (Refer back to page 178.)*
4. *Change the wording of Fig. 8.8 (page 179) to show how the closure of a large source of employment or the decline of a staple industry has a reverse multiplier effect – the multiplier working backwards. (For example, change 'location of new industry' to 'decline of industry', etc.)*

C. Conclusion

Although government intervention has met with much criticism, in a mixed economy such as Britain's it is probably fair to say that it has on the whole helped those areas to which it has been applied. Government policy for the regions hinges around the extension of spatial margins to profitability and the improvement of the image of the regions concerned. The section on mental maps in Chapter 6 (pages 123–30) indicated the difficulty development areas have in overcoming their 'Coronation Street' image. The way in which the former Cumberland County Council (now part of Cumbria) tried to project itself is shown in Fig. 8.11 and emphasizes strongly the environmental, as well as governmental advantages of the 'New Cumberland'. While the Cumberland of the advertisement may look very attractive, it is worth remembering that each other region in a development area is trying to attract industry, too, by improving its image to the potential industrialist.

It should be pointed out that government policy aims to decentralize office employment as well as employment in manufacturing industry. Tertiary and quaternary employment in some government establishments have already been decentralized, an interesting example being the location of the vehicle licensing centre at Swansea in South Wales. Within the country as a whole, however, employment in tertiary industry has become more localized in the last ten years, despite the work of the Location of Offices Bureau which tries to persuade offices to locate out of London. Whether non-government tertiary industry will, in fact, move away from the South East remains to be seen. The following piece of verse, written only partly with tongue in cheek, focuses amusingly upon several important elements of government regional policy.

Industry grows where the grass is greener.

Industry grows where the grass is greener
And the sun shines brighter and the rain falls sweeter.
The managers know what their wives want most —
And it isn't spoil heaps or slums or frost —
It's shops and schools and friends and amenity,
But Mintech — BOT says: 'It is our duty
To send you North, and West, and to Wales.
In nether regions you may find gales,
But take heart, and car, to a National Park!'

The government hope that new industry
Of quaternary type will also flee
To these same regions, that research may grow,
But a look at the map shows that R & D now
Is by the fair Solent, Bucks, Berks and Harlow.
Enterprise Lancaster woos them away
Up North to the Lakes, with the fells and Hallé.
The North's good for football — it's not good for ballet,
So R & D man with his wife and family
Stay in the South where there's *warmth* and prosperity.
Huntington lives! The climate determines
Where industry grows, not Mintech mandarins![13]

Glossary
Mintech — The Ministry of Technology
BOT — The Board of Trade
R & D — Research and development
Huntington — Ellsworth Huntington, geographer and environmental determinist (1876–1947) who stressed the importance of climate and its effect on human behaviour.

Good grants or good locations: a simulation model

In 1966, 63 new factory buildings were set up in South Wales. Some were immigrant factories, others were new firms, new local branch plants or factory extensions. Where might we predict they would locate? This exercise attempts to simulate the location of these factories for a region which in 1966 presented an interesting choice for the industrialist considering locating in the area. On the one hand much of interior South Wales was eligible for government assistance — Special Development Areas covering the 'poorest' locations — and the remainder of this area possessed development area status (Fig. 8.12). The coastal belt of the South East, however, was in 1966 unassisted as far as regional policy was concerned but, with access to the M4, the newly constructed Severn Bridge and the major towns and amenities of South Wales, it possessed many things in its favour. What is more, the south-east coastal belt is less wet and suffers less from the landscape exploitations of the Industrial Revolution than the valleys to the north and west.

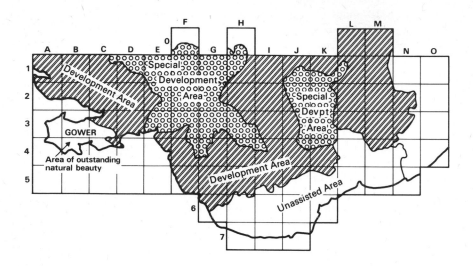

Fig. 8.12. Regional assistance in South Wales 1966. This map does not reflect *present-day* distribution of government help. South East Wales now qualifies for Intermediate Area status.

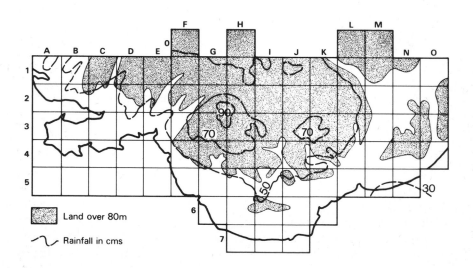

Fig. 8.13. Rainfall and relief, South Wales.

188

Figs. 8.13 and 8.14 illustrate further aspects of the area's regional geography (relief and rainfall, and towns and major roads respectively). The reader will observe that each of these three maps has been superimposed on an identical grid. Each cell of the grid possesses a probability of attracting one or more of the 63 new factories to it. The question is: can we weigh up the probability for each cell in order to predict where the factories will locate? (We should, strictly speaking, talk of *postdicting* since we are looking at a past period, rather than the future.)

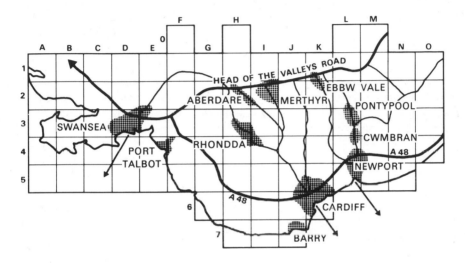

Fig. 8.14. Communications and main towns in South Wales.

A probability matrix

For simplicity we may isolate four factors as influencing industrialists locating within South Wales.

    (a) Government aid: the extent of government aid is shown in Fig. 8.12 and has been strongly emphasized in this chapter.

    (b) Communications and access: we have commented on the importance of market access for modern industry (pages 47 and 135) and access to local and national markets.

    (c) Local population: this provides not only the labour force but also, for some industries, a local market and the amenities and facilities of modern urban life.

    (d) Environment: by this we refer not only to the physical environment but also to the man-made environment which ranges from slums to new towns.

The selection of these four factors is highly arbitrary and the reader may think others should be added or that some should be replaced.

Table 8.8. (Weightings for factors used in simulation)

Factor	Weighting	Notes
(a) Government aid	8	This means that a cell chiefly made up of a Special Development Area would score 8 on this factor while a Development Area cell might only score, say, 6. An unassisted area would score nil though a cell *near* a Development Area (which implies the availability of surplus labour) might score 1 or 2
(b) Communications Access	10	A motorway site would obviously score much higher (9 or 10) than a cell some distance from a motorway
(c) Local population	6	Nearness to a large town means nearness to labour, amenities and linked activities. A cell on a large town would score more for this factor than a cell in the middle of a rural area
(d) Environment	5	Heavy rainfall and rugged terrain would score low on this factor while flatter land, drier weather and more pleasant urban and industrial environments would score more

Having decided on our location factors, it is clear that one may be more important than another. It is necessary, therefore, to allocate weightings to each of the factors. Again, the reader should feel free to disagree with the author's choice of weightings which are outlined in Table 8.8.

The basic idea which the model will now be used to demonstrate is that of *Probability* and how chance or random factors can be built into such a probabilistic model. The model predicts the probable distribution of plants and recognizes a choice among several locations. The 'best' locations have the highest probability of being chosen, though, as we will see, chance factors can take factories to unlikely places.

Running the model

Each cell is now allocated a score for each of the four factors. These scores should be entered in each corner of the square, starting with the government aid score in the top left hand corner and working in a clockwise direction down the list of factors. The four scores should then be added up to give a total score for each square. This has been done in Fig. 8.15. For example cell A1 scores 6 on the government factor, 3 on the communications factor, 1 on the population factor and 0 on the environment factor giving a total score for the cell of 10.

The penultimate step is to convert Fig. 8.15 into a probability matrix by allocating the squares, reading from left to right and starting with square FO, with a range of consecutive numbers. Cell FO, for example, possesses a score of seven. Thus this space would possess seven numbers (in this case 1–7 – see Fig. 8.16). Square G6, on the other hand, scored 20 and would therefore possess 20 numbers (1114–1133) in the probability matrix. The map of South Wales, converted into a probability matrix is shown in Fig. 8.16. The essential point to remember here is that as any one random number has the same chance of being called as any other, the greater the range of values in any cell, the greater probability that cell has of attracting industry.

Using random number tables, identify the first 63 numbers (of four digits) which appear in them and locate them in the appropriate cells on an overlay superimposed on Fig. 8.16. If the first random number called was 0530, put a dot in the square containing numbers 529–550. The 63 points represent the predicted distribution of the 63 factories which located in South Wales in 1966, based on the factors which went into making up the probability matrix. The 'chance' factor is built into the model by using the random number table. The predicted distribution is shown in Fig. 8.17.

While the exercise does, of itself, illustrate the idea of probability in arriving at a distribution of points, it is tempting to see now how well the weighting adopted here accurately predicted the *actual location* of the 63

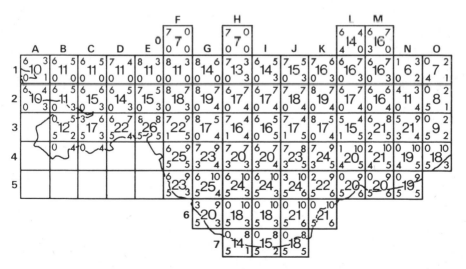

Fig. 8.15. Total and factor scores for each cell.

factories. Unfortunately, although the *precise* location of all the plants is not known, it is known how they were divided up among the 3 sub-regions of South Wales. Table 8.9 compares the actual number locating in each sub-region with the number predicted by the above model.

					1-7		8-14				15-28	29-44		
45-54	55-65	66-76	77-87	88-98	99-109	110-123	124-136	137-150	151-165	166-181	182-197	198-213	214-219	220-226
227-236	237-247	248-262	263-276	277-291	292-309	310-328	329-345	346-362	363-380	381-399	400-416	417-432	433-443	444-451
	452-463	464-480	481-502	503-528	529-550	551-567	568-583	584-599	600-616	617-633	634-648	649-669	670-690	691-699
					700-724	725-747	748-767	768-788	789-810	811-834	835-854	855-875	876-894	895-912
					913-935	936-960	961-984	985-1008	1009-1032	1033-1054	1055-1074	1075-1094	1095-1113	
						1114-1133	1134-1151	1152-1169	1170-1190	1191-1211				
							1212-1225	1226-1240	1241-1258					

Fig. 8.16. The map of South Wales converted into a probability matrix.

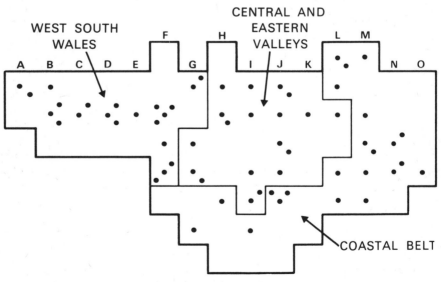

Fig. 8.17. The predicted location of the 63 factories.

Clearly, our choice of weighting was satisfactory though it is impossible to assess the precise success of the model in predicting the exact siting of firms within the region because of the unavailability of data.

Table 8.9. Predicted and actual factory numbers for sub-regions

Sub region	Actual	Predicted
West South Wales	19	22
Central and Eastern Valleys	20	18
Coastal belt	24	23
Total	63	63

ASSIGNMENT

Take another region of Britain northwest of the Tees–Exe line, e.g. North West England, North East England or Central Scotland:

1. *Draw maps to show (see Figs. 8.12–8.14):*
   (a) *Development area; special development area; intermediate area; unassisted area status;*
   (b) *Physical environmental factors;*
   (c) *Communications and main towns;*
   (d) *Any other factors you wish to show.*
2. *Prepare and justify weighting for these factors (Table 8.8).*
3. *Work out a grid, similar to that on Fig. 8.15, giving factors and total scores in each cell.*
4. *For a given time period assume 50 factories are set up in the region of your choice. Work out a probability matrix and use random number tables to predict where the factories are likely to locate.*

   Unless you have data for the number of factories actually commencing business in the time period of your simulation, it will not be possible to see the extent to which your simulated pattern mirrors reality. This should not detract from the value of undertaking this simulation, however, as the random and probabilistic elements in the model will still have been stressed.

Key Ideas

A. *Stages in the Cycle of Industrial Development (pages 152–8)*
1. Industrial regions tend to pass through a *sequence* of: infancy, youth, maturity and, in some cases, senility.
2. Senility may be prevented by *continued maturity* in the case of some regions.

H

3. Where senility occurs, there is the possibility of outside help leading to *rejuvenation*.
4. In Britain today regions in need of rejuvenation lie mainly to the north-west of the *Tees–Exe line*.

B. *Regional Disparities* (pages 158–68)
1. *Regional disparities* are marked features of the economic and social geography of the UK.
2. Broad contrasts exist between the relatively wealthy *growth* regions and the relatively poor *declining* regions.
3. Criteria for recognizing degrees of *economic health* include (a) income; (b) employment; (c) diversification of industry.
4. Not all these criteria, however, *correlate* with each other as accurate indices of economic health.

C. *Government Intervention* (pages 168–87)
1. *Government intervention* is required if regional disparities are to be ironed out.
2. *Government policy* is based on taking work to workers in regions of relatively high unemployment by a variety of measures.
3. These measures include both *incentives* (grants to go to development areas; advance factories) and *controls* (refusal to grant industrial development certificates).
4. In economic terms, government policy can be thought of as *extending firms' spatial margins to profitability*.
5. The economic success of such policies depends in part on the working of the *regional multiplier* effect, which means that government expenditure in a region is assumed to create a regional income greater in amount than

Fig. 8.18. Go south, young man (Source: *The Penguin Private Eye*, Penguin, 1965)

the initial government expenditure – new investment leading to a variety of infrastructural changes which in turn attract more industry and provide employment for a wider area than the place in which a new factory was sited.

6. Government policy tends to work more *successfully* when the country as a whole is going through a period of prosperity, though the greater need is in times of difficulty.

7. Government policy, while to some extent ameliorating the difficulties of the 'declining regions', has not been effective to the extent that the *growth industries* are still naturally attracted to and remain concentrated in the growth areas.

Additional Activities

1. Take a mature and a senile industrial region of Britain and analyse the factors which have led to this contrasted state of affairs.

2. Contest the view that government help to the development areas is producing an 'uneconomic geography' of those areas. (Refer to C in the Reading section below.)

3. Refer to the Cumberland advertisement on page 185.
   (a) What important spatial element is missing from the Cumberland advertisement?
   (b) Why might some industrialists prefer to locate in a more expensive, more congested part of Britain than Cumberland?
   (c) What kind of industrialist might benefit most from a move to Cumberland?
   (d) Make a list of the disadvantages of Cumberland for industrial location, illustrating them by a sketch map.

4. If all unemployed workers like the one in the cartoon (Fig. 8.18) took the advice given by the Citizens' Advice Bureau:
   (a) what would be the effect on the south?
   (b) what would be the effect on the town in which the Citizens' Advice Bureau is located?
   In answering use concepts from this chapter.

5. Put yourself in the place of the Minister responsible for regional development. Write a short speech attempting to convince a group of industrialists in Essex that they would benefit from a move to Northumberland.

Reading

A. Any titles in the *Industrial Britain* series, published by David & Charles.
B. RAWSTRON, E. & COATES, B., *Regional Variations in Britain*, Batsford, especially Chapters 3 and 4.

C. (i) LEE, D., *Regional Planning and the Location of Industry*, Heinemann, 1970.
*McCRONE, G., *Regional Policy in Britain*, Allen & Unwin, 1969.
(ii) HOUSE, J. W., *The UK Space*, Weidenfeld & Nicolson, 1973, Chapter 1 and Chapter 4, pp. 252–68.
(iii) HALL, P., *Urban and Regional Planning*, Penguin, 1974, chapters 4, 5 and 6.

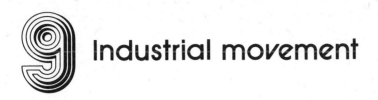 Industrial movement

A. Types of Move

1. Seed beds for factory growth

The simplest kind of move is the birth of a new factory, which is often associated with the initiative of a small-scale businessman who possesses limited capital and very little experience in locational decision making. The search for an initial location will, therefore, be neither rigorous nor comprehensive and will rarely involve the industrialist leaving his home town.

Since most initial entrepreneurs formerly worked in the same kind of enterprise in the same kind of industry in which they are now trying to 'go it alone', this lack of rigour in locational analysis results from a lack of funds rather than a lack of knowledge about the industry.

The initial decision about where to set up a factory is influenced by the desire to be near existing contacts and social ties. Such contacts and ties form a kind of *seed bed* for factory growth. Such seed beds are most likely to exist in large cities and specialized industrial areas and may contribute to the relative ease with which a new factory establishes itself in the same area where many others of similar or linked types already exist.

An actual example of the births of new enterprises in the post-war period is provided by the West Midlands conurbation. Here it has been shown[1] that conditions in the north-west of the conurbation seem to favour the establishment of new firms while conditions in the south-east of the conurbation do not. This latter zone lacked the sub-assembly activities and juxtaposed and interrelated processes of the north-west zone. The close linkages between industries in the north-west presented an incentive to form new enterprises either by setting up a completely new firm (by a man gathering a few of his mates together and going it alone), or by the development of branch plants.

2. Death beds

A second type of move is the converse of that described above, namely the death of an industrial establishment. Many new firms remain in business for a

197

relatively short space of time; lack of experience, too much risk or too much caution on the part of the entrepreneur, or perhaps a poor location outside the spatial margins to profitability may contribute to the closure of a factory.

Much heavy manufacturing (such as iron making) closed down in the inter-war years as the raw material inputs on which they were dependent became too costly to mine. Such closures are illustrated by the former iron works on the northern outcrop of the South Wales Coalfield, where local ore became too costly in competition with ore from overseas sources.

The geography of the death of factories is relatively undocumented. Pred's model (pages 112–18) certainly takes the death of plants into account in explaining the present-day industrial landscape in terms of the learning and imitation of successful location decisions. What seems less clear, however, is whether certain areas possess higher factory death rates than others.

It is known that as firms get larger and take over smaller firms, control moves from the periphery of the industrial package (see page 26) to the centre. Moreover, when branches of the enterprise close down it could be hypothesized that those branches furthest from headquarters (which is often in the south-east of England in the case of the large industrial corporation) are the ones which close down first.

For example, in 1951, of the main breweries in South Wales only two New-port breweries were controlled by firms outside the area. The rest had head-quarters in Wales. By 1972, however, outside firms controlled most of the region's brewing capacity, mainly from London. In addition, many breweries which had been taken over by UK corporations had closed down, the decisions having been made in far away London.

3. Branch plant development

Rather than move lock, stock and barrel, many firms prefer to set up branch plants. The range within which a branch may be located is wide. There seem to be sound reasons for a branch plant staying as close as possible to the parent firm so that management ties and contacts can be retained; at the same time there may be equally sound reasons for moving some distance away from the parent, for example, to serve regional markets or to open up new markets which were previously untapped.

Some firms adopt a policy of setting up branches within the daily travelling distance of the parent plant in order to ensure close management control. This can be illustrated by the case of Clark's Ltd., the Somerset shoe firm. Fig. 9.1 shows how the growth of the manufacturing package has taken place mainly within daily travelling distance of the firm's headquarters. Note that the branches have gradually diffused away from Street as the firm has, over time, extended its area of operations.

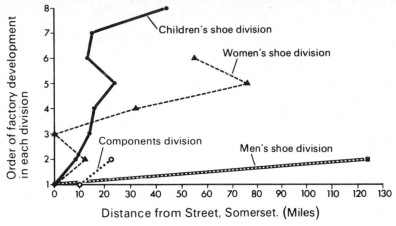

Fig. 9.1. The spread of Clark's factories from Street, 1939–67.

4. Lock, stock and barrel moves

The most literal kind of movement is, of course, where the plant closes down at one site and opens up at another. In the case of a small firm, it may move round the corner to a new location within the city. This kind of *intra-urban move* is dealt with towards the end of this chapter (pages 203–09). A much larger enterprise may decide to move beyond the suburbs of its present city location or even move to a new region altogether. It is with this kind of *inter-regional move* that section B below is chiefly concerned.

5. Potential mobility

A firm or enterprise is said to have potential mobility when the bonds tying it to its current location are relatively weak. Large firms are likely to be more mobile than small firms since they can *internalize* the important economies of scale thus making them more independent of suppliers and other links found to be essential to the smaller firm. It should be noted, however, that most moves are really compromises since, as we have said (page 119), most firms would probably prefer, if possible, to expand *in situ*.

B. The Dual Population Hypothesis

Two kinds of macro-scale movements can be identified in Great Britain. This 'dual population hypothesis'[2] consists of:

1. Long distance; inter-regional

These cover large-establishment-type moves from the central regions of Britain to the peripheral areas of higher than average unemployment. The availability of labour seems to be a major factor for such moves. In addition, the government inducements discussed in Chapter 8 (pages 174–5) are available in many of the peripheral regions (see Fig. 8.6, page 171), which also happen to be scenically attractive to members of senior management.

Thus, for Cornwall, Wales and the northern region of England, migrant firms from other regions have been estimated to account for 27.5%, 25.9% and 18.5% respectively of the total manufacturing employment. It is significant that 83% of all post-war moves to the periphery have been made up of branch plants.

The importance of these moves (see Fig. 9.2) is reflected in the fact that between 1946 and 1966 the peripheral areas received over 900 manufacturing establishments providing employment for 346 000 workers. Whether any one peripheral region is as good as another for a firm moving from, say, the south-east, is open to question. A firm in London, for instance, might first look at the nearest assisted area. Really remote areas (remote, that is, from the major markets of Britain) such as Central Scotland, may be at a disadvantage in this respect, therefore, compared with such areas as South Wales and Lancashire, because of distance from markets, from main concentrations of particular industries (such as light engineering in the West Midlands) and from the point of view of making personal contact with suppliers and customers.

2. Short distance; intra-regional

These tend to be small-establishment moves within the south-east – West Midlands axis and make up the second element of the dual population hypothesis. Many of these moves form part of what is termed *industrial overspill*. This involves the movement of people and industry out of conurbations and across the surrounding Green Belt to theoretically self-supporting new or expanded towns. Such overspill has occurred because it is assumed that the London or West Midland conurbations contain too many people and insufficient land to meet acceptable planning standards. Successful industrial overspill is determined by the matching of population movement with job movement – otherwise the overspilled workforce would simply 'leapfrog' the Green Belt, and produce further problems for the city region in question. The firms which are encouraged to move should be those which are not secured tightly to the conurbation centres through linkage.

These moves also contrast with the first type in that they tend to be complete relocations, the main location factor appearing to be the need for retaining proximity – not necessarily to the conurbation centre, but nevertheless to the conurbation, from which they have moved. 57% of moves to the South East and East Anglia between 1945 and 1966 were made up of complete transfers, many of which were to the new and expanded towns.

There appears to be *sectoral bias* to the movement of firms out of the London conurbation. Fig. 9.3 shows the origins of factories moving from

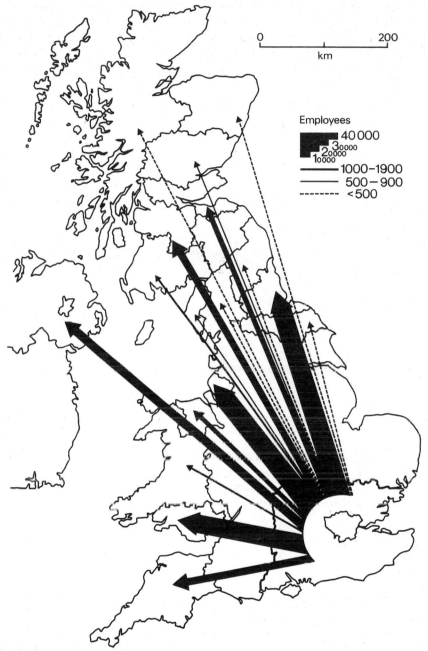

Fig. 9.2. An example of long distance movement; manufacuring movement from the South East to peripheral areas, 1945–1965. (Source: 'Industrial movement and regional development in the United Kingdom', *Town Planning Review*, **43**, 1, 1972, p. 3–25)

Greater London to four of the London new towns. Notice how firms moving to Stevenage mainly moved from north London, those to Bracknell from west London, those to Basildon from the east and those to Crawley from the south. In the early stages of New Town development the Greater London Council *encouraged* firms to move to the most accessible town, but more recently migration has been controlled by economic rather than by legislative factors.

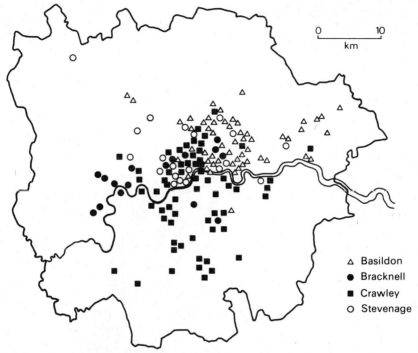

Fig. 9.3. Origin of factories moving from Greater London to four New Towns. (Source: C. M. Brown, 'Industry in the New Towns of the London Region', in J. E. Martin, *Greater London, an Industrial Geography*, Bell, 1966, p. 239)

Certain factors supposedly pulling firms beyond the green belts may be more apparent than real. For instance, in the case of the industrial overspill from the Birmingham conurbation, it has been shown that:
   (a) rents and prices of factory premises in overspill areas are *not* lower than those in the conurbation;
   (b) the majority of workers are often unwilling to move beyond the green belt, away from their old haunts and alternative job opportunities;
   (c) the conurbation may not *appear* so congested as the planners think. B. D. M. Smith notes that 'many people find city life attractive and find the city facilities and services much more adequate than those presently or likely in the future to be available in other areas';[3]

(d) the identification of the mobile firm may prove difficult and some firms may, in fact, be wrongly assessed. Some conurbation firms may have bought land alongside their factories for future expansion, only to be left with useless investment if they have to move as part of overspill.

ASSIGNMENTS

1. For Fig. 9.3 (page 202), can you suggest why a north London firm might prefer to move to Stevenage, rather than to, say, Crawley? Why should such short distance movers wish to retain contact with the metropolis?
2. With reference to your own industrial/urban region, or one near to you, show the extent to which it has been or is associated with simple moves (seed or death bed), branch plant, long distance or short distance moves.

C. Intra-Urban Industrial Movement

1. The importance of intra-urban movement

In the preceding sections we have considered industrial movement at the macro-scale, emphasizing that moves may be intra-regional or inter-regional. Most industrial moves are over quite short distances, however, and are actually within the urban area. Indeed, for small plants, employing perhaps fewer than 20 workers, the level of scale of the location decision is basically an urban site choice since such firms are unlikely to consider moving to distant regions. Because such small firms outnumber large firms (see page 18), the majority of location decisions are, in fact, intra-urban location decisions.

2. Generalizations about intra-urban movement

(a) A sectoral bias exists in industrial movement at this scale, as it did at the city-region scale (see Fig. 9.3 page 202). Fig. 9.4 illustrates how the establishment of branch plants or the actual lock, stock and barrel move of a firm is hypothesized as being within the same sector of the city as the parent plant or former location. The central axis of the sector (the 'axis of search') is a straight line drawn from the CBD, through the initial plant location, to the urban edge. In Fig. 9.4, a factory located at X is unlikely to set up a branch at U or move to U. Clearly this model assumes a considerable distance across the metropolis. Thus, in order to retain links with either parent plant or former contacts and avoid disrupting the residences of the workforce, new locations are located as conveniently as possible with regard to the previous location. Because the distance across smaller towns may act as less of a friction on movement such a model is unlikely to apply to towns of medium to small size (say, below 300 000).

(b) *Distance moved is closely related to the size of the firm* Smaller firms move shorter distances within the metropolis than large firms. Again, we have seen the same thing at a different level of scale in our discussion of inter-regional movement (page 199). Larger firms can not only afford the cost of moving the greater distances but, as we have seen, they are more independent of the suppliers, buyers and sub-contractors than the small firm for whom these kinds of linkages in the inner city are most important.

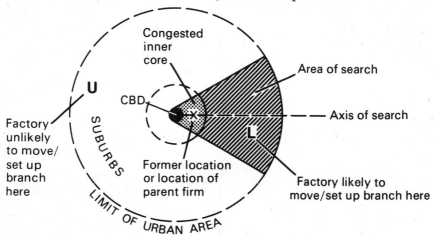

Fig. 9.4. Area of search for new sites in the metropolis shows a sectoral bias.

(c) *Suburbanization of industry* Although births of firms in cities are more likely to occur at the centre than in the suburbs (see page 62 for reasons), the major trend in intra-urban industrial movement is that of suburbanization.

The suburbanization trend is overwhelmingly seen to be the case for the major British conurbations, as shown in Table 9.1. Decentralization from the centre to the outer conurbation seems especially strong for manufacturing industries such as clothing, timber and furniture, paper, printing and publishing. The extent of such changes can be quantified by using the decentralization index which we examined in a different context on pages 79–80. The decentralization index in this instance shows the percentage shares of total conurbation employment in three conurbation zones – the centre (x), the rest of the central city (y), and the outer conurbation (z). The formula for calculating the index is:

$$\frac{(X \times 0) + (Y \times 1) + (Z \times 2)}{2}$$

A score of 0 means that all employment in a given activity is concentrated within the conurbation centre while a score of 100 means that the activity is totally concentrated in the outer conurbation. By comparing decentralization scores for different years we can observe the temporal as well as the spatial

Table 9.1. Conurbation decentralization scores for manufacturing industries. 1961 and 1966. (Source: G. C. Cameron & A. W. Evans, 'The British conurbation centres', Regional Studies, 7, 1973, p. 51).

| Order Heading | Conurbation | | | | | | | | | | | |
| | London | | South East Lancashire | | West Midlands | | Central Clydeside | | Merseyside | | Tyneside | |
	1961	1966	1961	1966	1961	1966	1961	1966	1961	1966	1961	1966
Food, drink and tobacco	67.6	71.8	86.4	87.1	67.2	68.7	57.5	62.5	60.0	62.3	59.5	64.8
Chemicals and allied industries	65.3	70.3	80.5	81.3	70.7	72.2	64.1	74.6	72.8	76.5	68.7	69.1
Metal manufacture	74.6	75.3	89.1	90.1	85.5	86.6	84.0	87.6	87.4	83.8	88.9	82.6
Engineering and electrical goods	78.6	81.9	85.7	87.1	70.0	72.9	79.7	79.8	59.9	58.3	76.7	79.6
Shipbuilding and marine engineering	79.5	84.6	92.7	95.5	69.4	93.4	63.9	65.3	82.4	83.3	87.8	88.9
Vehicles	92.5	92.3	93.8	96.7	63.6	63.6	81.2	86.0	52.1	75.0	69.0	78.4
Metal goods not elsewhere specified	68.0	71.0	79.4	84.3	74.7	76.8	73.5	75.8	66.4	67.0	77.6	79.6
Textiles	57.0	59.3	93.4	92.7	72.6	73.6	76.3	80.0	46.8	48.8	90.3	91.6
Leather, leather goods and fur	41.6	45.5	86.0	87.9	86.9	91.5	49.5	45.0	71.6	79.1	24.1	51.5
Clothing and footwear	43.0	46.7	67.5	73.4	76.6	80.5	37.7	44.4	43.5	47.4	84.0	84.6
Bricks, pottery, glass, cement, etc.	72.2	73.7	88.2	88.2	88.2	86.7	74.4	75.3	67.9	70.2	89.1	92.6
Timber, furniture, etc.	70.4	74.4	78.3	82.4	70.9	79.7	59.0	61.2	50.3	56.3	75.8	82.0
Paper, printing and publishing	34.1	37.3	65.1	68.3	56.6	60.0	42.4	45.6	48.8	52.0	53.8	66.8
Other manufacturing industries	75.1	77.3	77.6	83.4	66.4	68.8	60.7	67.0	53.0	56.0	88.4	95.5

changes in urban manufacturing location. Table 9.1 shows decentralization scores for manufacturing industries in six British conurbations for 1961 and 1966.

Fig. 9.5 shows how for London, South East Lancashire, and Tyneside the majority of scores are higher for 1966 than for 1961. Had all the symbols in the diagram fallen exactly on the 45° line the scores would have been exactly the same for both years. The higher scores for the latter year indicate, of course, decentralization in these industries. You may be able to observe a similar trend also taking place in smaller towns.

The redevelopment of inner cities has been accompanied by the voluntary and planned outward movement of industry, for purposes of expansion, for the accommodation of single-storey premises and to satisfy the demands for greater car-parking space and landscaping. In addition, the inner city may no longer be the most accessible part of the city. Congestion and the consequent high costs of movement in inner city locations contrasts with suburban sites' access to cheaper land, motorways or even airports.

At the same time one of the most important factors causing the decentralization of industry may be the increased demand in the central city for office space. It seems that offices still need central city locations more than industries. In addition, many central city areas have been subjected to extensive road improvements which have meant that many small workshops have been demolished and forced to suburbanize. Such small enterprises are often unable to afford the rents for new premises in the central city and new space has subsequently been occupied by offices.

3. Suburbanization; a social problem?

But what happens if the employees of inner city industries are less mobile than their workplaces? Poorer workers tend to live nearer their places of work than the more affluent members of management – the suburbanites. Thus one might expect more workers at a given city workplace to make short journeys to work while the more affluent minority made long-distance journeys from the suburbs. We have already used the term *friction of distance* to describe the effect of distance on movement (see page 142). A 'distance decay' pattern is produced on a graph showing number of workers plotted against distance travelled to work. It has been argued by Professor Arthur Getis[4] that in many towns in the USA there exists, around a given workplace, a 'frictionless area' (see Fig. 9.6) extending up to about three to six kilometres from the place of work. All other things being equal, all distance zones (shown by concentric circles in Fig. 9.6) within the frictionless area will contain a roughly equal number of workers. This means that workers do not care very much what distance they live from their workplace providing that it is within their 'critical isochrone'.

After the critical isochrone is reached the normal friction of distance effect sets in and the number of workers/distance curve begins to fall away steeply.

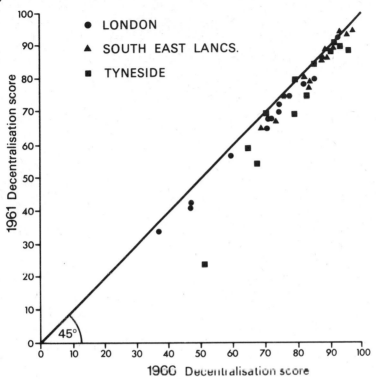

Fig. 9.5. Decentralization scores for manufacturing industry in three conurbations, 1961 and 1966.

What are the social implications of all this? Remember that in the USA the black ghettos, like the traditional workplaces, are near the CBD, in the 'zone in transition'. Professor Getis has written:

> When new workplaces are located in suburbs, the ghetto resident who finds barriers to migration to areas outside the ghetto is unable to compete for the new jobs. The new workplaces are not within the critical isochrone of the ghetto residents. This means that densities in the ghetto remain high; welfare rolls and unemployment increase as industry abandons the central city. The remaining unnecessarily high densities close to the centre of the cities cannot be explained by high accessibility to the CBD as present theory would have us believe.[5]

The respective journey to work patterns of blacks and whites has been analysed for several cities in the USA, notably for Detroit by the geographer Donald Deskins.[6] He has shown that in 1880 the whites still lived in the

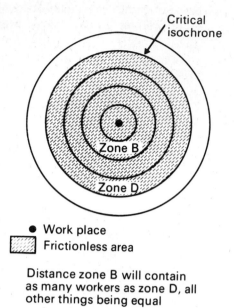

Critical
isochrone

Zone B

Zone D

● Work place
▨ Frictionless area

Distance zone B will contain
as many workers as zone D, all
other things being equal

Fig. 9.6. The critical isochrone. (Source: A. Getis, 'Residential location and the journey from work', *Proceedings of the Association of American Geographers*, **1**, 1969, pp. 55–9)

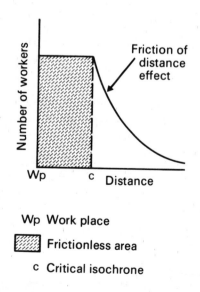

Friction of
distance
effect

Number of workers

Wp   c   Distance

Wp Work place
▨ Frictionless area
c Critical isochrone

Fig. 9.7. The frictionless area and distance decay pattern. (Source: As for Fig. 9.6)

central locations, close to their CBD-oriented workplaces and the blacks occupied the less favourable peripheral locations. Fringe residential areas were still undesirable. But between 1900 and 1953 negro worktrips were shorter than those of whites since during that period there had occurred a white flight to the suburbs, following the transport revolution in intra-urban travel. Blacks infilled deteriorating inner city property and the CBD remained the focal point of urban industrial life. By 1960, however, a rapid decentralization of industry was taking place with industry now moving to the suburbs. The workplaces were now increasingly beyond the critical isochrone of the black workers as white suburbanites now had the shorter journeys to work. The blacks were unable to move to the suburbs because of relative poverty and prejudice. Many of these suburban jobs were inaccessible by public transport which was still orientated towards the CBD. In Indianapolis as in other US cities, 'of the low-skilled job opportunities, clerical jobs which the inner-city residents are least capable of filling are located nearest to their place of residence as well as being the most accessible by public transit.'[7] You will now be able to see the social relevance of the decentralization of industry and an important application of the critical isochrone concept.

The suburbanization of industry is also occurring in Britain and there are signs that a similar problem is beginning here. For example, in 1971 nearly all Inner London boroughs had more than 7% of the economically active men not working – a higher figure than in some development areas.[8]

One final point about the suburbanization of industry is that, if employment does become more and more peripheral in location while services stay at the centre, rents (if they depend on accessibility) may level out across the urban area. This means that we may have to re-examine some of our classical urban models (page 57) which are based largely on the assumption that the central business district is the most accessible area of the city.

ASSIGNMENTS

1. Fig. 9.8 shows some examples of intra-city industrial movement in Toronto. To what extent does Fig. 9.8 support the model of intra-metropolitan industrial movement shown in Fig. 9.4 (page 204)?
2. Which industries possess the lowest decentralization scores in each of the conurbations noted in Table 9.1? Can you suggest why the locations of these industries are more concentrated? (Refer back to page 63 if necessary.)

D. Movement and Linkage

The dual population hypothesis (page 199) showed that the 'short-distance moves group' is linked relatively firmly to the metropolis. We should now try to relate the earlier discussion of linkage to that of movement. Industrial linkage has two principal implications for industrial movement studies: first, linkage can act as a 'brake' on movement and, secondly, linkage patterns may change with movement – old ones may be severed and new ones created.

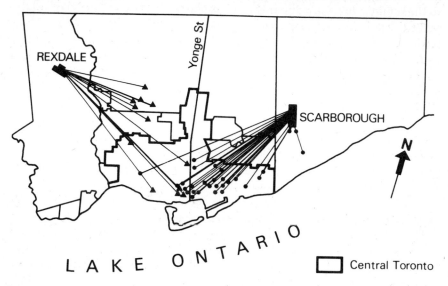

Fig. 9.8. Intra-city industrial movement in Toronto. Each symbol represents a previous location of a manufacturing firm. (After: J. Kerr & J. Spelt, *The Changing Face of Toronto, Memoir II*, Department of Energy, Mines and Resources, 1966, p. 140)

1. Linkage as a 'brake' on movement

The importance of linkage ties as far as mobility is concerned has already been noted (page 200). Some consideration, however, should be made of the *scale* of the linkage network under discussion. Local linkage, where it can be shown to exist, would logically seem more of a restraint on movement than regional scale linkages. Close contact with certain forms of sub-contractors is vital for the successful functioning of many small firms and it does appear from several research workers that it is for the small firms that such strong local linkages are the most binding. M. J. Taylor and P. J. Wood have written that 'certain types of firm in the West Midlands conurbation appear to depend on local connections overwhelmingly and it is difficult to imagine how they could have been founded or would continue to operate elsewhere'.[9] It may be, however, that as firms expand and grow in scale, they outgrow their dependence on the local region – a situation we discuss below. The fundamental problem of deciding how dependent a firm is on the local region is a continuous one facing the government in its move to decentralize industry.

2. Linkage changes with movement

Once a firm has decided to move it is theoretically possible that an existing or potential linkage network could have some bearing on the destination chosen. On one hand, a firm might be attracted to a location because of new linkages which it might develop there with local suppliers and purchasers. It is equally possible, however, that a firm, having been 'forced' to look for another site, may seek to retain existing linkages as a priority and thus locate as near as possible to those links. The former possibility rarely occurs since it is unlikely that a moving industrialist would know much about linkage in other regions or that firms to whom local linkages are important would be decentralizing. With regard to the retention of existing linkages, however, we have already noted that this is alleged to be an important component of the dual population hypothesis (pages 199–203). Thus in the mid-1960s it was found that 53% of the industrialists in London's New Towns did not entertain the idea of a location more than 50 kilometres from London. Such contact with the metropolis may be especially important in the case of information linkages.

But what about moves of over, say, 50 kilometres? Do these moves create important new linkages for firms in the receiving areas? The answer seems to be overwhelmingly 'no'. Of the new plants which have located in Northern Ireland since 1950, 80%, including most of the larger ones, showed remarkably few material linkages with firms in the region. Instead they retained their old ties with firms elsewhere.[10] Similar findings have been shown for East Anglia and the northern regions of England. Table 9.2 shows the proportion of migrant firms to these two regions which made more local purchases from the region than they had made before they moved there. It is clear that for the majority of firms 'no change' was the most common response, 49% for East Anglia and 67% for the Northern Region. Where firms do develop new local linkages they are mainly of the sub-contracting type, and purchasing and selling links remain outside the area in which they have recently located. Such findings suggest that in the short term at least, linkage may have been over-emphasized as a constraint on movement and that the cumulative causation model (page 179) may, in some cases, be more imagined than real.

Table 9.2. Linkage changes with movement. (Source: M. Moseley & P. Townroe, 'Linkage adjustment following industrial movement', *Tijdschrift voor Economische en Sociale Geografie* **64**, 1973, pp. 137–44)

	East Anglia	Northern region
Firms with more local purchases	14 (17%)	6 (11%)
'Other changes' (non-local)	27 (32%)	11 (20%)
No change	41 (49%)	36 (67%)
No answer	2 (2%)	1 (2%)
	84 (100%)	54 (100%)

E. Can industrial movement be predicted?

In attempting to understand the basic factors which affect the movement of industry, geographers have tried to formulate models which might enable them to predict why, how and to what extent industrial movement might occur, given certain simplifying assumptions. Let us first simplify the measures of attractiveness of a given region to the potentially mobile firm. Fig. 6.10 (page 121) showed that a relatively large number of 'pulls' can be considered, but for purposes of convenience and simplification we assume that industrialists look at two key elements of a region's attractiveness:

  (i) distance away from existing location (the accessibility factor in Fig. 6.10);
  (ii) the availability of workers (i.e. the level of unemployment).

A fundamental question arising from the consideration of these two variables is whether a region which may be inherently more attractive in terms of available workforce, but further away, exerts the same pull on industry from a given area as one which is inherently less attractive but nearer. You may have already spotted the analogy with the pull of gravity (available workforce) and a resistance (distance). Geographers have borrowed the physicist's terms and called the following formula the Gravity Model:

$$Mij = \frac{Aj}{dij}$$

where Mij is an index of the predicted volume of industrial movement between origin area i and destination area j;

Aj is a measure of the intrinsic attractiveness to mobile industry of destination area j;

Dij is the straight line distance measured between the approximate manufacturing centre of the relevant origin and destination areas.

Thus, given the distance between, say, South East England and various peripheral areas of Britain and the levels of unemployment in those areas, how good is the gravity model for predicting the amounts of employment created by migrant firms? Consider Fig. 9.9.

This diagram clearly shows the relationship between the predicted migration indices and the actual employment created by migrant firms from South East England to the various peripheral areas, between 1945 and 1965.

To be fair, it should be noted that this was the most successful version of the model. The correlation coefficients, while strong, were less so for movement from the Birmingham conurbation and the Greater London Council area than for the movement from South East England. At the same time, it should be noted that the measures of distance and attractiveness are rather crude. But this does represent a pioneering piece of work, using the gravity model in industrial geography whereas it has been more frequently utilized in urban and transport geography. The Cambridge geographer David Keeble concludes, 'spatial variations in migration to the peripheral regions do seem significantly to be related to distance and labour availability, when these are combined within a simple gravity model.'[11]

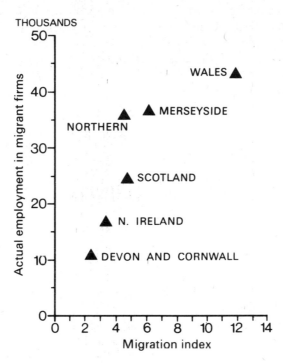

Fig. 9.9. United Kingdom: predicted migration indices and actual migrant employment in the peripheral areas; movement from South East England, 1945–65. (Source: D. Keeble, 'Employment mobility in Britain' in M. Chisholm & G. Manners (eds.) *Spatial Policy Problems of the British Economy*, Cambridge University Press, 1971)

Key Ideas

A. *Types of Move* (pages 197–9)
1. A firm is born when a new business sets up for the first time. Such births usually occur in *seedbeds* – areas where linked activities are found, usually in large cities.
2. A firm dies when its business closes down. Closures may occur through poor location but equally significant may be such factors as lack of business expertise, take-overs or mergers.
3. The setting up of a new establishment of the same firm is called *branch plant development.*

4. Total movement of the enterprise is called *lock, stock and barrel* movement.

B. *The dual population hypothesis* (pages 199–203)
1. The dual population hypothesis states that in Britain since 1945 two main types of industrial movement have taken place – excluding intra-urban industrial movement.
2. The first element of the dual population hypothesis consists of *long distance*, inter-regional, large establishment, lock, stock and barrel moves.
3. The second component consists of *short distance*, intra-regional, branch plant moves.
4. Such latter moves consist partly of *industrial overspill*, movement out of conurbations to new and expanded towns beyond the green belt.

C. *Intra-Urban Industrial Movement* (pages 203–09)
1. Numerically, short distance moves within the urban area constitute the majority of industrial moves.
2. A *sectoral bias* appears to exist in the movement patterns of firms in large cities.
3. The general trend in the western city is towards the *suburbanization* of industry.
4. Social problems may be created by decentralization of industry if a former inner city workplace moves beyond the *critical isochrone* (a line drawn at a distance from the workplace, beyond which distance begins to have a marked effect on the numbers travelling to that workplace) of its work-force.

D. *Movement and Linkage* (pages 209–11)
1. Strong local links may prevent or inhibit a firm from moving.
2. When short distance moves are undertaken, many pre-existing links are retained.
3. Long distance moves seem to have limited effects on the creation of new links.

E. *Predicting Industrial Movement* (pages 212–13)
1. The *Gravity Model* has been employed to predict the amount of industrial movement between two areas.
2. A region's attractiveness to the firm is thought of in terms of its availability of labour and its distance from the firm's existing location.
3. Given these variables, Keeble has shown that the Gravity Model usefully predicts the amount of industrial movement from the South East to the peripheral areas of Britain.

Additional Activities

1. Draw a diagram like Fig. 9.5 (page 207) to show decentralization scores for 1961 and 1968 for manufacturing industries in the West Midlands and Merseyside conurbations (data in Table 9.1 page 205). What conclusions can you draw from the graph?

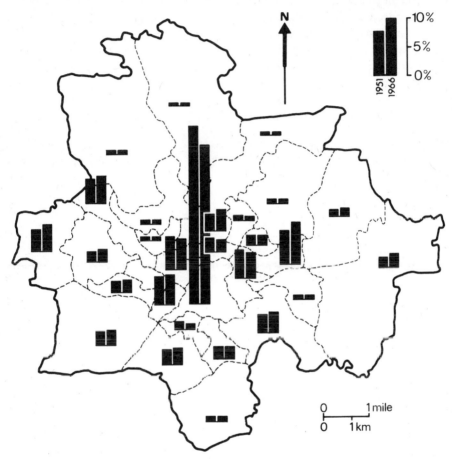

Fig. 9.10. The changing percentages of manufacturing employment in the urban sub-regions of Leeds. (After: R. L. Mackett, 'The estimation of employment in small areas within the city', *Working Paper 29*, Department of Geography, University of Leeds, January 1973)

2. Study Fig. 9.10 which shows the changing percentages of manufacturing employment in the urban sub-regions of Leeds. Write an explanatory account of what the map shows, making use of the concepts covered in this chapter.

3. With reference to any basic text on statistical methods (e.g. R. Hammond and P. McCullagh, *Quantitative Techniques in Geography*, Oxford University Press, 1974) review your knowledge of the Spearman Rank Correlation technique. Apply this technique to the data presented in Fig. 9.9 (page 213). What does your result suggest to you?
4. Test the 'critical isochrone' concept (page 208) for a large workplace (your school?) located in a large urban area. Data required include time or distance travelled to work for each worker. A large, economically heterogeneous sample should be used.
5. Attempt to summarize in the form of three diagrams, the changing relationship between workplaces and residences for blacks and whites in large American cities. Use three different symbols in each diagram to represent (a) main concentrations of workplaces, (b) residences of blacks and (c) residences of whites. Draw one diagram for each of the years 1880, 1950 and 1965.

Reading

A. KEEBLE, D., 'Industrial movement and regional development in the United Kingdom', *Town Planning Review*, 1972, pp. 3–25.
B. GETIS, A., 'Residential location and the journey from work', *Proceedings of the Association of American Geographers*, 1969, pp. 55–9.
C. BROWN, C. M., 'The industry of the new towns of the London Region', in MARTIN, J. E., *Greater London: an Industrial Geography*, Bell, 1966, pp. 238–52.

10 Conclusion

The previous chapter concluded on a relatively optimistic note for those geographers wishing to promote their subject as a social science. One of the main aims of science is prediction and, in that industrial geographers are able to predict at a very general level, their subject may indeed be called a social science – albeit an embryonic one. It is unlikely, however, that geographers will develop laws but rather 'law-like statements'. This is the result of the vagaries of human nature and the large number of variables which interact in producing human behaviour, and thus the decisions which influence industrial location. A major purpose of this book has been to demonstrate that, in the search for explanations of industrial location, a variety of approaches may be adopted. Because industrial geography is a rapidly developing field, it is almost impossible to say that there is a 'correct' approach to explanation. It has been emphasized, for example, that what applies at one level of scale may be inappropriate at another; that what seems logical at one time period appears inapplicable at the present day; that 'economic man' approaches contrast with those which try to accommodate the 'human' and 'chance' factors. We have accepted that the role of local and national government, the linkages between plants and the movement patterns of plants all complement the availability of inputs and access to markets in 'explaining' industrial location patterns. If the reader now feels more inclined to question simplistic explanations of industrial location, this book will have served its purpose.

References

Chapter 1

1. TAAFFE, E. J., 'Introductory economic geography; selected themes or thorough coverage' in BALL, J., STEINBRINK, J. & STOLTMAN, J. (eds.), *The Social Sciences and Geographic Education*, Wiley, 1971, pp. 154–63.
2. ABLER, R., ADAMS, J. & GOULD, P., *Spatial Organisation: the Geographer's View of the World*, Prentice Hall, 1971, p. 14.
3. WATSON, W. W., 'Geography – a discipline in distance', *Scottish Geographical Magazine*, 1955, 1–13.
4. COX, K., *Man, Location and Behaviour*, Wiley, 1971, p. 371.
5. HAGGETT, P., *Geography: a modern Synthesis*, Harper & Row, 1972, p. 461.

Chapter 2

1. Quoted in HAGGETT, P. & CHORLEY, R., 'Models, paradigms and the new geography', in CHORLEY, R. J. & HAGGETT, P. (eds.), *Models in Geography*, Methuen, 1967, p. 20.

Chapter 3

1. WARREN, K., *The British Iron and Steel Sheet Industry since 1840*, Bell, 1970, pp. 2–3.
2. MORRILL, R., *The Spatial Organisation of Society*, Duxbury Press, 1970, p. 6.
3. ESTALL, R., 'Some observations on the internal mobility of investment capital', *Area*, 1972, p. 194.
4. MORRILL, R., *op. cit.*, p. 8.
5. ISARD, W., *Location and Space Economy*, MIT Press, 1956, p. 8.
6. THOMAS, T. M., 'Geographic and economic factors in the siting of a major integrated steelworks', *Tijdschrift voor Economische – Sociale Geografie*, 1964, pp. 185–96.
7. *Ibid.*
8. WATTS, D. G., 'Milford Haven and its oil industry' *Geography*, 1970, pp. 68–9.
9. WHITE, G. F., 'Industrial water use; a review', *Geographical Review*, 1960, pp. 412–30.
10. ESTALL, R. C. & BUCHANAN, R. O., *Industrial Activity and Economic Geography*, Hutchinson, 1961, p. 55.

11. HALL, J., 'Industry grows where the grass is greener', *New Society*, 4 Feb., 1971.
12. WARREN, K., *The American Steel Industry 1850–1970*, Oxford University Press, 1973, p. 5.
13. WALLWORK, K., 'Map interpretation and industrial location', *Geography*, 1967, pp. 166–81.

Chapter 4

1. ISARD, W., *Location and Space Economy*, MIT Press, 1956, p. 280.
2. PRED, A., 'The intrametropolitan location of American manufacturing', *Annals of the Association of American Geographers*, 1964, pp. 165–80.
3. RODGERS, H. B., 'The West Midlands and Central Wales', in MANNERS, G., *et al.*, (eds.), *Regional Development in Britain*, Wiley, 1972, pp. 198–9.
4. HALL, P., 'Industrial London: a general view', in COPPOCK, J. T., & PRINCE, H., (eds.), *Greater London*, Faber, 1964, p. 235.
5. PRED, A., *op. cit.*

Chapter 5

1. WEBER, A., *Theory of the Location of Industries*, (trans. C. FREIDRICH) Harvard University Press, 1926.
2. SMITH, W., 'The location of industry', *Transactions of the Institute of British Geographers*, 1955, pp. 1–18.
3. *Ibid.*
4. *Ibid.*
5. KENNELLEY, R. A., 'The location of the Mexican Steel Industry' in SMITH, R. H. T. et al. (eds.), *Readings in Economic Geography*, Rand McNally, 1968.
6. LINDBERG, O., 'An economic–geographical study of the localisation of the Swedish paper industry', in SMITH, R. H. T., *et al.*, *op cit.*
7. Quoted in HAGGETT, P. & CHORLEY, R. J., 'Models, paradigms and the New Geography', in CHORLEY, R. J. & HAGGETT, P., *Models in Geography*, Methuen,
8. LÖSCH, A., *The Economics of Location*, Wiley, 1967.
9. CHRISTALLER, W., *Central Places in Southern Germany*, Prentice Hall, 1966.
10. WOOD, P., 'Industrial location and linkage', *Area*, 1969, pp. 32–9.
11. WEBER, A., *op cit.*, p. 16.

Chapter 6

1. WATTS, H. D., 'The location of the sugar beet industry in England and Wales, 1912–36', *Transactions of the Institute of British Geographers*, 1971, pp. 95–116.
2. RAWSTRON, E. M., 'Three principles of industrial location', *Transactions of the Institute of British Geographers*, 1958, pp. 132–42.
3. SMITH, D. M., 'A theoretical framework for geographical studies of industrial location', *Economic Geography*, 1966, pp. 132–42.
4. RAWSTRON, E. M., 'Where x then abc; thoughts upon a comprehensive theory of the geography of production' in OSBORNE, R. H., *et al.* (eds.), *Geographical*

Essays in Honour of K. C. Edwards, Department of Geography, University of Nottingham, 1970, pp. 242–7.

5. REISER, R., 'The territorial illusion and the behavioural sink; critical notes on behavioural geography', *Antipode*, 1973, pp. 52–7.

6. STAFFORD, R., 'An industrial location decision model', *Proceedings of the Association of American Geographers*, 1969, p. 142.

7. TAYLOR, M. J., 'Location decisions of small firms', *Area*, 1970, pp. 51–4.

8. McDERMOTT, P., 'Spatial margins and industrial location in New Zealand', *New Zealand Geographer*, 1973, pp. 64–74.

9. PRED, A., *Behavior and Location*, Gleerup, 2 vols., 1967 and 1969.

10. BOAS, C., 'Locational patterns of American automobile assembly plants, 1895–1958', *Economic Geography*, 1961, pp. 218–30.

11. WEBBER, M., 'Sub-optimal behaviour and the concept of maximum profits in locational theory', *Australian Geographical Studies*, 1969, p. 4.

12. CLAUS, R. J. & CLAUS, K. E., 'Behavioural location theory; a review and discussion of Pred's dynamic location theory', *Australian Geographer*, 1971, pp. 522–30.

13. EVERSLEY, D. E., 'Social and psychological factors in the determination of industrial location', in WILSON, T., (ed.), *Papers on Regional Development*, Blackwell, 1965, pp. 102–14.

14. KEEBLE, D., 'Employment mobility in Britain', in CHISHOLM, M. & MANNERS, G., (eds.), *Spatial Policy Problems and the British Economy*, Cambridge University Press, 1971, pp. 24–68.

15. THOMAS, T. M., 'Geographic and economic factors in the siting of a major integrated steelworks', *Tijdschrift voor Economische en Sociale Geografie*, 1964, pp. 185–96.

16. GOULD, P., & WHITE, R., 'The mental maps of British school leavers', *Regional Studies*, 1968, pp. 161–82.

17. TOWNROE, P., *Industrial Location Decisions*, (Occasional Paper, 18), University of Birmingham Centre for Urban and Regional Studies, 1971, p. 66.

18. GOULD, P. & WHITE, R., *Mental Maps*, Penguin, 1974, p. 178.

19. ABLER, R., ADAMS, J. & GOULD, P., *Spatial Organization: the Geographer's View of the World*, Prentice-Hall, 1971, p. 218.

20. BLACKBOURN, A., 'The spatial behaviour of American firms in Western Europe', in HAMILTON, F. E. I. (ed.), *Spatial Perspectives on Industrial Organization and Decision Making*, Wiley, 1974, p. 254.

Chapter 7

1. TAYLOR, M. J. & WOOD, P. J., 'Industrial linkage and local agglomeration in the West Midlands metal industries', *Transactions of the Institute of British Geographers*, 1973, pp. 127–54.

2. WOOD, P., 'Industrial location and linkage', *Area*, 1969, pp. 32–9.

3. TAYLOR, M. J., 'Local linkage, external economies, and the West Midlands and East Lancashire conurbations', *Regional Studies*, 7, 4, 1973, p. 397.

4. ANDERSON, J. & GODDARD, J., 'Some current approaches to human geography in Sweden', *Discussion Paper*, 33, London School of Economics Graduate School of Geography, undated, p. 19.

5. SMITH, D. M., *Industrial Location: an Economic Geographical Analysis*, Wiley, 1971, p. 504.

Chapter 8

1. THOMPSON, J. H., 'Some theoretical considerations for manufacturing geography', *Economic Geography*, 1966, pp. 336–65.
2. ESTALL, R., *New England: a study in Industrial Adjustment*, Bell, 1965.
3. RAWSTRON, E. M., & COATES, B., *Regional Variations in Britain*, Batsford, 1971.
4. *Ibid.*
5. SMITH, D. M., 'Identifying the grey areas: a multivariate approach', *Regional Studies*, 2, 1968, pp. 183–93.
6. CHISHOLM, M. & OEPPEN, J., *The Changing Pattern of Employment*, Croom-Helm, 1973, p. 79.
7. ALLEN, K. J., 'The regional multiplier: some problems in estimation', in ORR, S. C. & CULLINGWORTH, J. B., (eds.), *Regional and Urban Studies: a social science approach*, Allen & Unwin, 1969, pp. 80–96.
8. HUMPHRYS, G., *Industrial Britain: South Wales*, David & Charles, 1973, p. 71.
9. TOWNROE, P., *Industrial Location Decisions, Occasional Paper*, 18, University of Birmingham Centre for Urban and Regional Studies, 1971, p. 92.
10. *Ibid.*
11. JONES, R. M., 'The direction of industrial movement and its impact on recipient regions', *Manchester School of Economic and Social Studies*, 1968, pp. 149–72.
12. SALT, J., 'Workers to the work?' *Area*, 1973, pp. 262–6.
13. HALL, J. M., 'Industry grows where the grass is greener', *Area*, 1970, p. 45.

Chapter 9

1. BEESLEY, M., 'Birth and death of industrial establishments; experience in the West Midlands conurbation', *Journal of Industrial Economics*, 1954, pp. 45–61.
2. KEEBLE, D., 'Employment Mobility in Britain', in CHISHOLM, M. & MANNERS, G., (eds.), *Spatial Policy Problems of the British Economy*, Cambridge University Press, 1971, pp. 24–68.
3. SMITH, B. D. M., 'Industrial overspill in theory and practice: the case of the West Midlands', *Urban Studies*, 1970, pp. 189–204.
4. GETIS, A., 'Residential location and the journey from work', *Proceedings of the Association of American Geographers*, 1969, pp. 55–9.
5. *Ibid.*
6. DESKINS, D., 'Race, residence and workplace in Detroit', *Economic Geography*, 1972, pp. 79–94.
7. DAVIES, S. & ALBAUM, M., 'Mobility problems of the poor in Indianapolis', in Peet, R., (ed.), *Geographical Perspectives on American Poverty*, Antipode Monographs in Social Geography, 1, 1972, pp. 67–86.
8. EVERSLEY, D., 'Rising costs and static incomes', *Urban Studies*, 1972, p. 350.
9. TAYLOR, M. J. & WOOD, P. J., 'Industrial linkage and local agglomeration in the West Midlands metal industries', *Transactions of the Institute of British Geographers*, 1973, pp. 127–54.
10. STEED, G. P. F., 'Industrial reorganization, firm integration and locational change in Northern Ireland', *Economic Geography*, 47, 1971, pp. 371–83.
11. KEEBLE, D., *op cit.*, p. 59.

Index

222

land reclamation, 35
Land Utilization Survey maps, 20–1
least cost model, 82
linkage, 139–151
linkage and movement, 209–211
locational quotient, 62–3, 65, 168
locational triangle, 83, 149
logarithmic scales, 18
Lösch (see market areas)

Main Order Headings, 11–14
map reading, 51
market areas, 100–3
market as a location factor, 47–8, 134, 136
material index, 84–6, 107, 154
mental maps, 123, 126–9
Minimum List Headings, 11, 16, 22
models, 4–5
movement of industry, (see industrial movement)
multiple nuclei model, 56–7

natural environment, 33, 41
non-economic man, 107

objective environment, 125
oil refining, 40

'packet' of manufacturing functions, 25–6
paper making industry, 95–97
perfect competition, 82, 100
photographic interpretation, 51
plants, 18
potential mobility, 119, 199
primary industry, 11, 153
probability matrix, 189, 192
problem regions, 152–8
pulls, 120–1

quaternary industry, 14

rank-size distribution, 18
regional disparities, 158–168
regional multiplier, 177–8
rent-surface, 35, 37

satisficing, 107, 119
secondary industries, 14
sector model, 56–8
sectoral bias, 200, 202–4
'seed beds', 197
simulation model, 187–193
sites for industry, 33–5
size of plants, 18
space cost curve, 109, 112–3
space revenue curve, 109, 112–3
spatial margins to profitability, 107–12, 114, 176–7, 186
spatial perception, 123
specialization index, 164–5
sphere of influence, 112–23
Standard Industrial Classification, 11–16
stepped freight rates, 99
suburbanization of industry, 204–9
sugar manufacture, 85, 107–8
sytems, 5–7, 24–6

tertiary industry, 11–14, 186–7
time-space activity, 44–5, 146
Trade and Industry, 21
transport, 21
transport costs, 83–4
transport type, 99

unemployment, 154–5, 157, 161–2

value/weight ratio, 133
Varignon frame, 84, 91–3

water use in industry, 39–41
waterfront industries, 67–9
Weber model, 82–101, 104, 107, 111, 149